Courage Under Fire

Courage Under Fire

Profiles in Bravery from the
Battlefields of the Civil War

WILEY SWORD

St. Martin's Press   New York

www.stmartins.com

Design by Sarah Maya Gubkin

Library of Congress Cataloging-in-Publication Data

Sword, Wiley.
    Courage under fire : profiles in bravery from the battlefields of the Civil War / Wiley Sword. — 1st ed.
        p. cm.
    ISBN-13: 978-0-312-36741-1
    ISBN-10: 0-312-36741-4
    1. Soldiers—United States—Psychology—History—19th century. 2. Soldiers—Confederate States of America—Psychology. 3. Courage—United States—Case studies. 4. Courage—Confederate States of America—Case studies. 5. United States—History—Civil War, 1861–1865—Personal narratives. 6. Soldiers—United States—Biography. 7. Soldiers—Confederate States of America—Biography. 8. United States. Army—Military life—History—19th century. 9. Confederate States of America. Army—Military life. 10. United States—History—Civil War, 1861–1865—Psychological aspects. I. Title.

E607.S95 2007
355.0092—dc22

                                                                                2007028302

First Edition: November 2007

10   9   8   7   6   5   4   3   2   1

To the women of courage in my life,

My mother, Genevieve Johnson Sword, 1909–1995,
who survived bipolar disorder

My wife, Marianne C. Sword,
who overcame breast cancer

Contents

PART ONE *The Face of Courage*

PART TWO *Physical Bravery*

PART THREE *Moral Courage*

Acknowledgments

As is usual, I'm grateful for the help of many who helped, encouraged, supplied materials for, and assisted in this book. Many of the original materials used for this book came from my ever-expanding collection of historic Civil War letters. Most such items were purchased from Internet sources. For a longtime writer who continues to adjust to the modern era of Internet access, I must admit that the resources available, information extant, and total spectrum of data that can be gleaned from electronic means is stunning. Much of this book was put together on the basis of Internet data, or was obtained from sources available and located therefrom. For an author who has seemingly traveled to the ends of the earth for research, who wrote his first book entirely in longhand and then had a dedicated secretary type it, this is a truly marvelous development. The time saved, the miles not traveled, and the hassle-free means at hand ensure a much more easily produced product. Yet, kindly people are indispensable. The help of those who read and suggested improvements, and others who offered various photographs, letters, or other significant items, is gratefully acknowledged. They are an essential element:

Richard A. Baumgartner, Huntington, West Virginia
Dr. Albert Castel, Hillsdale, Michigan
Alain Houf, Belgium
Paul Larkin, North Falmouth, Massachusetts
John H. Lewis II, Suwanee, Georgia
Mark W. Johnson, U.S. Army
Dave Roth, Columbus, Ohio
Mary Younger, Dayton, Ohio

Also, the materials supplied by various institutions were important, and I thank these institutions for their generous help:

Charles S. Peace Collection, Navarro College, Corsicana, Texas
Georgetown University Library, Washington, D.C.
Ohio Historical Society, Columbus, Ohio
Southern Historical Collection, University of North Carolina, Chapel Hill, North Carolina
U.S. Army Military History Institute, Carlisle Barracks, Pennsylvania
Bentley Historical Library, University of Michigan, Ann Arbor, Michigan
Yale University Library, New Haven, Connecticut

Special thanks are due to my editor at St. Martin's Press, Michael Flamini, also to George Witte, editor in chief, and their staffs, particularly Vicki Lame. Dr. Albert Castel, Hillsdale, Michigan, read the manuscript and was very helpful with suggestions. Of course, my wife, Marianne, was most understanding in sacrificing her time, and as usual supported the project with her love and personal commitment.

Preface

WHY THE CIVIL WAR
OR ITS COURAGE?

It seems strange to many why some persons look to the past and study its history and people with such fervor and intensity, especially the American Civil War. My own mother once remarked: "Why are you so concerned about something that occurred more than a hundred years ago, and can't be changed or doesn't affect your life now?" In my adolescence I merely quipped: "Because I find it so interesting."

Today, if I were to answer that question I might add a little more perspective: The Civil War was perhaps the central crisis, the crossroads of our nation's destiny; it determined whether we would be split apart and form various nations much like the fate South America experienced, or remain a united nation with the advantages of combined resources and population. It essentially resolved for this nation the age-old question of where ultimate authority rested: at the state or national level. It brought into full perspective a defining crisis of the soul, of whether any people so dominant, so advantaged, could "own" the lives of other human beings.

These were truly the material and pragmatic aspects that were fought over. Yet the Civil War was more than that; it was both a crisis of and a study in human existence. The combined lessons of that war were without equal in the history of mankind. It was in condensed essence the old versus the new, both in implementation of technology stemming from the Industrial Revolution, and in perspective about the nature and meaning of our lives. Death, an almost accepted, commonplace element of life, was, in the wake of the gruesome horrors of the Civil War, transformed into a vile, unacceptable condition—other than from old age. How we look today at the specter of death stems in part from the agony of so many (more than six hundred thousand) young Americans dying so soon amid such grim carnage.

Further, there were essential insights into mankind's destiny—of progress toward a role beyond the mundane, old-world "reactive" existence of the past. The "proactive" elements of our future rationale were beginning to take root and become apparent. To act with greater knowledge and understanding was to implement an enhanced learning curve of reason. It was an era of enlightenment, yet also one of personal drama, of the oft-repeated will to do and/or die amid the great issues of mankind.

Hence the role of courage. The ability to control one's emotions, body, and behavior amid the greatest of all stress—the imminent risk of death—is a fascinating phenomenon. The power of reason is why we exist beyond all other animate life as a reflection of God's supreme earthly creation. As a historian, I believe the courage personified by our nation is its defining quality. To this point, our history is a never-ending saga of people surmounting adversity with the highest of valor amid some of the severest tests of life. Even today, the events in Afghanistan and Iraq have their correlation in the common bond of courage displayed by our soldiers. The enactment of valor in combat is timeless in its nature, and the relevancy is obvious: we think much the same as our ancestors did, and value those experiences that define our lives. The Civil War was but one heightened aspect of the demand for courage that shaped our destiny. Yet it remains among the greatest stories of our nation.

Remembering the essential question my mother once posed, and that which thousands of others ponder: the Civil War is but a window to view the essence of life. The more we understand about the crucial elements of our past, the more we care. The more we care, the more we will perpetuate those ideals for which so many sacrificed their lives. We owe it both to ourselves and to future generations that our forefathers' courage is never, ever forgotten.

PART ONE

The Face of Courage

1

TO OBEY ORDERS OR NOT

August 3, 1864, was not proving to be a good day for Frank Curtiss. He was sweating profusely because the Illinois lieutenant colonel faced a big problem. He had been ordered by the senior (brigade) commanding officer, Brigadier General Joseph Andrew Jackson Lightburn, to take his regiment, the 127th Illinois Infantry, and charge the fortified Rebel lines across an open field near Atlanta, Georgia. Curtiss knew what was in store. His skirmishers had already attempted to attack the enemy's pickets across the same field. They had started off with a yell, aiming at the dusky brown line of improvised earthworks. Halfway across the field, it seemed as if all hell had exploded in their faces. Ten Confederate cannon, firing deadly shotgunlike blasts of canister, had raked the sprinting lines of blue-clad soldiers. Minié balls had zipped about like angry swarms of bees. Seven of fifty men were downed in an instant, and the remainder had scattered in confusion back to the Union lines.

Before the attack Curtiss's palms were sweaty. Now the oppressive Georgia heat added to the ache in his heart. If he took his men out there again, perhaps not a man would survive. Yet Curtiss carefully considered the situation: Lightburn was waiting impatiently, his brigadier general's stars glistening on gilded shoulder straps. Obviously the austere and gruff West Virginian saw little merit in Curtiss's hesitation. He wanted that Rebel skirmish line captured.

Frank Curtiss was no fool. A veteran combat officer with extensive experience, he knew the consequences of making the attack: heavy losses for an insignificant gain. A thousand thoughts raced through his mind. Lightburn was known to be bucking for a second star and division command, especially since his superior, Major General Morgan L. Smith, was ill and on the verge of leaving the army for home. Moreover, Lightburn was aware that the Army of the Tennessee's new commander, Major General Oliver O. Howard, was personally present, watching for good results. Lightburn thus wanted bold action that might impress his seniors.

Frank Curtiss wanted only to keep his men alive. They deserved better than to have their lives thrown away in a useless frontal assault that could accomplish nothing to compensate for an outright slaughter. From Arkansas Post to Dallas, Georgia, these men had fought valiantly and suffered accordingly. Their lives were precious, more so than the prospect of a new star for old Lightburn—whom the boys said they "hated worse than a Rebel" for his self-serving ways.

Curtiss's expression turned grim. Common sense opposed Lightburn's orders, but it equated to a dire choice: his arrest for disobeying orders, or the death of many of his men. Thus the decision was both simple and complex.

In Frank Curtiss's mind there really was no choice. He refused to make the attack.

Lightburn's reaction was like that of a stricken grizzly; swiftly Curtiss was placed under arrest, his sword was confiscated, and the distraught officer was sent to the rear to face dismissal from the army.

Lightburn now angrily turned to the next regiment in line, the 55th Illinois Infantry. The result was the same. The captain commanding (the senior officers were casualties) decided he, too, would not make such a forlorn attack. When the third regiment's commander also hesitated to charge, Lightburn had these officers arrested and was seen galloping off in a huff, apparently damning the ill luck that had brought him command of such independent-minded units.[1]

Great moral courage was comparatively rare on the tactical battlefield prior to 1864; experience, if not the ability, was wanting. Knowing what was tactically right or wrong was generally a by-product of personal experience, and hence had to be learned. Yet acting upon that same knowledge frequently involved an extraordinary dilemma. At what point was the right to be implemented, and at what cost? The lessons of three years of increasingly vicious warfare had clarified the means and the issues. Those in the ranks knew, as survivors, what their service had taught: what was or wasn't practical or possible. Often at issue was a myriad of counterpoints, from what was good judgment, to the implementation of selfish motives or bureaucratic initiatives, to a use of common sense. It was a familiar bane of common soldiers and their units' officers: coping with the perceived bungling of high-ranking commanders. Those who seemed to know the best were those with the most to gain or lose—their lives. Decisions by those not at risk often involved a far different perspective.

"Cannon fodder" was an outmoded concept even in 1861. "Theirs not to reason why, / Theirs but to do and die" implied a universal theme of compliance amid ignorance. Yet in the mid-nineteenth century the masses were not essentially stupid. With the Industrial Revolution had come an equally fundamental educational revolution. Ordinary people were no longer largely uneducated and thus complaisant amid their relative ignorance. From religious institutions to the military, the implications were enormous. The masses, able to read and write, and stimulated to think by rapid means of communication, were as a maturing apple tree, ready to bear quality fruit where only the yield would be affected by the climate and conditions. Being told what to do now involved a more sophisticated approach—that of rationale. While there were those who relied upon traditional methods to obtain results, they often were less successful than the innovators, the leaders who studied, reasoned, and adapted.

By 1864, the crux of the matter was the evolving war of technology, in which attitudes and traditional concepts were subject to the relative overall wisdom that was applied. Management of the battlefield centered on a new criterion—personnel conservation and efficacy in action. In its most basic meaning, this translated into use of common sense rather than staid, all-but-obsolete textbook concepts. The world was changing. New technology had altered the methodology of war. Thinking had to keep pace. It was a fascinating challenge to those in control—how well could they adapt?

To the men who fought in the trenches during the later stages of the war, the matter of their life or death thus had a new focus; would their lives (being increasingly precious) be truly valued by those in command? Would they be given a fair chance to survive in combat, consistent with the altered, more deadly conditions of modern warfare? Because of the widespread use of more lethal weapons technology, this meant fighting smart.

FROM TODAY'S PERSPECTIVE

In achieving victory in battle, the basic reliance for ages has been on military discipline. As such, the focus has always been on the one essential maxim: "Obey orders." Yet in a "why" context, is it enough to be told what to do on the basis of rank? Perhaps in ordinary circumstances, yes. But ultimately, if human life is the essential value, are there times when risking one's life is to be weighed against the viability of the endeavor? Traditionally, superior rank has been given full discretion in such matters, but at what point does a higher consideration have sway? Frank Curtiss thought he must act in refusing an order based upon his knowledge and personal experience; he saw the situation at Atlanta on August 3, 1864 as resulting in a useless sacrifice of life. To refuse Lightburn's mandate was contrary to the oath he had taken to obey the lawful orders of his superiors, but he viewed his moral courage in doing what was "right" as saving the lives of countless numbers of his men. Was it justified? Or, in reverse perspective, was Lightburn's tactical ignorance—or perhaps ulterior motive—in ordering the attack defensible under the scrutiny of hindsight? If correct in a technical sense, were his actions in a practical sense justifiable? Even in today's military, should a subordinate officer be denied the chance to alter the course of action, given explicit orders contrary to the moral ethics of right versus wrong—such as to sacrifice without due gain the very lives of his men? The answers are not easy, even as we examine cause and effect. No explanations or solutions will be satisfactory, but it is a fundamental human quest to seek an understanding of what is ultimate wisdom.

This book, while often focused on the tactical battlefield, examines decision making as a consequence of personal perception and applied moral resolution. Differences in thinking may be based upon extent of knowledge, but ultimately the results sometimes defy conventional rationale (because, essentially, we are not invariably smart enough to correctly perceive and manage all factors large and small). While an analysis of some of the Civil War's key decisions in forethought and their subsequent consequences is necessarily limited by the passage of time and inherent loss of data, we can in a larger sense stimulate thought, raise internal questions, and inspire deeper reasoning. Indeed, if we are to learn from the past, our understanding must encompass as much of the whole story as is possible—that is, the thinking as well as the doing.

What went through the mind of certain individuals caught up in life-or-death circumstances is generally difficult to determine. However, put into perspective from the historical clues that exist, often a meaningful if subjective analysis is possible. If we are to better understand our lives and the meaning of such, the past hopefully holds clues in its many recorded lessons.

II

THE REASON WHY

Sam Wolcott had always felt a need to be one of the boys. Cognizant of his patriotic duty and what was at stake in reuniting the nation, the Salisbury, Connecticut, youth had enlisted along with his buddies in the 7th Regiment Connecticut Volunteer Infantry in the fall of 1861. The 7th, as it turned out, was an elite and special regiment, having been organized by a future general, Alfred H. Terry, and it would eventually serve with distinction in the assault at Fort Wagner in July 1863. In October and November 1863 the regiment's status was changed; it was equipped as "boat infantry" for the specific purpose of leading an amphibious night assault on Fort Sumter, South Carolina. The army would not rely on the navy's marines; the army's attitude seemed to be that which caused one veteran soldier to comment: "a Marine [is] that non-descript whom neither soldiers or sailors lay claim to."[1]

Although the 7th Connecticut trained hard at Folly Island, South

Carolina, and was specially equipped with some of the first Spencer re-
peating carbines manufactured, the project was ultimately given up as
impractical. In the spring of 1864 the regiment was reassigned to Virginia. Through it all, Private Samuel W. Wolcott had been quite fortunate, earning a noncombat assignment in Hilton Head, South Carolina
as a clerk on mustering duty. His friends in Company F kept him informed by letter of the intense fighting in Virginia as Major General
Benjamin F. Butler's Army of the James crept onward up the peninsula
toward Richmond.[2]

Wolcott was not pleased. Thoughts of missed adventure, and being
unable to prove his manhood, clouded his mind. Even worse were his
fears of not being an equal among his peers in dangers met and conquered. It burned at his very soul, and Wolcott explained to his mother
in an emotional letter what he intended to do:

Office Com[missioner] of Musters
Hilton Head, S.C. June 12, 1864

My Dear Mother:
Your letter of the 5th ult. is before me; it having been received
at twenty minutes past ten a.m. yesterday. . . . And now I want to
write you a short essay on—I don't know what, unless it is
patriotism. *I think when I was home you were telling me of a*
woman who had sent five *sons to the war, and felt very sorry that*
she had but no more to send. I guess you have forgotten her.
Now, just imagine me, a soldier here away from my regiment,
with hardly anything to do, and in good health, while the
thousands of Union soldiers are marching, working, and fighting
almost incessantly amid the clays of Virginia. Have not they
friends at home who sympathize with them and would, if possible,
shield them from harm? Is their interest in the country greater
than mine? Or, am I better than they? But, you say I may get shot
if I go there. Are there not thousands of the best men in the
country exposed to the same danger? And will not the same God
watch over me there as here?

*I do not believe that I am a coward. If I am, I shall find it out
in Virginia. And the sooner I know it the better. I should be
ashamed to remain here until the expiration of my term, and then
return to Connecticut with the other boys, many of which could
name a score of fields where they had met the foe and with honor
to themselves and cause. But if I were questioned, what should I
say? No, mother, instead of telling me to remain here, tell me to go
to the front and there help achieve our liberties. And when the war
is over, or my time expires, you will not be ashamed to greet me,
knowing that I shrank from no duty.*

    *Yesterday I received a letter from one of the boys of my company
(Wallace E. Norton [Co. F]). At the date of his letter, May 29th, he
had been in four engagements since he landed in Virginia. In the
last one, as a corporal, he carried the state flag, the staff of which was
shot in two in his hands and a charge made upon it to effect its
capture. But he bore it safely from the field. And [do you] think if he
lives to see the end of the war he will soon forget that day[?] As a
partial reward for his bravery they made him a sergeant, and
doubtless there are hundreds of others as brave as he, who in doing
their duty are bringing honor for themselves. Not that the honors won
by the few make up for the mauling of the many. But when the work
is to be done, I think that none but cowards will shrink from bearing
their part. And believing this, I should go to Va. on the next boat if I
could. But I cannot get away, and shall have to remain here until the
first of next month, when I will write to you, if well, from the regt.
Now don't borrow unnecessary trouble about me, nor ask me even to
avoid the dangers which as a soldier it is my duty to share.*

    Most affectionately,
    Saml. W. Wolcott

Sam had his way. Within a few weeks he was with the 7th Connecticut at the front near Bermuda Hundred, Virginia. During the operations
at Deep Bottom, Virginia, August 16, 1864, the 7th Connecticut suffered
severely, losing seven killed, twenty-five wounded, and four prisoners.

Yet Sam's fears about his mettle were unfounded. He was no coward. Private Sam Wolcott, who had so ardently sought a place with his comrades at the front, was among those killed that day.[3]

Devotion to duty had its risks as well as its rewards. Was his death in battle random fate, or perhaps his destiny? His mother's grief did not differentiate. Ironically, Wolcott's friend Sergeant Wallace E. Norton, who had initially sought combat service, was soon assigned to quartermaster's duty and survived the war.

The "thrill" of combat was perceived as an incentive by many, at least in the conception. To boldly fight the enemy, to make him flee, and to smell the dizzying elixir of victory—it seemed indelible as a perception of combat glory. Further, who could resist the inspiring martial pageantry, and the campfire talk about battle's fierce ardor? Twenty-one-year-old Horace B. Ensworth, of Oswego, New York, was one of those caught up in the furor when he wrote home in the spring of 1862, a few days before going into battle for the first time. A private in Company B, 81st New York Infantry, the rough-and-tumble Ensworth regarded his forthcoming trial by fire with confidence, and even a bold audacity.

April the 20 1862

Dear Father and sister. I take my pen in hand to write a few lines to you. W[e] are all well at present; . . . We are to Fairfack [actually, Warwick] *Court house now. That is ten miles from the place called Yorktown, where the Rebel troops are. We shall see fun before long. We all want to see it badly. That will tell what the 81st is [made of]. The boys say that it [is] raining damned hard [so] I guess I will put on my jacket. We are tougher than pig tale [tail] lightning. We are bare foot[ed] and when the sun comes out it scalds the hide. All say we gained a great victory last night. Our troops took 3,000 Rebels last night. I think if we could get a chance at a Southerner we would suck his blood. I suppose what makes us all so fast [is] we don't get any more than we want to eat. We marched 12 miles the other day. We had the heft of five pecks of wheat on our march. If a man had told me that I could make a pack horse of myself [I would have scoffed]; but a man don't*

[know] till he tries it. I had to throw my boots away. Some throw
their coats away, but I hung [on] to mine. The balloon [Professor
Thaddeus Lowe's] went up yesterday morning. It raised up almost
one half mile and last night they commenced fighting. . . . We
have the shadow of a piece of mule for meat to eat. It makes a
man tough. . . . I could get my discharge a spell ago if I had
wanted, but I am bound to see it through. If I can keep my health
then I don't care a damn for old Jeff [Davis] and his whole tribe
together. [That's] All for the present. Yours truly, Horace B.
Ensworth, Casey's Division, 3rd Brigade, Fortress Monroe.[4]

On May 31, the 81st New York suffered heavy casualties at Fair
Oaks and Seven Pines, Virginia, and Private Ensworth began to comprehend the implications of battle. Little more than two years later he had
the misfortune to be in the disastrous charge at Cold Harbor, Virginia,
June 2 and 3, 1864. Here the much reduced 81st suffered 215 casualties,
and the effect on Ensworth was dramatic. The remarkable contrast in his
attitude well reflected the metamorphosis from recruit to combat veteran.

Fort Harrison, Va. Dec. 1st 1864
Dear Father, . . . Well, father, I suppose that hell will be to pay
now before long, for every man that is able to carry a rifle has got
to take one, and the 18th and 1st Corps is consolidated together,
and I am not sure but I think that it is called the 24th Corps.
Father, I begin to think that they are not a going to leave a man
[alive], for that old [Gen. Ulysses S.] Grant has got to charge from
here to Richmond, and charging is played out with me. I never
will make another one as long as I belong to the 81st Regt. Well
they can, all of them, talk about what a fine thing it is to be in a
charge and get out of it all right, but being at home and [talking
about] making a salient charge, or being down here and charging
upon the Johnnies, is two different things in my way of thinking.
Well, father, I do not know, but I think that there will be some
pretty hard [fighting] done down here in this department before
many more days pass off. It has every appearance of it now from

*the signs of our own men and the Johnnies too. Well, father, since I
commenced to write this letter I have had to go out and drill. We
have to drill 4 hours every day and we are on picket every 2 days,
so you see what we have to do down here in the Southern country.
There is a good many of our army that is a running away to the
Rebels so [as] to get sent off to the foreign countries, and besides
there is a great many of them that is enlisting into the Regular
service and taking the bounties and a going to the old countries in
order to save themselves from going through the next coming
campaign. I have [made] several applications for to go with
different ones. I think that I shall live just as long to stay as I
agreed to, as I should. To desert from my home, my country, and
my friends, I might have an easier time, but what would be
thrown in my parents' faces every time that they, "Was[h] Engine"
[Washington—i.e., the establishment], got mad. I will stay where
I belong, or go [out of service] honorably. Well, father, I suppose
that you have got my boots ready to send by this time. I tell you
that I am barefoot and my pants is nearly gone. Write soon and let
me know the news of the day. direct to Horace B. Ensworth, Co.
B, 81 [NY] 1st Division, 1st Brigade, 18 Corps."*

Ensworth was fortunate. He was promoted to corporal and then sergeant in 1865, and survived the war, being mustered out in August 1865.[5]

In the euphoric foreglow of entering military service with high expectations, who could conceive what the actual realities would be? Said
one enlightened soldier, it wasn't that being in the army was so much
different than he thought it might be; it was just that there were "a
great many things (viewing it as I did from a distance) that I couldn't
see."

Indeed, combat was really only an infrequent and small facet of the
total military experience, especially in the early years of the war. Aside
from the physical realities of prevalent sickness and inclement weather,
boredom, tedium, regimentation, martial tyranny, and a lack of freedom
of expression and action all wreaked havoc with the volunteer soldier on
both sides. The perception had not been the reality: being in the military

was far more "reptilian" in nature than many had imagined. Common sense was far less prevalent than rank, discipline, and the capricious whims of men far up the command chain. Being told what to do was preconceived as being founded on the wisdom of experienced leadership. In practicality it was frequently on the basis of abstract reason. Personal considerations gave way to a dogma of manipulative indifference; the army way was steeped in regulations and bureaucratic inefficiency. The men were mindless; therefore they might be treated as cogs in a machine and mechanically manipulated. So ran some of the logic.[6]

The extent of tyranny within the military mind-set was predicated largely on the regular establishment, where regular-army discipline was fear-induced. One enlisted man who had been talked into joining the regulars in 1862 after his volunteer unit was disbanded found a remarkable difference in attitudes between the two, at least at the company level. "I don't like the regular service so well as the volunteers; we can't have so many privileges," wrote Private Isaac B. Jones of the 3rd Battalion, 18th U.S. Infantry. "The Regulars are exceedingly strict. The army regulations have to be carried out to the very letter. And you know the military law is the most tyrannical thing on earth."[7]

It wasn't that every regular officer was a brutal tyrant, but that the vices of army life were often accentuated by the training and difficulties associated with the regular establishment. Prewar contentiousness, fostered by the difficult prospect of promotion, politics, and even alcoholism, ran its course in human relations, further ingraining standoffishness and suspicion within a more harsh, regimented routine. The men were too often regarded as the dregs of society, unable to find more gainful employment among civil pursuits, hence, misfits, morons, or malcontents, mindful only of a firm guiding hand. Regular army practices, such as placing a sergeant with a fixed, leveled bayonet behind a deployed battle line to prevent the men from running away in combat, carried over into the volunteer service. The regulars were noted more for their discipline than for their spirit; thus spread a belief that the American volunteer soldier needed not spirit but discipline to achieve the greatest prowess in combat.

This concept quickly melded with the initial methods of fighting the war. By discipline the men could be made to stand up manfully in the ranks and fight shoulder to shoulder against a foe disposed to the same tactical concepts. Instead of a guideline for courage, it proved largely to be a formula for disaster.

III

"TO WIN GLORY ENOUGH"

DAVID W. NORTON, CHICAGO, ILLINOIS

It hurt a lot, but the ache came from within—a constant, gnawing agony that conveyed a thousand bitter thoughts. It was both devastating and humiliating. She had been his ideal: bright, witty, and a little saucy—a comely brunette with lilting eyes and a beguiling smile. From the beginning they had hit it off well; Mary was full of life and teeming with energy. David, a moderately successful twenty-four-year-old sales-man from the East, was devoted and considerate, catering to her every whim. Their relationship had been progressively endowed with love, and he was already thinking of marriage. Yet the events of April 1861 loomed large in their lives. Mary T. Dodge had shuddered at the thought of David going off to war. His ardor seemed divided; the war was a chance to "enlist in the glorious cause of our country," and also to serve one's ambition. "If we have any good fighting, I mean to have a higher rank than at present—if there is one to be had by doing one's duty," he proclaimed shortly after joining the 1st Zouave Regiment of Chicago as a sergeant. Mary was indifferent. Instead of military glory, she saw only separation and loneliness. There was no fun in keeping an austere vigil for a departed lover, especially as there were so many eligible bachelors wishing to court her. Popular and a local celebrity in Dodgeville, Wisconsin (named for her prominent grandfather, Henry Dodge), Mary soon found solace in another man's arms.

Within a few months David Norton learned the bitter truth; Mary T. Dodge was betrothed to another man! In anguish he poured out his soul to his mother back in Massachusetts:

> *My fortune has been the same in this case as in most things since I came west. My [relative] poverty put it out of my power to win [her], and another richer and perhaps more suitable man has carried off the prize. His attentions and the wishes of rich and aristocratic friends were able to carry the day against me. It happened sometime since, but I have not before felt like writing on the subject, even to you. I now can write, and I believe I could talk the matter over with you as cool as any other subject, . . . but I don't think the edge is blunted, but only sunken out of sight of outsiders. I may appear to all as is usual, . . . but I don't think you will be likely to have a daughter-in-law on my account in some time to come. . . . Mother, I believe I have lost the prize to gain which a life might be spent. I shall now strive to win glory enough to fill the void. I wish for nothing else now than to make a name that my friends and country may be proud to point to. I have no confidence that I shall succeed in this aim much better than in my past aims. But what is life without some higher aim than to [just] live? I am almost selfish enough to wish that I did not love and respect Mary so much as I do. Of course, you will not mention any of the personal part of this letter. The facts of the case cannot be changed and the less said about the matter hereafter, the better I shall be pleased. I . . . do not wish [it] to go any further.*[1]

David W. Norton's burning ambition masked his deep anguish. His star-crossed love affair inspired a determined, almost all-consuming obsession to achieve great success. If not good enough to win Mary, by God, he would show the world there was no inferiority in his makeup. Promoted to lieutenant and then captain by diligent effort that involved almost incessant study and work, Norton proudly wrote home that he had achieved all of this within four months of enlisting. Already looked upon as an up-and-coming leader, Norton turned his thoughts again to the military glory he so ardently coveted. His regiment, redesignated the 42nd Illinois Volunteer Infantry, was shipped off to the wilds of western Missouri in September 1861. Here Captain Norton found belated comfort in being the first of the 42nd's personnel to engage the enemy, although his aggressiveness led to a tiff with the unit's major. "I have the honor of the first shot for the Douglas Brigade [i.e., 42nd Illinois Infantry]," wrote David in a revealing letter home.

> *I went out day before yesterday and surprised a small camp of*
> *Secesh [i.e., Secessionists/Confederates] and took five prisoners and*
> *14 horses & mules. None of my boys were injured. It was the first*
> *expedition from our regiment, and I feel proud of my boys. . . .*
> *The joke of the affair is that Maj. Roberts sent one of his pets,*
> *Capt. Vardon with his whole company, to take this [enemy] squad.*
> *Maj. Roberts would not authorize me to do the same thing that he*
> *ordered Capt. Vardon to do. I had the best guide and went straight*
> *to the camp, about 12 miles, took it and returned to my camp the*
> *same night. What I did, I did on my own responsibility.*[2]

Although a minor incident, the future political consequences were foreseeable:

> *I was sick [one] night, and the doctor reported to the major that I*
> *had the bilious fever and that I could not be moved. But I had*
> *never yet allowed my company to march without being at their*
> *head. I told the doctor I should go, and began to dress accordingly,*

when the major came to my tent and ordered me to remain behind—nominally to take charge of the camp and sick, but really because he thought it dangerous to move me in a lumber wagon, for he and the doctor thought that they had a sick capt. . . . They were rather anxious to get me on the sick list, not that they wanted me to suffer, but only because I had always made fun of them for getting tired or "played out," as we call it. . . . Well, the regt. marched from camp and I stayed behind in obedience to major's orders. In the afternoon one of the officers came back to camp and said the regt. was to march at daylight [the] next morning and to proceed to St. Louis immediately. I thought from that that they must want to send us immediately into Kentucky, and having no notion of being [left] behind, I got up and had a horse saddled and started at sundown to ride to the other camp—about 12 miles. It was hard work to ride, and took me about 5 hours to go to the camp. The next morning when the major saw me, he threatened to put me under arrest for not obeying his orders. But when I told him that I understood that he was to march that morning, he laughed at my conceit for thinking the regiment could not get along without me, and called me a fool for running the chance of making myself sick. While I was talking to the major, the doctor came to report that he had succeeded in getting an ambulance to send for me. He was surprised and angry at seeing me, and said I had signed my death warrant that time sure! He said I was as sick as any man in the regt., and had the bilious fever, but I knew better. So he got angry and so did I, and he insisted I was sick, and I that I was not, and so ended the affair. We did not march until the next day. I was hardly able to march, but would not ride because I would not acknowledge that the dr. was right. I actually drove sickness from my tent, and have been in first rate health ever since. That one day is the only day that I have not been in command of my company since we left Chicago. I am fat and saucy—so say my superior officers, for my old habit of saying what I think at all times and in all places has not left me yet. In fact, camp life just suits me. I believe I weigh more now than at any other time since I was at home. My time is fully occupied with affairs of my company, for I have the whole to do excepting what can be trusted to my non-commissioned officers. My lieutenants are of very little use to me, as they are either sick or lazy all the time.[3]

Norton was "a brick," as many would say in using the popular jargon of the times. Indeed, he was just the sort of man who could be relied on to do the toughest job well, but was considered an unpredictable personality, and sort of a "loose cannon" who usually spoke his mind. Bravery was a byword to Norton when facing danger, and he was the kind of leader the men could understand, for they knew he wouldn't ask more of them than of himself. Norton's great courage and determination were clearly evident when the 42nd Illinois was required in September 1862 to march from Alabama to Nashville, Tennessee. Norton noted:

One day when our regt. was rear guard, and we had charge of the [wagon] train, I was riding along the train attending to getting all who were unable to march placed on the wagons. Suddenly, as I rode quickly along, a whole volley was fired at me from a bluff which overlooked the road. The buckshot fell around me like hail without one ball striking me. One hit my sword, & on the horn of my saddle. I got ten or fifteen of the sick and footsore men off the nearest wagons, and gave my Secesh assailants as much fight as they wanted. We killed one man and three horses, and captured one man. We could not follow them when we had routed them, for they had horses and we had none. Our train was attacked several times during the day, and . . . I had a good deal of fun and excitement during the day. As the attacking force was scattered in small squads, we had no trouble in making them skedaddle without calling for any assistance from the regiment. . . . Our regiment really doesn't know enough to be afraid of anything—that is what other regiments say of us.[4]

As his men learned, it was a sentiment equally appropriate to Captain David Norton. Norton's involvement in a spirited skirmish near Nashville in November 1862 was a classic of what might be expected from such an aggressive personality.

The day before the first troops arrived the Rebels attacked us at 2 o'clock at night & it took us until 2 o'clock P.M. to beat them back from our picket lines. We only lost five or six killed, and perhaps 50 wounded, while, according to the reports of the citizens, the Rebels must have lost from 50 to 100 killed, & many more wounded. . . . I had the pleasure of shooting one Rebel myself. My company was employed as skirmishers, and one of my boys fired twice at a Rebel without hitting him, and I was a little mad at it, and took a rifle from one of my boys and shot at him myself. I hit him in the leg, and he was carried back to the rear into the woods. I was skirmishing for more than an hour, and the shots were flying very close around, but our luck is so good that not a man of my company was shot, although shots fired at us hit several men in the rear of us. My company received the compliment of being the best skirmishers the general had ever seen under fire. Of course I was proud of the praise, as it was given in the hearing of a large group of officers who were behind us while we were actually engaged. . . . I think it was in earnest. At the time it was said, I was under a perfect storm of balls, & charging up a hill to drive the enemy skirmishers from behind a hedge, to allow our artillery to advance across an open field while the Secesh were covered by the hedge. I can't account for their not hitting some of us. According to tactics, I should have been in [the] rear of my skirmishers, but when the balls began to fly pretty freely, it seemed cowardly for me to stay in the rear and order my men to go forward when it appeared to be certain death to enter that open field. So I went up on the line, & every man said he would keep as near the enemy as I [did]. I advanced on the run through the field & drove the Secesh from their position. The day after our fight, . . . the advance of Gen. Rosecrans' army arrived, & the Rebels skedaddled.[5]

His self-confidence was contagious, and Norton gloated that his men trusted him implicitly. Indeed, by the fall of 1862 he had the entire division aware of his capacity. Due reward came in the form of an assignment to the staff of Brigadier General John M. Palmer, the hard-fighting division commander who, although a politician and not a West Pointer, was earmarked for higher responsibility. Norton was highly pleased; he wrote the folks at home on November 19, 1862: "I am proud to inform you that I have been selected by Brig. Gen. Palmer for the position of inspector general of his division. When you consider that there were about 350 officers to select from, you will realize the size of the compliment."[6]

Norton may have had reason to reconsider the merit of this "compliment" when about a month later he was with Palmer during the furious Battle of Stones River. As a member of Palmer's staff, he was on duty from 4:00 A.M. on December 30 to 10:00 A.M. on Jan. 1, and amid the "fury" of the heaviest enemy attacks. "The way the balls flew crossways [i.e., from various directions] is more than I can express," later wrote the amazed Norton. "When I looked at the general's face after I returned from carrying an order and saw how calm and steady he looked, I almost was guilty of tears, for I did not believe that one of us, sitting there on our horses, could by any chance escape. Imagine each snowflake in a heavy storm as bullets, and you will get a faint idea of how promiscuously the balls were flying. Yet not one of the staff were hurt. We were in range of three lines of [enemy] fire for some two hours, and how we all escaped is a wonder." Convinced that "this division [Palmer's] saved the day" at Stones River, Captain Norton was bitter that "thus far almost all the credit has been given to divisions and generals who did not do the best fighting." Yet Palmer was unconcerned—"[he] says it will all come out right," noted Norton, who added, "I hope it may, for the sake of the gallant officers and men of this division who feel very sore on the subject."[7]

David Norton had always wondered about what it would be like to experience major combat; would he have the mettle to carry out his convictions amid the firestorm of a big battle? Earlier, at Farmington, Mississippi, on May 9 during the Corinth Campaign of 1862, this nagging thought had bedeviled him, as he recorded at the time: "I always thought I should be frightened . . . on getting into a real battle, but I was not. To be sure, when the first few shots flew by me, I thought of home, . . . but after that, I was only in fear for my men. I thought all the time that I ought to be with each & every man to see that he took proper care of himself."[8]

The subsequent fighting at Stones River had only reaffirmed his faith that his fate was in God's hands. Indeed, through it all, Norton had survived unscathed. The thought of being mortally wounded had surfaced frequently during the war, but David was always quick to reassure his family that the danger was overstated. Prior to Chickamauga, Norton had sought to calm the rampant fears of his mother:

We shall probably have a battle with Bragg in the course of 4 or 5 days and I want to again impress on your mind that all who go into battle do not get hit, and that all who are hit are by no means killed. You will probably hear and read of our being defeated, killed, wounded, etc. two or three days before you hear of the actual result of the fight—if we have one. I have little doubt that we shall finish Bragg's army this time, for our army is in the very best of spirits and in splendid fighting order. We cannot have so hard a fight as we had at Stones River, and I was not hurt then— although you did not hear from me for some days. Now, if you hear that we have a fight, don't imagine that I am wounded or killed. I will telegraph (if possible) or write you immediately after the fight is over. If I am hurt, I have made arrangements to have you informed of it instantly. If you do not hear from me as soon as you would like to, do not worry any more than you are obliged to. . . . We have great confidence in Rosy [General Rosecrans], and that is half the battle.[9]

At Chickamauga, Norton, riding by Palmer's side, was thrust into the thickest action. Although Norton had chided: "Don't be afraid of my getting hurt; I shall not hunt for any honorable wounds—I'd rather keep an honorable whole skin," on September 20 he suffered a disabling wound. Struck by a round musket ball in the right shoulder, Norton was visited by his brother a few months later, who noted: "[It] came very near breaking the shoulder blade." Yet he had rapidly recovered, and was found "large, strong, fleshy, [and] weather beaten," even remarking to his brother that "his health is perfect."[10]

Palmer also had taken a wound in the subsequent skirmishing around Chattanooga—in the buttocks—but was now a major general and corps commander, and Norton was elevated to the rank of major. "The future is a big thing," wrote Major Norton in a letter home, and he optimistically predicted that the nation was about "to see the beginning of the end of this rebellion."[11]

Encouraged by the prospect of further promotion as recommended by Palmer, and even a commission in the regular army, David Norton seemed almost eager for renewed military campaigning in the spring of 1864. Thoughts of his old flame, Mary Dodge, may have been repressed, but beneath it all there was an awareness of impending destiny. "You will probably hear of a large battle by this army soon," he confided on May 6, 1864. "If the Rebs [are] to whip us, they will have to improve on their fighting qualities more than I will allow to be possible, [for] we know by experience [their capabilities]," he sarcastically wisecracked.

The Rebels were found ensconced in the Georgia mountains near Dalton as the campaign against Atlanta opened in May 1864. Norton had reasoned: "I shall not be in half the danger on the corps staff that I was in at Stones River and Chickamauga, [when then] on the division staff." In fact, he predicted: "The coming summer will see the end of all heavy fighting of this war," and the "re-election of President Lincoln will kill the last efforts of the Rebel leaders. [For] the people know that he will never give up as long as a Rebel is in arms, and they well know that they cannot hold out for another four years."[12]

By May 20, following nearly a month's fighting, Major Norton was even more sanguine: "We have had a hard campaign thus far to be sure," he wrote home, "but it has been very pleasant nevertheless." The Rebels had become "frightened," he asserted, for "they had a very strong position and were well fortified [at Resaca, Georgia] but their hearts failed them, I suppose, and they ran again." In a country resplendent "in its summer dress"—beautiful wildflowers were in abundance—his thoughts turned to the sublime. In better times "this would be paradise itself," he reasoned. His mood seemed ebullient and almost whimsical. Gaily, he foresaw as a culmination of the present successful campaign a personal leave of absence to come home in June or July. "All I can say is that I expect to come home within the coming three months," he added. "Keep up a good heart."[13]

His prediction was all too true.

By mid-June his coffin arrived at his old Boston home in the custody of another of General Palmer's staff officers.

It had been a dreary, rainy morning on June 3, 1864. Palmer with several other 14th Corps generals and their staffs were scouting the Confederate lines in the vicinity of Pickett's Mill, Georgia. Unknowingly, as they sat on horseback in the rear of the picket lines of the 14th Ohio Infantry, they loomed large in the sights of Confederate riflemen who had crept forward unnoticed and waited patiently at close range for the appearance of a suitable target. Amid a sudden burst of gunfire, Norton went down, but Generals Absalom Baird and Palmer escaped by bolting with their horses to the rear before the Confederates could reload. How they survived was a mystery to all who had witnessed the ambush. "[They] would have been killed . . . had not Providence been merciful, and the Rebels less skillful in arms than they were discreet [in stealthily getting there]," wrote an Ohio colonel.[14]

Palmer's "so narrow an escape" was not shared by his senior aide. David Norton expired within minutes, never having realized that the bullet he took was meant for his commander. There was little to be said; a few stunned officers told of the sad event, one relating in his report that "it was on my [skirmish] line that the much lamented Maj. D. W. Norton was killed." Although Norton had once accused Palmer of being "much too careless of himself" in combat, he was the one who had suffered an "exposed" death, a virtual "sitting duck" for a nearby enemy rifleman.[15]

But the war went on. The grieving parents took little solace in the armies' rapid evacuation of the region where their son had died, or the

restoration of quietude to the beautiful country where Norton had rev-
eled in the flowers only a few days earlier. In the end there were only a
few grim relics of their dead son for them to savor: his last letter home
with a recent photo of a beaming David resplendent in his new major's
uniform, and two silver dollars found in his uniform pocket when shot.
These items seemed outrageous, a far too meager remembrance of one
so promising and so gallant. Flesh and blood had vanished, and in their
place there were only these mute curios.[16]

David W. Norton had died in one of many battles amid a never-
ending war. His profile in courage was high; yet his military glory was
rather typical, being very short-lived. Once the object of admiration and
even envy for his stunning courage, in the end Norton was but another
of the conflict's many faceless victims. The war prevailed; within a few
months his memory was confined to a few—mostly family and close
friends. Even John M. Palmer, the general who was his benefactor, virtually forgot him when, years later, he wrote his memoirs without any
mention of Norton.

The void that had been Norton's life when jilted by his intended
wife, Mary Dodge, had been fulfilled. There were no public funerals,
grieving masses, or even fretful constituents devastated by the loss of
one so brave and valuable. A soldier who aspired, Norton had found
only everlasting obscurity.

This message was well recognized by many soldiers who dared and
had survived, but now knew that the risk exceeded any reward. Captain
James A. Sexton, 72nd Illinois Infantry, after viewing in 1864 the
hideously mutilated dead in the earthworks ditch at Franklin, Tennessee, noted that it was one of the Civil War's most grotesque bloody
spectacles. Sexton was outraged, and wrote: "I feel like one who wit-
nesses a bitter wrong; a monstrous injustice. Call it glorious to die a horrible death, surrounded by an awful butchery, a scanty burial by . . .
[enemy] hands, and then total oblivion, name blotted out and forever
forgotten—where is the glory?"

Another soldier, Private James P. Campbell of Company D, 79th
Illinois Infantry, had similar intense thoughts after the scything his regiment had taken at Chickamauga. In bitter reflection he wrote:

I saw whole brigades cut to pieces at a single charge, and even divisions melted away like snow. Our regiment lost about half of our men. It will not take more than one such scratch [event] and the history of the 79th [Illinois] may be written in full for it will be [counted] with the things that were. And what of this history? The regt. may be remembered, but those that composed it will be forgotten before the flesh drops from their bones. Talk to a soldier about the glory of dying for his country (as some of our northern newspapers do) and he will point you to the ditches on the field of Chickamauga—and ask you what glory you can see in three or four hundred dead bodies piled in one narrow ditch. The fame of dying in battle is not prized very highly by a soldier. But talk to him of peace and of home, and you will animate his whole soul.[17]

It was just that stark. All the fighting and dying was reduced to a common understanding—that glory wasn't the answer; neither was the adventure or spirit of this endeavor. It was the prospect of a better future, of the mundane and uneventful—peace in a quiet time frame. "It is to save their country and get home to their family again that motivates the soldier to do his duty," reasoned Private Campbell.[18]

His thoughts speak volumes in perpetuity.

IV

THE FACE OF COURAGE

Frazar A. Stearns was twenty when the Civil War began. A junior at Amherst College, where his father was president, Frazar had determined to risk his life for his convictions. "If I knew I should fall [in battle] it would not change my determination [to do my duty]," he told a friend on enrolling in the 21st Massachusetts Infantry in 1861. Commissioned a first lieutenant and acting as adjutant, Stearns was possessed of an inner fire, a compelling need to accomplish. Yet he was burdened by dire thoughts of an impending personal ordeal and perhaps death in the army. Having already lost his mother and a girlfriend whom he had intended to marry, death was a visible and ever-present specter. Fatalistic yet religious in perspective, he coped with his fears by reassuring himself: "It is not such an awful thing to die, though to the flesh it seems hard. The end [purpose] of life is not to live, but to do what God wants us to do."[1]

In approaching his initial experience in combat, at Roanoke Island,

North Carolina, in February 1862, Lieutenant Stearns considered how he would react. "I hardly know whether I have courage or not. I cannot go into danger without excitement, though I never shrink from it. I once read of a soldier who, pale and trembling as he marched firmly on right up to the cannon's mouth, was pointed out to Napoleon for his timidity. 'Not so,' said the Emperor, 'he is a brave fellow; he both knows his danger and does his duty.' If anything like that is courage, I have it," concluded the youthful Stearns.[2]

On February 8 he was in the heat of combat, where during a frontal assault across a hundred yards of open ground "the bullets poured like rain." Lieutenant Stearns was in front, where the danger was greatest, and was wild with excitement. "We could see the enemy running [away]; I never in my life saw a sight so magnificent. I never was so thrilled." Then it happened. Stearns in rapid sequence was hit by two missiles. "I was hit twice," he later wrote, "first by a ball which passed within one-quarter inch of my spine, made a little furrow in my neck, and passed through my shirt, vest, coat, and overcoat. The other, a buckshot, entered my cap, passed through and hit me on the right forehead. A stunning sensation, a feeling of faintness, and I sank on the ground. Then I revived, and crawling a few steps I found I was all right, though blood was streaming down my face." Stearns jumped to his feet and continued on in the charge, contributing to the dramatic victory soon won by General Ambrose Burnside's troops.[3]

He had been most fortunate that day, he later realized. Combat was a frightening experience, and once the adrenaline subsided twenty-four hours later, he began to feel the pain of his wounds. The thought of what he had faced was sobering: "The bullets whistled all about me, . . . yet none hit me until the very last. [It was] as if God wished to show me how kind he was to me." Indeed, Stearns was shaken. "I cannot but hope God will grant that I return in safety home," he confided.[4]

Little more than thirty days later he would face a second trial in battle, at New Berne, North Carolina, and shortly before that event he wrote home to his father warning him: "Remember that at any hour or any moment may bring you news that I am killed or dangerously wounded. If either, then God's will be done; and I hope I may always be prepared." Undoubtedly, Stearns was frightened by the prospect of another hard battle. Yet he was resolute in the firm determination to do his duty. He had once admonished his sister when confronted by a difficult crisis: "Do just exactly what your conscience tells you is right. There is only one right and one wrong to anything, and you must decide for yourself, by the help of God."[5]

At the Battle of New Berne, North Carolina, on March 14, 1862, Adjutant Stearns was in the forefront of a charge across the railroad into the old brickyard. As he was yelling to his men to rush onward, a bullet from an Enfield rifle struck him on the left side, passed through his lungs, and exited his body below the collarbone on the right side. Stearns collapsed to the ground. A nearby corporal ran to his side. "Oh, God," Stearns groaned, then lapsed into unconsciousness.[6]

He lived about two and a half hours. Shortly before noon he died without a struggle, aged twenty-one years and eight months. Highly lauded by his comrades and commanders, Lieutenant Frazar A. Stearns never knew of the grief his death inflicted upon his family, or the pride his father took in writing of his courage in a memorial volume he privately published a few months later. His son's courage was not that of indifference to danger, but the courage of principle and will overcoming fear. He wrote: "A resolute soldier rather than a blindly daring one, he had expected death, but did not flinch." This was the full definition of courage, he added: "courage and a high sense of honor."[7]

Courage is frequently defined by familiar words, danger and fear are suppressed by a virtue—of doing what is brave and also right. While some might conceive that it is fearlessness in the face of danger, true courage is more the overcoming of adversity despite one's fears. Indeed, it is the practice of valor while being under and mindful of the threat of dire personal injury. The ability to perform and/or achieve in the face of disaster is a self-defining, if sometimes elusive, quality. Yet the cousins of courage are found to be recklessness and even stupidity. How we act and what we do in times of stress are crucial within one's mind. No matter the opinions of others, we individually best understand the implications of our words and actions. Either we are displeased with ourselves or self-congratulatory.

Usually, the risk and the reward are apparent at the time of our most critical decisions. We are taught to make our decisions objectively, basing them on logic and facts, or perhaps by overcoming the emotional aspects of a situation to reach a reasonable course of action. Yet in the heat of action, be it in deadly combat or sudden, intense situational stress, the ordinary mind is not so rational, so all-encompassing in sorting out the myriad factors. Our reactions, based upon instinct, life values, and a sense of duty or a job to be done, typically vary.

Recent studies have shown the mind of most of us to be more nearly numbed than inspired by the sudden, unexpected encounter with mortal danger. Many, when encountering an unfamiliar deadly circumstance, are overwhelmed by the processing of situation-related information. Our mind's reflex is often disbelief, then a reliance on reflex. When struck by a bullet, the body may feel at first only a stunning blow, but the mental process is quickly stress-reactive. An immediate awareness of what has happened often infuses mental shock; denial—"Is this really happening to me?"—is followed by "What do I do next?" Unless the individual has been mentally prepared or "stress oriented," the tendency is to "shift into low gear" in an attempt to process unfamiliar problem-solving criteria. Not knowing what to expect, stunned and bewildered, many rely on an animal instinct of involuntary paralysis in an attempt to survive. In the face of a predatory attack, many animals freeze, which is a survival mode, for some predators won't eat nonstruggling prey—stillness is evidence that something is wrong with the victim, sickness or an unwholesomeness that might harm the predator. The result of such paralysis is a slowing down of the reactive process, physical lethargy, and a mental evasiveness that dulls the awareness then needed. Perhaps 75 percent of the survivors of the attack on the World Trade Center Towers on September 11, 2001, were at first utterly bewildered.[8]

Crisis training or a mental rehearsal of pending misfortune often provides the best preparation for confronting death or dire injury. Yet the human mind is complex. Inculcated beforehand with the need for valor in confronting a deadly situation, the soldier's reaction to danger is often driven by a simple goal-based objective—the performance of an assigned task. While the prospect of people being under stress is endless, and dire ordeal is likely in the future, the role of courage in the past enables us to better understand some of mankind's most fundamental crisis behavior.

The essence of courage was examined by a pioneering study in the World War II era, *The Anatomy of Courage,* by Lord Moran, a combat-tested military doctor during both world wars. Lord Moran's premise was that a man's character defined his courage in the broadest sense, but no individual's reservoir of courage was limitless; self-control in the face of danger was expended, much as the spending of a person's capital. The consciousness of doing what was "right" was the controlling factor in a soldier's actions in war, not fear or courage, asserted Moran.[9]

The play upon one's mind of fear—and all normal men fear death or severe injury—encompasses a wide range of emotions and circumstances, all of which must be managed by personal discipline in the form of self-control, counseled Moran.

In ages past courage seemed to involve a different circumstance, relative ignorance, or an unfeeling lack of concern about danger. This state of mind derived from the masses' lack of education in the Old World, where expectations for the common man were for much travail and ordeal in the form of war and death. A relative lack of fear of death or injury seemingly resulted from the vacant mindlessness of not knowing any better. The so-called dolt or yokel was in essence the "cannon fodder" of yesteryear. The rank-and-file soldier's commonly witnessed fearlessness in battle was said to be rooted in this higher threshold of fear, whereby few were taught to reason about their dire circumstances.[10]

In a more modern era, the progressive thinking (hence concern about injury) of the common soldier was self-evident with the evolution in battle tactics. Teaching based on Napoleonic models said that soldiers marching to attack in line, shoulder to shoulder with others, derived and provided mutual support in the feeling of "togetherness" in coping with a common danger. The massed union of bodies moving together across a battlefield in a drill-practiced, disciplined maneuver would negate the primitive instincts of flight, reasoned the analysts. Knowing that the man next to you was undergoing (and surviving) the same dangerous circumstances, and feeling his physical presence there with you, was a powerful source of mental strength to steel the mind against fear.[11]

By the era of the American Civil War, the transition from a cannon-fodder mind-set to a discipline of persuasion and of leadership in firing men's souls with both willpower and reason was in vogue. To educated soldiers, leadership involved the ability to define, clarify, and achieve objectives based upon common sense and the intelligent commitment of manpower. It was not enough to say, "Do it"; it was more important to say, "For this reason we are going to do such, and here's how." Yet the old thinking died hard.

In many early Civil War encounters, commanders attempted to achieve victory by resorting to the tried and traditional methods of the past. Antietam had become a name synonymous with wholesale slaughter, a one-day combat that resulted in more than twenty-six thousand casualties—the war's bloodiest single day. This carnage was largely the result of stand-up–style combat tactics involving massed battle lines in linear formation making frontal charges across largely cleared ground. Said a wounded soldier of the 15th Massachusetts, a unit badly cut up in the West Woods fighting, "The Rebs fight like devils. . . . I tell you, war is not so funny as I thought it was before I came out here. I will be glad when I get out of this [situation]."

At the Battle of Fredericksburg in December 1862, the Union army under Major General Ambrose Burnside again attempted massive assaults in linear formation across mostly open ground in the face of major enemy forces whose center was protected behind a stone wall. The men who had fought at Antietam and other major slaughter grounds knew the dire prospects involved. But they were the survivors who still relied upon what they had been taught for countless hours on the drill ground. Battle-line discipline was used to fortify their mind-set of strength in numbers. The touch of the comrade's elbow, the collective confidence of togetherness, an electric current of being united in a common tactical effort with irresistible ardor and physical fellowship, were supposed to inspire steadiness.[12]

At Fredericksburg, however, all quickly went awry. In the words of one New York captain, "The way they pitched shot & shell at us was horrid. The air was filled with shrieking, bursting shells." Ordered to lie down to escape the slaughter, he saw the enemy run forward a section of artillery, which soon blasted the prone Federals with twenty to thirty rounds of canister. "It was like sowing bullets broadcast," noted the captain. "How any of our regiment escaped was miraculous." Trapped beneath the enemy's guns and compelled to wait out the fighting until the army withdrew after horrendous casualties (nearly thirteen thousand), Burnside's men were devastated. Once they reached safety the sickened Union captain wrote, "Words cannot express how intensely disgusted I am with this show. It is the damnedest humbug that ever was carried on."[13]

After helplessly watching his regiment virtually melt away under the merciless Rebel fire during their exposed assault up Marye's Heights, Private Emmet Irwin of the 82nd New York Infantry wrote that Antietam was but "child's play" compared to the naked helplessness he felt at Fredericksburg. Burnside's massed assault resulted, he said, in "a human slaughterhouse." He proclaimed it "one of the most foolhardy movements of the war," and as a result he wrote home saying that he might seek a discharge, for he didn't feel like fighting again "unless forced into it." "I feel as if I had gone through all these hardships and dangers, witnessed scenes too direful for the pen to tell, and all for what—naught!" Irwin wrote in despair. His estimate of "the incapacity" of the army's numerous commanders made him believe that he should follow the advice of a comrade's wife: be sick once in a while, especially at about the time there was to be another fight. This would be a good plan, he considered, "particularly if I thought we were to be led into another Fredericksburg affair."[14] Private Irwin wasn't alone in his mounting disrespect for traditional methods and inexpert commanders.

The frequent lack of innovative approaches to fighting had resulted in a shocking number of casualties in the manner of stand-up, compact-battle-formation fighting. Management of men on an unprecedentedly huge scale of combat involved learning the lessons of a new, relatively sophisticated manner of fighting. Simplistic approaches to combat led increasingly to failure; to inspire men to perform under fire, the commander had to understand their minds.

The natural fear of a man educated to know and envision the consequences of danger was paramount. Dealing with a reluctance to deliberately expose one's self to death or severe injury was crucial in achieving victory in battle.

The need for courage was obvious, but the primal level of courage (fearlessness) in soldiers was, as Lord Moran enumerated in his study, limited to a very few. Moreover, there was a limit to what could be expected of the ordinary soldier, concluded many combat veterans as the Civil War progressed. Their ability and willingness to do their duty under fire, regardless of their fear, were fundamental to selecting viable battle objectives. Thus, sagacious management of combat exposure, inspired reasoning in the inducement to battle, and preparedness in what to expect were essential to the well-being of the men and their cause. Respect for any man who braved the dangers of the battlefield was inherent, but how the combatants were asked to fight was critical.

Robert Nevill, a private in Company E, 103rd Ohio Volunteer Infantry, was somewhat surprised to hear from his wife, Mary, at the beginning of the Atlanta Campaign in 1864, that she despised cowardice and accordingly admonished him to act with the utmost courage. "Courage! What a word that is," he replied in a letter home. "I am really glad that you, my dear, see fit to exhort me in every letter [you send] to play the part of a courageous man; 'Husband, [act] just as though your honor, your happiness, and future life of our darling [child] was at stake.' So it does [is], my dear. And honor, and a thanks to you, my dear wife, for that bugle note, 'courage.' Trusting in God, I'll try to be [such]."

Yet, Nevill was not a fool, or reckless in his combat behavior. He had seen enough killing in frontal infantry assaults, including one he participated in at Resaca, to know that charging fully exposed across open ground was "terrible work." The way to beat the Rebels, he knew, was "to out general them," which should collectively be "our duty." Aware that the corpse-strewn battlefields he had experienced and gawked at in astonishment were missing his own badly mangled body only by the grace of God, he was mindful that the next time he might not be so lucky. As many "feel so overjoyed at the idea of piling up a thousand Rebels in a heap, for my part I don't wish them all that loss of able sons," Nevill wrote. In reasoned perspective he continued, "I don't feel like exulting over the awful slaughtering of our foes, . . . [even though] they must suffer the consequences [of not giving up the fight]." Nevill had learned from his experiences in the fight at Resaca that no man,

Yankee or Rebel, should have to endure the special hell of "killing one another" while openly exposed in a cleared-field frontal charge. His own "naked" vulnerability, as well as that of others, was fully apparent.[15]

Nevill's views were significant. A soldier had a profound need to cope in his mind with personal extermination, or perhaps with a horrendous, pain-laced wound that would incapacitate a man for life. The horribly mangled corpses and wounded littering the battlefield were a severe negative stimulus. Thus it was important to feel that one's exposure would not be unwisely or unnecessarily mandated by officers in command. Fighting well meant fighting wisely. It reinforced the all-important will to fight with courage in the physical effort. That courage was a virtue—a discipline involving moral values whereby self-control would dominate the instinct for self-preservation and personal safety—was foremost in view.

V
—————

TWO WARS IN CONCEPT

Facing the prospect of death on the battlefield involved a dire and stressful uncertainty, but at least amid all the worry there was the rampant hope of one's survival. Prevalent in this ongoing mind game was usually a positive—or negative—outlook. Soldiers with less experience of being under fire generally had more concern.

Prior to combat, a soldier's mind usually was laced with apprehension, the consequence of a natural awareness of one's vulnerability and mortality. Fear of the unknown was perhaps the greatest worry for many soldiers. Once battle's stern array was encountered, however, the mental perspective seemed radically altered. Indeed, when in combat, reflected a soldier, there was no time to think of anything but the task at hand. The physical activity of deployment, maneuver, and performing duties such as loading and shooting usually absorbed one's immediate thoughts and produced a lack of "real-time awareness." In fact, enduring combat was to many an unexplainable, rapid-paced experience, likened by some to groping through a fog. Essentially stress-driven, it loomed as an intuitive, cope-as-best-you-can ordeal. For some, trust in God, superstition, or just plain luck seemed to provide the best hope for survival.[1]

The common soldier of the 1860s was far better educated than his predecessors. He knew more about his surroundings and the complexities of life, and his increased skills were fostered by a sharp rise in inventiveness, communication, and self-awareness. Moreover, he was stimulated by a deep hunger for knowledge, enhanced meaning in life, and even adventure.

Before it was experienced, combat often seemed compelling if dangerous. "Seeing the elephant" was a popular expression of the time, meaning enduring combat. The term had derived from the traveling circus; at each new town it visited, local boys would be hired to water the awesome and often mean-tempered elephants. There seemed to be a compelling spirit of adventure and fascination with "the creature," but when in close proximity to those trampling feet and probing trunks, said one experienced water boy, "you won't like it a damn bit."[2]

Few truly enjoyed combat; the terrors were too grim, and the immediacy of danger was too contrary to the desire for survival. War's visage was perhaps grand to behold, but when it came to personal exposure, the awareness of one's mortality was usually self-effacing. A nameless grave in the dirt of some godforsaken field, flesh rotting away, and one's existence completely obliterated; it was a hard fate to ponder. No matter what the circumstances, good or bad, the result was grotesque. What enduring honor was there in an ignominious death and a hasty burial, a fleeting death notice to the family, then one's name all but vanished and soon forgotten forever?[3]

Displaying personal courage required overcoming much. Just thinking about the dire consequences of death or severe injury promoted caution, not risk taking. Yet the repeated exposure to war's horrid scenes generally inured many to the stark and paralyzing emotions of otherwise repulsive battle carnage. The psychological mechanism required to sustain one's mental well-being generated an ability to put into perspective the gruesome scenes and awful emotions.

Within the awareness of what was reality—even if one's demise was perhaps in the offing—the rational mind tended to generate receptors for survival. The rationale for enduring danger was usually steeped in a "current status" perspective. If another soldier or friend was dead, it was him, not you. Your existence was the reality, and hope for such continued. While intending to avoid to the extent possible the circumstances that led to the other's demise, there was a basic belief in self-survival. The random chance of death or injury was just that—a happenstance that was beyond full explanation. A trust in God's protection might serve as a mental shield, but few were so convinced of divine intercession as to recklessly expose their bodies during combat. What was practical within the evolving code of accepted battlefield behavior usually served as a guiding premise for personal conduct. As the war continued, that which was considered proper behavior generally became more conservative. Taking one's chances did not involve foolish bravery. The need to display extreme courage was assessed personally and practically, as determined by varying circumstances.

While many displayed uncommon valor on the battlefield, this was often counterbalanced by those who didn't. There was a practical explanation for much of this. War was then so deadly, owing to technological innovations following from the Industrial Revolution, that what was once routine battlefield exposure was now virtually suicidal. The stand-up-in-ranks, shoulder-to-shoulder, in-the-open method of confronting an enemy was severely outmoded. Tactics that had been practiced with success as late as the Mexican War of 1846–48 were suddenly impractical and highly dangerous. The great killing fields of the Civil War in 1862 not only shocked the nation but produced a glaring paradigm shift in attitudes. The risks one might take and expect to survive altered both tactics and the conception of courage. What once had been regarded as manly courage was now considered reckless, foolish behavior. In the Civil War the widespread use of the rifle-musket, firing a more accurate,

higher-velocity minié ball,* improved artillery projectiles, and even re-
peating rifles had ensured that a deadly "fire zone" would be faced at extended ranges during the often-utilized frontal assaults.[4]

The human-cannon-fodder concept of shock tactics, of columns attacking en masse to breach a critical point, had ultimately been proved
to be not only extremely bloody but largely ineffectual.[†] The attacking
lines could not often get to within close range of the defensive positions
without incurring devastating and unacceptable casualties. Soldiers were
demoralized by the failed assaults, and lost confidence. In turn, the lack
of confidence often resulted in future lackluster performance due to a
conservation or modification of personal effort.

At the heart of the matter was the changed battlefield, not a fundamental absence of courage or discipline. If a man was to risk his life in
battle, the circumstances had to allow for at least a fair prospect of survival. Since efficacy in action was the basis for an individual's effort,
tactics were the key element—not only in winning in combat, but in
mentally sustaining the soldier as an effective fighting instrument. No
matter what the generals proposed, combat veterans knew through their
own experience what was or wasn't viable on the battlefield. Getting the
soldier intact to the place where he could effectively fight the enemy was
the primary requisite. It was an unwritten but essential understanding of
what was needed to be able to accomplish the soldier's task of winning
battles. If simple in expression, it was complex in the accomplishment.

---

* This bullet was comparatively new 1850s technology, adopted in 1855 by the U.S. Army,
but originally devised by Captains Claude-Etienne Minié and Henri-Gustave Delvigne of the
French army. Rather than a round ball, it used a cylindro-conoidal-shaped lead bullet with a
large hollowed base to provide for expansion into the rifling grooves upon firing. This pre-
vented the propelling gas from escaping around the circumference of the projectile, increasing
velocity and adding to the accuracy by forcing the relatively soft lead bullet's base into the rifling grooves. The result was a tight, straight spin.
† There are a few analysts who assert that shock tactics were not outmoded in the American
Civil War, and that the rifle-musket did not revolutionize tactics (because of the alleged short
range and long duration of many firefights). See Paddy Griffith, *Battle Tactics of the Civil War*
(1987). As in any perspective, this is much a matter of interpretation of evidence and judgment. "Close-range" combat in 1864–65 seems not to be due to a lack of weapon effective-
ness, but rather a resort to altered tactics (especially in timbered terrain) so as to deal with the
deadly new efficacy in firepower—such as going prone behind natural ground cover and fighting further "protected" by quickly improvising breastworks whenever possible.

Too many decision makers lacked the perspective, know-how, and ability to achieve effective troop dispositions and exert a maximum impact on the battlefield. Fundamentally, common sense mattered the most. Doing the smart thing in combat meant understanding "the animal"—what worked, and what didn't.[5]

THE LESSONS APPLIED

Perhaps a wiser if bedeviled veteran officer, one of General William T. Sherman's men, said it best in June 1864: fighting this damned war wasn't anything like it used to be. "At the outset of the war, a man who would get behind a log or stone was jeered at by his fellow [soldiers]," wrote Major Robert P. Findley of the 74th Ohio Infantry. "And the officer who would have stood behind a tree on the skirmish line, cut off his [shoulder] straps to avoid being a target for sharpshooters, and not have exposed his person by standing upright and in exposed positions, would have been stigmatized as a coward. But now, of the officer or soldier who won't take these precautions, if killed or wounded, the expressions of the soldiers are, 'I don't pity him, he had no business exposing himself unnecessarily.'"[6]

Findley had learned the essence of Civil War combat. Common sense and good judgment were the vital means of survival. "It is the duty of an officer to take every precaution to preserve his own life and that of his men, consistent with the performance of his duty," continued Findley with the conviction of a long-suffering veteran, "and if an officer will expose himself unnecessarily, he cannot consistently require care on the part of his men."[7]

They didn't teach such practical wisdom at West Point. It was a battlefield reality, learned by bitter experience—at least by those daily exposed to the more accurately fired bullets and shells. On the other hand, there were those who remained committed to old ideals and traditional thinking. "Some yet have the idea that it will gain them a reputation for bravery," acknowledged Findley, "and expose themselves accordingly." Unfortunately for thousands of soldiers both North and South, that conviction remained prevalent among far too many senior officers—especially those not usually required to brave the dangers of the altered, more modern battlefield.[8]

The American Civil War was really two wars within one in the manner it was fought. During the initial years the tried-and-true tactics of prior wars, including Napoleonic "linear" concepts, were often used. This was usually in strong contrast to the methods (and results) of the last two war years.

Yet if the soldiers were quick to learn the practicalities of tactical combat involving new, sophisticated weaponry and improved defensive means, their leaders were too often influenced by other objectives: the chance for promotion, notoriety, or glory, and sometimes even an end to stalemate or tedium. The controversy and conflict in purpose and means transcended the broad sweep of battle. It provided an ongoing question that often affected the high drama of the 1864 Civil War battlefield. How would each person respond to "foolish" or unreasoned orders, such as to make an unsupported attack against a fortified enemy position obstructed with nearly impenetrable defensive barriers? Thus combat had become a matter of the mind as much as that of rote discipline and physical courage.

Therein lay the essential story. Too many had died foolishly or in vain on the battlefield. Did one have to prove blind obedience to one's commanders, and be shot or die without recourse; or was there a better way? Privates allegedly weren't supposed to think as officers did. Even if not technically "educated," who knew best on the modern battlefield? In fact, those who had the most to lose—their lives—proved to be keen observers of the new reality. Their battlefield education was founded on a practical experience that few if any military textbooks taught.

The controversy thus accentuated the focal issue of what was proper—blind obedience or reasoned reassessment—in a new era of far greater battlefield danger. The consequences, both personal and practical, had been intensified by the advent of a highly effective "killing technology." This was the new reality. Too often, coping with these altered circumstances involved the use of only traditional, textbook methods by the commanders. What was well perceived by the soldiers who were to do the fighting—the need for innovative thinking, such as loose-order battle formations—was frequently relegated to a secondary consideration by the generals. If the wisdom of tactical expertise was evident to the soldiers, it often seemed that their commanders were slow to recognize the demand for informed or "smart" orders on the battlefield. Belatedly, William Tecumseh Sherman privately admitted after various futile efforts that he had learned that his soldiers would not attack strong breastworks. "Our men will charge the parapet without fear," wrote Sherman in September 1864, "but they cannot the abatis and entanglements, which catch them at close range."[9]

Within these few words lay a bitter chronicle: the hard lessons and issues of the 1864-style fighting as a reflection of the broad change in warfare from even a year earlier. Sherman's comment encapsulated key elements of the new era of warfare. In the Atlanta Campaign, Sherman's men, and also Johnston's and Hood's, fought, bled, and died as few others had prior to 1864. That year's battlefield was the culmination of two years' prior combat; of new thinking, of new methods, and of a new "horrific" destruction. Initially the horror belied the means. Yet soon the war's methodology was in focus. It was the way of the future, created by a sudden, unheralded swath of bloodletting. To survive was to adapt.

Through it all, one central question remained: Could the mind match the ongoing technical evolution—at least among those who counted the most, the decision makers? It made for a fundamental challenge amid the high drama of some of the war's most decisive combat. If our life is at stake, we are taught, we should do our best to survive. Some of our forefathers appear to have reasoned differently, minimizing the heavy risks involved while emphasizing the potential gain. Others were more mindful of human value. Their stories exemplify how both brilliantly extraordinary and rather ordinary Americans coped.

VI

ORDEAL AT ATLANTA

Lieutenant Colonel Frank S. Curtiss, noted Sergeant Andrew McCornack of Company I, 127th Illinois Volunteer Infantry, was in a tight spot. Having refused to make an isolated attack across the open field near Atlanta on August 3, 1864, with his small regiment, "saying that he would not take his boys in to get them all killed, [that] he would rather be arrested than have his boys all killed," McCornack observed that big trouble was now brewing. A surly General Joseph Andrew Jackson Lightburn, promoted to division commander from brigade command on August 5, wanted Curtiss peremptorily dismissed from the service. His disobedience of orders was flagrant and his cowardice extreme, according to Lightburn. Indeed, the angry brigadier saw to it that the matter was given prompt attention. Within a few days the matter was resolved at corps and army headquarters. General Field Orders No. 8, August 6, 1864, announced the verdict. "For disobedience of orders and misbehavior before the enemy on the 3rd day of August 1864, Lieut. Col. Frank S. Curtiss, 127th Regt. Ill. Infy. Vols. is hereby dismissed the service of the United States subject to the approval of the President." The order was issued by Major General Oliver O. Howard, the new commander of the Army of the Tennessee and the man who had ordered Lightburn to advance his troops. It hadn't helped that Howard had been present at the time of the incident and witnessed the unwillingness of Curtiss to get his picket lines forward, as Lightburn had directed. Curtiss was made to look bad, especially when a separate special skirmisher force had succeeded in advancing their lines on the division's left flank. Thus it was apparent somebody would pay the price for this ugly circumstance.[1]

It was a fascinating controversy. Had Frank Curtiss refused to advance on the basis of cowardice? Or had he acted with strong moral courage—as an experienced combat commander he knew the hopeless nature of the attempted assault, and valued the lives of his men more than his own career?

In the 127th Illinois there was little debate. "The boys are all very sorry [for Frank Curtiss]," said Sergeant McCornack, who had well established his own reputation for bravery, winning the Medal of Honor for the "Forlorn Assault" at Vicksburg, May 22, 1863. "[The men] say all the duty they [will] get out of them [now] will be small. He was like a father to his boys, and a braver man never trod American soil. It's a pity, but [it] can't be helped now. [I] hope old Lightburn will see the day he will be sorry for it."[2]

Frank S. Curtiss was a veteran officer with much combat exposure, and as might be expected, he didn't go down without a fight. On August 8, two days after the dismissal order, he wrote a letter to General Howard, seeking a formal investigation into the matter and offering his version of the August 3 events.

According to Curtiss, that day he did not technically disobey orders, nor commit any misbehavior before the enemy. Discretion was given to him personally by General Howard, said Curtiss, and he had been told "he need not advance" due to the critical circumstances Curtiss had outlined. Later, when a staff officer of the corps commander

(General John A. "Black Jack" Logan) insisted he attack, Curtiss again discussed the matter with his brigade commander, Colonel James S. Martin. Martin said the orders were peremptory—but that Curtiss would be supported on his flank by the 55th Illinois Infantry. When that regiment failed to advance, said Curtiss, it was madness to attempt to attack with his regiment, which had by this time been reduced to twenty men, since his five companies on the right had withdrawn back to camp when replaced by skirmishers from another corps (without his prior knowledge).[3]

Curtiss was basing his hopes on a technicality, that Howard, as commander of the army, had verbally given him discretion that outweighed any of his subordinate commanders' insistence. Also, because of the noncompliance by another unit, his attack orders were invalid. The question was thus larger than that of disobedience; did an experienced combat officer have a right to override a superior's direct orders based upon the "good of the service"—avoiding unnecessary bloodshed for what appeared to be no practical or viable purpose?[4]

It was thus a moral dilemma as well as a question of compliance with the oath of military law. Doing the right thing in the ultimate sense was in essence predicated on what proved to be proper based upon subsequent events and knowledge. Obeying direct orders was simple: do what you are told by a superior commanding officer. Yet Frank Curtiss was a battle-wise, intelligent, reasoning man, mindful of his responsibilities as a commander to do what was possible and to protect the lives of his men. Was it possible to comply with the dictates of one's conscience and still obey orders in this circumstance?

Tom Taylor thought so. The major of the 47th Ohio Volunteer Infantry was in virtually the same situation as Curtiss on that sultry August 3 at Atlanta. Major Taylor commanded a select force of skirmishers assembled for the same purpose of attacking the enemy-held line on Curtiss's left flank. The equally experienced Taylor had fought with skill and bravery from Vicksburg to Atlanta and, like Curtiss, contemplated the severely distressing orders to attack with minimal troops a formidable enemy line defended by infantry and artillery. Obviously, it was not only a heavy risk, but a bitter order to obey—one that would cost many lives. Yet Taylor's reaction and reasoning were explained fully in a letter to his wife a few days after the events of August 3.

Wednesday morning [August 3, 1864] our skirmish line advanced and drove the enemy from their skirmish pits. About an hour afterward the enemy charged the line & retook the pits. At noon a staff officer came up and informed me that I would have my regiment ready to move at 2 P.M. and retake the pits. I protested against taking the regiment up, and went and saw the brigade and division commanders. I knew the reception we would get and told them that the regiment was already small and instead of running it alone into the jaws of death, I preferred a detail from the brigade so that the loss would be equalized. I told them that I would go wherever directed, regardless . . . but if I could avoid it, my men should not [have to face impossible odds]. The regiment was [then] excused, and a detail made of thirty-two, or three, companies. I was instructed as to the signals—three shots in rapid succession from [Captain Henry H.] Griffith's 4th Division battery. The 4th Division [General William Harrow's] on the left were to cooperate. I had charge of [the men of] our brigade [Lightburn's], & Lt. Col. [Frank S.] Curtiss of the 1st Brigade [James S. Martin's, on the right]. The hour set was three.

I had my lines arranged—the assaulting line; the first support and fortifying line, the 2nd, 3rd, 4th, and 5th supporting lines, and a line in the old pits to halt stragglers from the front. I passed down the lines & gave the instructions & showed them the ground and the best way to advance and told them the signal, and then made them lie down. But could I be still? Could I lie down? No! The anxiety of my mind was so intense that I could not rest, but step after step, and pace after pace, wore away the minutes. And I was listening for the signal when I got word that it [the attack] had been postponed one hour. Another hour of painful suspense, made more disagreeable by a severe thunderstorm, dragged slowly by. Presently the quick boom! boom! boom! burst upon our ears, and instantly the loud "forward, double quick, march!" resounded through the wood, and that line of brave men dashed forward and hurled themselves upon the enemy, who made a stubborn stand. . . .

Seeing the first line falter a little, the second moved [up] with tools, and these [two lines] combined broke the [skirmish] line of Rebels, and our men went rushing down in their rear. They [the Confederates] attempted to rally, and away went my third line. This completed the rout, and we captured most of them in our front. Word [then] came to me that the First Brigade [Curtiss] had not advanced, and [that] my right would not go forward on account of a furious cross fire. Away I went, exhorting, driving, pulling, and pushing, shaming them, etc. until I took them clear up and over the point of a hill. Men groaned with fear, some supplicated, begged, etc., but the officers helped finely, and I brought them up, but the 1st Brigade did not advance, and I had not enough men to drive the Rebels from their front. I then massed three or four companies and endeavored to take their [skirmish] line and charge them by the flank, but on each flank we had a hollow to cross and a hill to ascend. These I found by actual experiment to be perfectly raked by the [Rebel] batteries and the enemy line of skirmishers and reserve[s] on the right of our brigade. I tried and tried again, but it was killing men in vain, and I sent a report up stating what I had done, and what I could not do. I then received an order to fortify, but I had already laid out my line and had very good works up.

I passed over the whole line and examined its strength and capacity for resistance. I went back [and] sent up the other two lines of reserves, and constructed my works so that both reserve and main [lines] could fire at once. Anon the enemy came in very heavy skirmish lines almost amounting to a line of battle, and three lines deep. As they always do, they came bravely and handsomely up, but oh! such a withering fire as greeted them. On my left was the 4th Division, with a skirmish line supported by 900 men. The whole commanded by Major [William] Brown of the 70th Ohio V. I. In the beginning of the war this would have been called a big battle.

Poor Brown—gallant officer and most excellent gentleman—fell mortally wounded. The first enemy line broke and moved off [to] the right flank. The second came up, and [then] a third, but how nobly our boys stood up to the work, and repelled them. Then I had three loud, defiant cheers given, and each man felt glad. Again I passed along the lines, made details for work, instructed officers, and encouraged men. I was almost everywhere. I was so anxious— the point taken is of great importance and I was determined to hold it. When I got it safe and saw the assaults of the Rebels repulsed, I went up to report [to General Morgan L. Smith] in person [and] was warmly greeted, thanked, etc. Logan told me yesterday that if that other brigade [Curtiss's men] had advanced our success would have been complete. Before I thought, I spoke and said yes, and [that] I thought they could have moved in the wood on their right, broke the [enemy] line by a charge, and then swept down in the rear of it. He said, "yes, yes, if I had a regiment I would have done it." Morgan L. [Smith] was not pleased with them [Curtiss and his men] and said he ought to place all [the 1st Brigade's] senior [officers] under arrest and place Col. [Wells S.] Jones in command of one brigade, and Major Taylor in command of the other, and then they would have [good] brigades. If I had the rank, I would not be an hour without a brigade [command]. My reputation is too good, and I am afraid for it.[5]

Tom Taylor had proven a point. By personal bravery and determination in the face of seemingly insurmountable odds he had succeeded when others drew back. His courage and valor were outstanding, and his accomplishment remarkable.

Ultimately, however, his sortie achieved little. Although the Union skirmish line moved forward a few hundred yards, the main lines remained relatively stable in the zone for three more weeks as the prolonged siege of Atlanta continued. Moreover, the intense if limited fighting over these skirmish lines had cost the Union ninety-five casualties, including two prominent officers killed. The immediate consequence of the 1st Brigade's failure to advance was an immediate shake-up in command;

beyond Curtiss's dismissal, on August 4, brigade commander Colonel James S. Martin was transferred to another brigade (where he commanded only a regiment), and replaced with Colonel Theodore Jones, who assumed brigade command.[6]

So who was right: Taylor for his physical courage in making the effort and proving the attack could be successful even if at a heavy price, or Curtiss for his moral courage in saving the lives of his men when the odds were seemingly impossible and the advantage to be gained minimal?

Not everyone agreed then, nor would it be likely to find a consensus of opinion today. How we view the decisions of others relates to our own conscience and experience.

Frank Curtiss had a difficult circumstance to confront in attempting to rescue his army career and official reputation. Both Lightburn, who assumed division command on August 5 from Morgan L. Smith, and Major General William B. Hazen, among the senior officers, were most adamant in insisting on Curtiss's dismissal. The case reached the adjutant general's office in Washington, D.C., in mid-August, and following a routine review, orders were published confirming the dismissal, "by direction of the President."

Yet this was before receipt of Curtiss's petition, which resulted in reconsideration of the case. On September 29, 1864, it was apparent that Frank Curtiss had been summarily dismissed without due process; by order of the president he was immediately reinstated, pending his trial by a general court-martial, should that "be deemed advisable." The attitude of the army's hierarchy remained negative, however. Major General Howard had unfavorably endorsed Curtiss's petition on August 10; Howard said that he (Curtiss) had stayed away from his regiment "quite a long time" and "seemed to me rather disposed to talk rather than act," and the skirmish line had not gone forward in his sector "as directed." Whether this was "from incompetentcy [sic] or willful disobedience of orders, I could not then determine," wrote Howard, who seemed to remember neither his conversation with Curtiss nor allowing him discretion in the matter. An investigation would be proper, added Howard, except that the pressing demands of the Atlanta Campaign required the entire attention of the officers involved.

By the time the paperwork was returned to Howard for action, it was late October. Howard directed that the 15th Army Corps convene a court-martial and try Curtiss, but circumstances led to further delay. A special board of officers was convened to investigate the case and report its recommendation. Since Lightburn was out of the division, having been incapacitated when struck in the head by a spent bullet on August 24 and reassigned to duty in West Virginia following his recovery, there were few officers present in late 1864 who felt compelled to pursue the case.

The findings of the board were "that there are no grounds for charges against this officer." Thus the matter was put to rest on April 1, 1865. Curtiss was formally restored to command of the 127th Illinois Infantry, and resumed command in time for the final war operations and the Grand Review of the Army in Washington, D.C. He was welcomed back by his regiment with open arms. Noted Sergeant Eugene A. "Casey" McWayne of Company E, "He was dismissed [from] the service illegally. All Gen. Hazen, who now commands our division, wanted of Curt [i.e., told him upon resuming his command] was that he should be as good an officer now as he was under Morgan L. and Giles A. Smith. So you can see how things are working in the army. This Gen. Lightburn that was then commanding the division had some spite against Curt."[7]

Courage, be it moral or physical, eventually seemed to find its own level in an individual's perception.

V_{II}

PAT CLEBURNE, A MAN
WHO UNDERSTOOD

As a profile in tactical wisdom there are few more graphic than the remarkable case of Patrick Cleburne, perhaps the Southern armies' best tactician. When analyzed as a matter involving the courage of his convictions, it provides an extraordinary insight into battlefield efficacy in action and mind.

Pat Cleburne was a most unlikely candidate for supremacy in combat management. Although originally Irish, Corporal Cleburne was an enlisted man in the British army, 1846–49, and had purchased his discharge and immigrated to the United States with members of his family in December 1849. Settling at Helena, Arkansas, he had become by 1861 a lawyer and a distinguished member of the community, a self-made man who remembered well the lessons from the British army. When war clouds appeared in 1861, Cleburne, who was captain of the local militia company, the Yell Rifles, relied on his previous military experience to fashion his men into a combat-ready unit. Cleburne had not only learned the mechanics of one of the nineteenth-century world's great military organizations but, even more important, had come to understand the perspectives and needs of the common soldier.

Pat Cleburne evaluated his personal experiences. His eyes informed him, but his mind analyzed what to do based upon calculated logic. His high intelligence and logical mind helped in determining what needed to be done to make a soldier both effective and content. This keen awareness later translated into using common sense and logic, rather than regulations, as guides. Cleburne sought to adapt to the myriad conditions he encountered. Flexibility, not rigid adherence to doctrine, was a natural consequence of his reasoning.[1]

Cleburne's spirit of independent thinking, combined with common sense, duty, honor, and ability, produced a remarkable leader. Yet greatness was not his birthright. His quiet, modest nature masked his enormous determination to succeed and his intense commitment to excellence. The driving will to accomplish was measured in Cleburne's mind by the practical results obtained. Overcoming adversity was a hallmark of his career, from learning to ride Thoroughbred horses to obtaining a law degree through part-time study. Before the war he had learned one of life's great lessons: The true enemy is fear itself. To conquer one's self-doubt is perhaps the greatest victory of all in life.[2]

Cleburne's previous military experience and civilian prominence ensured that he would have a chance to excel as a leader of men. Elected as the original colonel of what was to become the 15th Arkansas Infantry, Cleburne was soon on the fast track to military prominence. Placed in command of a brigade at Bowling Green, Kentucky, in the fall of 1861, he was by March 1862 a Confederate brigadier general. What lay behind his rise to prominence was hard work, determination, competence, and an energy unimagined by many. An astounded observer, Basil Duke, noted in 1862 how Cleburne was personally occupied "from morning until night superintending squad, company, and battalion drill." "I have seen him in the hottest days of August instruct squad after squad in the bayonet exercise until I wondered how any human frame could endure the fatigue that this exercise must have induced," he remarked. Tired or

not, Pat Cleburne took "great interest in everything connected with tactics, and personally taught it all," said Duke. This enormous effort, plus a
wisdom in methods, quickly paid off for the inspired Cleburne. He demanded much of those who served under him, but always asked more of
himself. His continual teaching imparted not only knowledge, but discipline and self-confidence. The result was the best-drilled regiment in
General Albert Sidney Johnston's Kentucky army. As a reward for its
proficiency, Cleburne's brigade was issued newly imported Enfield rifles,
then in small supply.[3]

Cleburne's intense preparation and effort proved to have a big effect
in his unit's first major combat—at Shiloh on the fateful days of April 6
and 7, 1862. Ordered to attack William Tecumseh Sherman's outlying
camps through a large swamp, his brigade, though split apart, made repeated attacks with dogged persistence. Badly bloodied by severe incoming fire and hampered by the marshy terrain, Cleburne's soldiers fought
tenaciously until Sherman's lines finally gave way. After pursuing the
routed Federals and confronting another enemy division, Cleburne's men
moved to within four hundred yards of Pittsburg Landing that evening
before being recalled by General P. G. T. Beauregard's orders. Then, on
April 7, Cleburne's brigade was compelled by the stubborn insistence of
General Braxton Bragg to make repeated charges across open ground.
When the fighting was over that evening, Cleburne's brigade had lost
1,013 men from its prebattle strength of 2,700, a 37.5 percent casualty
rate. This was the highest loss of any brigade in the Confederate army,
and Cleburne was highly praised by his commander, Major General
William J. Hardee, and others for valor and conspicuous gallantry.

Yet what mattered the most to Cleburne was his severe losses, the
lessons of the battlefield, and improving the prospect of winning the
next fight. Shiloh was "a battle gallantly won and as stupidly lost," reflected Cleburne in considering the senseless piecemeal frontal assaults
against the Hornets' Nest and other positions. Pat Cleburne's discerning
mind had identified critical aspects of combat that needed changing if
the Southern soldier was to prevail in what was obviously a radically
new era in fighting. Having early lost control over batteries of artillery
that were redirected elsewhere by the artillery staff, Cleburne sought to

clear lines of authority so that he would never suffer for want of artillery support because of split command responsibilities. The Irish general had also learned the value of personal reconnaissance of the ground to be fought over. Never would he allow his units to be committed to attack without prior knowledge of the topography they were facing. As was apparent to Cleburne, tactics, not grand strategy, meant the most in winning a battle among roughly equal combatants. If you were going to beat the other fellow in battle, you must fight smarter. More intelligent management of the battlefield translated into refined tactics.[4]

This supreme tactical awareness became a guiding principle of Pat Cleburne's combat success. The terrible price paid by his men at Shiloh was a lesson well learned. Thereafter he would seek to utilize common sense and higher intelligence rather than traditional methods. Trained soldiers were too precious as military assets to carelessly throw away their lives on the battlefield. Everything needed to be done to protect them and reduce their exposure within the framework of the mission to be accomplished. Conversely, the enemy must be made to pay the highest price possible once Southern troops were committed to the fray. In order to achieve this, Pat Cleburne devised several brilliant tactical innovations based upon his personal perceptions. A company of select sharpshooters was organized to pick off enemy leaders and, especially, Yankee cannoneers. He foresaw that this would both create confusion and interfere with sustained artillery fire, which often was the most damaging to attackers.[5]

However, identifying and utilizing the best shots among his men wasn't enough for Cleburne. Going beyond the ordinary, he solicited and obtained some of the very finest technology in small-arms weaponry, the deadly accurate Kerr and Whitworth sniper rifles. They were so costly and difficult to obtain that in 1862 only about a dozen were in the entire Confederate army. These rifles were deadly killers in skilled hands at ranges of up to a thousand yards.

Moreover, Cleburne carefully refined his ideas of how to successfully attack a large or imposing enemy battle line. He knew that piecemeal assaults involving isolated attacking units were typically unproductive and unwise. Yet he foresaw that senior commanders schooled in the theories of Dennis Hart Mahan and Antoine-Henri de Jomini (Napoleonic-era tacticians of linear assault) would continue to utilize the tactical offensive in Southern battle plans. Thus he boldly addressed the problem of getting his men into the best position to win a fight without first taking heavy losses.[6]

Because of improved weapons technology, a factor far too many Southern generals ignored, the situation on the battlefield had vastly changed since the Mexican War. The new minié ball–firing rifle-musket, being more accurate, powerful, and effective at extended ranges, had made an enormous difference in fighting battles. The old West Point–taught reliance on the tactical offensive—massing columns of troops against a single targeted point and overwhelming it with a heavy column—had been shown to be impractical in Civil War combat.[7]

The basic problem was that attacking columns couldn't get within effective striking distance without losing too many troops. Heavy casualties suffered by an attacking column usually resulted in either a premature withdrawal, or insufficient strength for a lasting penetration once the enemy line was breached. Disorganization due to wooded terrain, poor unit-to-unit communications, and (as the war evolved) the likelihood of facing a fortified enemy line made successfully executing a large-scale assault even more difficult. Yet Cleburne repeatedly coped with these dire circumstances and was largely successful in attack after attack. The reason for this related to his innovative common sense.

During the Perryville, Kentucky, fighting of October 8, 1862, Pat Cleburne led a successful charge with his brigade against a seemingly impregnable enemy position. The enemy was entrenched behind a breast-high rock wall atop a ridge and was supported by numerous batteries. A direct attack against this same position by another brigade, Bushrod Johnson's, had just failed, with heavy loss of life. Yet Cleburne was ordered to face the same bleak odds and make the same attack with fewer men. Pat Cleburne responded with his characteristic battlefield ingenuity. By first sending the 15th Arkansas regiment to creep forward along a stone wall that ran at right angles to the enemy's line, Cleburne was able to compel his Yankee opponents to drop back toward the ridge's crown. Aware that Union brigadier general William H. Lytle's troops could not then see fully down the slopes, Cleburne ordered a brilliant tactical maneuver. After first deploying a strong line of skirmishers in front of his own main battle line, Cleburne ordered all of the brigade's flags forward into the advanced skirmish line. When the charge began, what happened was vividly described in Cleburne's own words: "The moment our flags, carried by the line of skirmishers, appeared above the crest of the hill, the enemy, supposing our main line of battle was in view, emptied their guns at the line of skirmishers. Before they could reload, our true line of battle was upon them and they instantly broke and fled, exposed to our deadly fire."[8]

This crafty battle plan was quickly recognized as genius of the first order. One of his captains wryly remarked: "Only such a man as Cleburne could inspire men to go up against such odds, and win, and he did." At the Battle of Stones River, Cleburne's men were compelled to attack some of the Union army's best troops in the vicinity of the Cedar Forest. An astounded captain of the U.S. Regular Army observed, "The enemy bore down upon us in three or four lines. Their front rank would fire and fall down and load, the rear rank firing over their heads. By this means they poured an incessant fire into us. They had the advantage of position, standing beneath the shadows of the pines enveloped in smoke, while we stood in ranks at the edge of the timber in bold relief against the light. They fired very low, and their shots told fearfully upon us. . . . [Thus] the order to retreat was given." Although the battle was later mismanaged by the Confederate commander, Braxton Bragg, leading to a withdrawal, Cleburne's men knew that they had won another tactical battlefield victory with high merit.[9]

Cleburne's innovative combat management had inspired a feeling of well-being and pride in his men. They were confident in themselves, aware that no matter how badly others bungled the battle, they were self-reliant and sure to beat the enemy in a fair fight. Pat Cleburne was the source of this inner worth, the mastermind who had made it all possible. If defeat and frustration were the lot of other elements of the army, Cleburne's troops could rely on their commander as well as themselves for a sustaining spirit. The Army of Northern Virginia had Lee and Jackson, but the Army of Tennessee had Cleburne for a source of pride and inspiration, and the anticipation of a better tomorrow. This later became a basis of the raw hope that propelled much of the army onward. Cleburne's mastery of tactical combat was the key. His men knew that Old Pat, as they often called him, wouldn't waste their lives unnecessarily in foolish stand-up-and-go-at-'em attacks. Indeed, his men, observed a captain on his staff, idolized him for both his competence and his personal caring. In justification of his high battle honors, by mid-1862 Pat Cleburne was commanding a division.

While the promotion vindicated the thirty-four-year-old Irish immigrant, his passion for high military achievement and his desire greatly to succeed transcended his unassuming nature and modest, quiet temperament. Blessed with great talent and a keen mind, Cleburne seemed to have before him the brightest of futures. Yet dark storm clouds, inherent in everyone's life to a greater or lesser extent, began hovering overhead in ominous portent.

Wounded at Richmond, Kentucky, in the fall of 1862 by a rifle ball that struck him in the mouth, Cleburne returned to duty two months later sporting a short, neatly trimmed beard to cover the scars. Soon he was injured again, taking several wounds at Perryville, Kentucky on October 8, 1862. Yet this was only the beginning of his burgeoning difficulties. While it was evident that Pat Cleburne possessed a rare ability to win repeatedly in combat, it was equally apparent that his greatest weakness was a severe political vulnerability. After Stones River, Braxton Bragg had asked for a candid opinion of his conduct in leading the army during the Kentucky Campaign. Cleburne dutifully but indiscreetly replied: "You do not possess the confidence of the army in that degree necessary to secure success." Politically, it was catastrophic for Cleburne as a rising star in the army's high command. Bragg didn't forgive those who failed to support him, no matter what justification they might have. During 1863, when Cleburne should have been promoted to corps command, he remained in limbo as a division commander under far less competent leaders.[10]

This was especially perplexing, for at Chickamauga, Chattanooga, and Ringgold Gap, Cleburne accomplished amazing feats of military success while greatly outnumbered. At Chickamauga, noted a staff officer, Cleburne "rode like a fury from brigade to brigade—horse and rider seemed frenzied alike—and the men responded to him." Cleburne was required on September 20 to attack, against his advice, a strongly entrenched enemy line. He carried out such a determined assault that, although eventually repulsed, it required Federal troops to be hastened from other points of the line. This ultimately led in part to the fatal gap that James Longstreet's attack exploited to win the battle. At Chattanooga, after being sent at the last moment by a flustered Braxton Bragg to defend North Missionary Ridge, Cleburne's men virtually won the battle before it was unexpectedly lost as a result of the famous charge by Major General George H. Thomas's soldiers up Missionary Ridge. Incredibly, Cleburne's four-thousand-man division alone repulsed Sherman's uncoordinated thrusts on North Missionary Ridge, even though thirty thousand troops were available to the Union commander. Repeatedly, Cleburne personally led counterattacks at critical points along the face of Tunnel Hill to keep Sherman's troops disrupted. Again, at Ringgold Gap as the Confederate army's rear guard, Cleburne defeated the swarming attacks by Joe Hooker's eastern soldiers, which saved much of Bragg's artillery and baggage train. For this brilliant action, Cleburne was awarded the Confederate Congress's formal resolution of thanks. Amazingly, however, Cleburne went no further in high command.[11]

Even following Bragg's removal after the loss of Chattanooga in late 1863, the seeming promise of Cleburne's rise to corps command quickly turned to ashes when he was apparently blacklisted for further promotion by the Davis administration because of his proposal to enlist blacks in the fighting army. Despite twice being awarded the Confederate Congress's vote of thanks for extraordinary battlefield achievements, Cleburne saw other, less able officers promoted over him. Incredibly, four corps command vacancies occurred in the Army of Tennessee within the span of eight months, and the best general, Cleburne, was summarily passed over.[12]

Earlier warned by his staff officers that the proposal to enroll slaves as soldiers might cost him the chance for promotion, Pat Cleburne never wavered. He considered such a move the South's only hope for independence. At worst he might be court-martialed and cashiered. If so, he said, he would enlist as a private in his old regiment, the 15th Arkansas, and still do his duty.[13]

This remarkable attitude and the will to do what was right, not what was politically expedient, were characteristics that both glorified his ultimate stature and sealed his tragic fate. While obviously disappointed, he continued to rely upon a favorite adage: "An honest heart and a strong arm should never succumb." This enormous moral and physical courage personified Cleburne's greatness as both a commander and a person.[14]

During the Atlanta Campaign of 1864 Cleburne and his men covered themselves with added glory. In the fighting at Bald Hill on July 21, during a holding action he called "the bitterest day's fighting of his life," and also during the critical Battle of Atlanta the following day, Cleburne was among his men. He would ask no man to go where he would not, and during a rush over the enemy's breastworks on July 22 he was seen in the forefront with drawn sword in hand, shouting, "Follow me, boys!" His extraordinary valor again cast him in the role of the army's outstanding fighter. Yet destiny beckoned.[15]

Following the fall of Atlanta on September 1, 1864, Confederate commander John Bell Hood, increasingly desperate, launched an uncertain offensive into Tennessee. Unfortunately, as Pat Cleburne perceived, the Tennessee Campaign of November and December 1864 was ill-fated from the start. At Spring Hill, Tennessee, on November 29 the bright prospect of triumph rapidly turned to dire frustration. Hood had ordered and executed a successful flank march around a major opposing enemy force under General John M. Schofield, only to discover the following morning that the elusive enemy had slipped past his deployed army in the middle of the night. Instead of destroying Schofield's trapped columns retreating from Columbia, Hood's forces spent the morning of November 30 in belated pursuit of the enemy, then retreating to Franklin, twelve miles farther north.

When his troops arrived in front of Franklin, the angry and frustrated Hood announced his plans for a massive frontal attack, even though Schofield's men were strongly posted behind stout breastworks. This was apparently retaliation against corps commander Frank Cheatham and division generals Pat Cleburne and John C. Brown, whom Hood blamed for the Spring Hill fiasco. They would be selected to make the assault in the center of the enemy's line, where the fortifications were the strongest and the concentrated enemy fire would be the heaviest.

An astounded and angry subordinate assessed the slim possibility of surviving the pending grand assault across two miles of open ground against the frowning rows of Yankee cannon and twenty thousand fortified infantry. Hood's attack—with only a few artillery batteries present for support—was tantamount to suicide, he warned. "There won't be many of us that will get back to Arkansas," somberly reflected one of Cleburne's subordinates, Brigadier General Daniel C. Govan. "Well, Govan," replied the grim Cleburne, "if we are to die, let us die like men."[16]

Despite the love of a waiting fiancée, Susan Tarleton, no matter what the cost or how bitter the grief, Pat Cleburne would do his full duty. If his men were required to make a forlorn assault against impossible odds he would be with them. No man was regarded as mere cannon fodder. His men were the essence of his victories in life. They were the true means of accomplishment. His bond with them transcended mortal life in the mutual display of the highest pinnacle of courage.

As always, Cleburne had the tactical battlefield in mind. He would arrange his attacking columns to reach their objective, the enemy's breastworks, with the least possible loss. Accordingly, he received permission to advance his brigades in column rather than in deployed battle lines. This would minimize the exposed front until the last moment, when he would change front to a deployed line of battle.

At 4:00 P.M. on that fateful November day, the Confederate army, more than twenty thousand strong, began marching toward the Union army's fortified entrenchments, more than two miles distant. With bands playing "Dixie" and "Bonnie Blue Flag," Cleburne's men surged forward beneath their distinctive battle flags, faded blue banners with white moon centers. The ground trembled under the tramp of thousands of marching feet, creating a sound, said an eyewitness, like the hollow rumble of distant thunder. Nearly twice the size of Pickett's Charge at Gettysburg in 1863, the Confederate assault at Franklin appeared like an oncoming avalanche of butternut and gray uniforms. Coveys of quail swirled skyward, and bounding jackrabbits scattered in fright ahead of the relentless sea of men. Moving across the entire breadth of open ground, the aligned ranks presented perhaps the war's most magnificent sight. It was worth a year of one's life to witness it, thought an awed observer.

The spectacle was but a grand facade masking the gruesome reality of death. Federal three-inch ordnance rifles shelled the advancing throng from Fort Granger, opening wide gaps in the gray ranks with each ear-shattering burst. Yet Cleburne's tactical deployment of brigades in column diminished their losses, so they were able to reach the forward enemy line with military formations intact. This gave them a fleeting chance to breach the defiant enemy line.

As Cleburne's men approached the breastworks in front of the Carter cotton gin, they found earth-covered parapets topped with head-logs and a wide, three-foot-deep ditch. A thick abatis fashioned of thorny Osage orange barred their progress even to the frontal ditch. Here all hell exploded in their faces. A blazing firestorm of musketry and canister leaped from the Yankee works. The solid plane of fire ravaged the Confederate ranks. "Never before in the history of war did a command of such small strength in so short a time kill and wound so many men," shuddered a Rebel officer. Cleburne had been correct. The prospects of breaking the enemy line were all but nil. Yet, reminiscent of Armistead's attack at Gettysburg, miraculously, at the very storm center, a Confederate rush overwhelmed the defenders. Enough men had been saved by Cleburne's tactical deployment to effect a breakthrough at the Carter house. Cleburne's and Brown's troops poured through the gap shrieking the eerie "Rebel yell."

Pat Cleburne was now on foot. Two horses had been shot from under him following the rush over the enemy's advanced skirmish line. Cleburne waved his embroidered kepi above his head and dashed forward on foot, disappearing into the great, swirling cloud of gunsmoke.

It was the end.

When they later found him, he lay lifeless with a fatal wound from a rifle ball just to the left of his heart. Like Cleburne, many of his men also met a tragic fate. Although a valiant rush by Cleburne's and John C. Brown's troops at the Carter house had created the momentary hope of victory, the enemy's reserves countercharged and secured the ground in bitter hand-to-hand fighting. Just as Cleburne had predicted, the Confederates couldn't penetrate the Yankee line in sufficient strength under such adverse circumstances to win the battle.

After nearly five hours of intense combat, with many of the Southern soldiers helplessly trapped in that blood-soaked outer ditch, the shooting mercifully stopped as the Union troops withdrew unhindered to Nashville. "The most furious and desperate battle of the war in the west," wrote General A. P. Stewart, had finally ended. The madness that had occurred at Franklin had wrecked the Army of Tennessee. The more than seven thousand Southern casualties ensured that the tragedy was fulfilled when Hood attempted battle at Nashville a few weeks later but lost much of the remnant of his army in the war's worst major battlefield defeat.[17]

By that point the Confederacy's fate was all but obvious. Perhaps the bitterest defeat of all was the loss of hope for a brighter tomorrow. Pat Cleburne had personified Southern hope as his army's brightest star. Cleburne's inspired management of the tactical battlefield reflected his extraordinary ability to make decisions with an ultimate awareness. After Franklin he was but a memory.

Beyond all the tragic suffering at Franklin and elsewhere, however, is an awareness that human life is overshadowed by mankind's indomitable spirit. Pat Cleburne had willingly sacrificed his life for a greater cause. He knew that no matter what the ultimate cost, our destiny extends only as far as our innermost values. The essence of his life, courage as a total commitment of heart and soul, reflects a personal investment in future generations of Americans. Indeed, his was a courage for all ages.*

---

* Today a visitor can stand on the outskirts of Franklin and gaze over what was formerly a blacktop parking lot and a pizza establishment, the very site where Pat Cleburne lost his life. The site was recently reclaimed from commercial development, and the old pizza building was torn down for a memorial park. This former outrage and the desecration of our heritage was remedied by the combined effort of concerned citizens, historical preservationist groups, and the city of Franklin administration. It is a victory in the modern sense for common sense in preserving our important heritage. Yet, that this situation existed well into the twenty-first century is perhaps a fitting reminder of our society's imperfect view of the past. It is also evidence of the work that yet remains, and the choices that face us.

VIII

WHAT DO YOU SAY WHEN YOU KNOW YOU'RE ABOUT TO DIE?

Life is mankind's most precious physical asset. Without life there physically is, before and after, nothing. It is both the means and the source. The soul may find solace in another realm, but the spark of physical life, once extinguished, is gone. This self-evident premise is the focus of our essential existence. We normally seek to do all we reasonably can to preserve our life. This instinct is primary and ingrained in the subconscious as well as the conscious mind, resulting in a keen awareness of life-threatening circumstances. Thus, when we perceive the imminent end to our physical existence, we tend to reflect with the deepest and most crucial rationale about the meaning of our life. It is both an emotional and practical catharsis, or sometimes a trembling of the soul about encountering the great mystery ahead.

While courage is not a requisite, given the time to scrutinize imminent death, the feelings of inner peace require self-examination and a commitment to die with dignity or else intense struggle. Faith has a key role in the process: faith that one has lived right, or else in relying upon an understanding of the continuance of our soul's existence as a matter of religious belief. How we meet the specter of death has much to do with our education, intelligence, and intuitive sense of being. But courage in facing death is intensely personal. There are those who would seem to embrace death in a physical sense as a means of escaping pain, distress, or misfortune. Yet the courage to let go gracefully in our mind, and with belief in an ultimate benefit in death rather than in a dire, all-obliterating demise, is a matter of the soul. We have little way of knowing the ultimate truth of how others face death, but we often have important evidence. The ideas and statements of others in confronting death are often only haphazardly recorded, being given verbally at bedside, or else in stressful physical circumstances that cloud full consciousness or means of lucid communication. Many individuals resist thinking about the essence of their death until the end threatens. It is often a painful and unpleasant prospect and a matter that is easily put aside until finally necessary to consider. While many seek to escape death's final reality, often we wish to leave as a legacy of our existence our perspectives on the end.

With death so much a part of everyday life during the Civil War, the gruesome lottery of personal demise affected nearly a million Americans, North and South. In four years of warfare the grim toll of military-related deaths accounted for about 2 percent of the nation's population, nearly all of whom were young. What was evident to those soldiers who were death's victims was the awful reality of warfare in determining their personal fate. Officially numbered only as a statistic or given cursory notice in the public records, theirs was a far different perspective in actually experiencing the event. In personal terms death not only was fraught with physical pain and agony, but was a source of deep anxiety and highly emotional. What they said and did at the time was usually an acute reaction, a final expression of the meaning of one's life and also, often, an exercise in courage.

DEATH ON THE BATTLEFIELD—WHY (NOT) ME?

Thornton F. Brodhead

Thornton F. Brodhead was at age forty the colonel of the 1st Michigan Cavalry Regiment. Headstrong and bold, he was a Harvard-educated lawyer who had served as a captain in the 15th U.S. Infantry during the Mexican War, earning a brevet for gallantry. His success in life—as a state senator and the postmaster of Detroit—marked him as a prominent public personality with a reputation as a competent, no-nonsense administrator. His participation in the Second Battle of Manassas on August 30, 1862, seemed typical of his personal commitment—and also of his intolerance of bungling leadership. When confronted by the approaching enemy after the Federal cavalry had been beaten back, Colonel Thornton Brodhead attempted to rally his men but was shot in the chest by the adjutant of the 12th Virginia Cavalry, Lewis Harman, when the colonel's surrender was demanded but refused. Brodhead knew he was mortally wounded, but remained bitter about the combat performance of Major Generals John Pope and Irvin McDowell, which he referred to as treasonous behavior. Brodhead's raw battlefield courage was matched only by his concise, well-measured comments from his deathbed.

August 31, 1862

> *My Dearest Wife:*
>
> *I write to you, mortally wounded, from the battlefield. We are again defeated, and ere this reaches you your children will be fatherless. Before I die, let me implore you that in some way it may be stated that General Pope has been outwitted, and that McDowell is a traitor. Had they done their duty, as I did mine, and had they led as I led, the old Flag would have waved in triumph.*
>
> *I wrote to you yesterday morning [before the battle]. Today is Sunday, and today I sink to the green couch of our final rest.*
>
> *I have fought well, my darling, and I was shot in the endeavor to rally our broken battalions. I could have escaped, but I would not*

till all hope was gone and was shot [being] about the only one of our forces left on the field. Our cause is just, and our generals, not the enemy's, have defeated us. In God's good time he will give us victory.

And now, good bye, wife & children. Bring them up—I know you will—in the fear of God, and love for the Savior. But for you and the dear ones dependent I should die happy. I know the blow will fall with crushing weight on you. Trust in Him. . . . Dr. Nash is with me. It is now after midnight & I have spent most of the night in sending messages to you. Two bullets have gone through my chest, and directly through the lungs. I suffer but little now, but at first the pain was acute. I have won the soldier's name, and am ready to meet now, as I must, a soldier's fate. I hope that from Heaven I may see the glorious old Flag wave again over the undivided Union I have loved so well. Farewell, wife & babes, and friends. We shall meet again.

Your loving Thornton

Thornton Brodhead's mettle was self-evident, but his intelligent perspective reflects the great dignity of his self-sacrifice. There was bitter resentment, to be sure—the inequity of his death in a losing role, the want of ability and courage on the part of others. Yet a belief in the eventual and ultimate victory of that which was right sustained him in his agony. It was his courage of the soul, not only his physical efforts, which marked him as a truly special man, to be duly recognized and honored.[1]

Major Sullivan Ballou

Major Sullivan Ballou was a man of intense feelings, an emotional person who groped for the essence of his life's journey. Aware that he would soon be facing battle's stern array, Sullivan Ballou thought about the consequences. The natural worry that something harmful might happen to him led him to consider the repercussions. He would risk leaving a young wife, their two children, and grief ever after—for there would be no more everyday contact or sharing of life's experiences together. Sullivan Ballou, like so many other soldiers, foresaw the possible personal consequences. Unlike most others, Sullivan recorded his thoughts and, as a contingency, wrote a profound letter to explain his sentiments.

It was midsummer 1861, and the Federal army of which he was a part was about to march to Manassas Junction, Virginia, to combat the Confederate forces under General P. G. T. Beauregard. A realist but not a pessimist, Ballou anticipated his survival in combat, yet he knew of the risk. He had a strange feeling—not a premonition about his fate, but a concern that matters might not go as he hoped. Not wanting to alarm his wife, yet seeking to communicate should the worst happen, he wrote the following letter but didn't mail it, knowing it would be found among his effects should he die. If he survived, the letter might be destroyed. Perhaps it was playing both ends against the middle. Yet he desperately wanted to soothe the pain and to confront the shock and grief that would inevitably occur if he were killed.

As a major in the 2nd Regiment Rhode Island Volunteer Infantry he was a prominent, highly regarded man, and already a success at the youthful age of thirty-two. His ability and intellect were evident in his prewar civilian role of lawyer and then his election as clerk of the state House of Representatives. A graduate of Brown University in Providence, Rhode Island, Ballou had married Sarah H. Shumway in October 1855, and in 1861 their family consisted of Edgar, age four, and William, age two.

It was a week prior to the First Battle of Manassas, or First Bull Run (as it was known in the North), and Sullivan Ballou was thinking of home, unaware of his personal fate, but mindful of the building impetus toward deadly combat of the two principal eastern armies. His pen began to convey what the mind regarded with distress:

July the 14th 1861

My very dear Sarah:
The indications are very strong that we shall move in a few
days—perhaps tomorrow. Lest I should not be able to write you

again, I feel impelled to write lines that may fall under your eye when I shall be no more.

Our movement may be one of a few days' duration, and full of pleasure—and it may be one of severe conflict and death to me. Not my will, but thine, Oh God, be done. If it is necessary that I should fall on the battlefield for my country, I am ready. I have no misgivings about, or lack of confidence in, the cause in which I am engaged, and my courage does not halt or falter. I know how strongly American civilization now leans upon the triumph of the [Federal] Government, and how great a debt we owe to those who went before us through the blood and suffering of the Revolution. And I am willing—perfectly willing—to lay down all my joys in this life, to help maintain this government, and to pay that debt.

But my dear wife, [is it right] when I know that with my own joys I lay down nearly all of yours, and replace them in this life with cares and sorrows—when, after having eaten for long years the bitter fruit of orphanage myself, I must offer it as their only sustenance to my dear little children[?] Is it weak or dishonorable, while the banner of my purpose floats calmly and proudly in the breeze, that my unbounded love for you, my darling wife and children, should struggle in fierce, though useless, contest with my love of country?

I cannot describe to you my feelings on this calm summer night, when 2,000 men are sleeping around me, many of them enjoying the last, perhaps, before that of death. And I, suspicious that death is creeping behind me with his fatal dart, am communing with God, my country, and thee.

I have sought most closely and diligently, and often in my breast, for a wrong motive in thus hazarding the happiness of those I loved, and I could not find one. A pure love of my country and of the principles [I] have often advocated before the people, and "the name of honor that I love more than I fear death" have called upon me, and I have obeyed.

Sarah, my love for you is deathless; it seems to bind me to you with mighty cables that nothing but Omnipotence could break, and yet my love of country comes over me like a strong wind, and bears me irresistibly on with all these chains to the battlefield.

The memories of the blissful moments I have spent with you come creeping over me, and I feel most gratified to God and to you that I have enjoyed them so long. And hard it is for me to give them up and burn to ashes the hopes of future years, when, God willing, we might still have lived and loved together and seen our sons grow up to honorable manhood around us. I have, I know, but few and small claims upon Divine Providence. But something whispers to me—perhaps it is the wafted prayer of my little Edgar—that I shall return to my loved ones unharmed. If I do not, my dear Sarah, never forget how much I love you, and when my last breath escapes me on the battlefield, it will whisper your name.

Forgive my many faults, and the many pains I have caused you. How thoughtless and foolish I have oftentimes been! How gladly would I wash out with my tears every little spot upon your happiness, and struggle with all the misfortune of this world, to shield you and my children from harm. But I cannot. I must watch you from the spirit land, and hover near you, while you buffet the storms with your precious little freight, and wait with sad patience till we meet to part no more.

But, Oh, Sarah! If the dead can come back to this earth and flit unseen around those they loved, I shall always be near you; in the garish day and in the darkest night—amidst your happiest scenes and gloomiest hours—always, always. And if there be a soft breeze upon your cheek, it shall be my breath; or the cool air fans your throbbing temple, it shall be my spirit passing by.

Sarah, do not mourn me dead. Think I am gone and wait for thee, for we shall meet again.

As for my little boys, they will grow up as I have done, and never know a father's love and care. Little Willie is too young to remember me long, and my blue-eyed Edgar will keep my frolics with him among the dimmest memories of his childhood. Sarah, I have unlimited confidence in your maternal care and your

development of their characters. Tell my two mothers, his and hers,
I call God's blessing upon them. Oh Sarah, I wait for you there!
Come to me, and lead thither my children.

Sullivan

The battle was fiercely fought. It was Sunday, July 21, 1861, and
Sullivan Ballou's regiment, the 2nd Rhode Island, was defending the
crown of Matthews' Hill, being hard pressed to hold the line. Their colonel, John S. Slocum, had already gone down with three wounds, and
Major Ballou, on horseback, was attempting to change the 2nd's alignment to let other regiments take position. Between the bursting shells
and volleys of musketry the hilltop was a fiery cauldron. Suddenly, Ballou and his mount were flung to the ground. A rifled cannon shot had
struck Ballou's mount and killed it instantly, while the major's leg was
mangled by the same shell. A quick glance suggested that Ballou was unconscious and dying, and he was left behind.

After falling into Confederate hands, Ballou was later attended to at
a makeshift hospital and lived until July 29. His death was protracted,
and thoughts of his waiting letter amid his left-behind army belongings
must have eased his mind. He was soon buried on the battlefield, and
his story should have ended there. But in the wild, often frenzied aftermath of the battle, Southern civilians or soldiers scouring the battlefield
for trophies dug up the body. Observing from the uniform that it was a
Yankee field officer, believed to be the despised Colonel John Slocum,
they mutilated and partially burned the corpse, then left the remnants
to decompose in the open. When, months later, Governor William
Sprague of Rhode Island sought to recover Slocum's and Ballou's bodies, he found from the remnants of a shirt collar that the desecrated
body was that of Ballou, not Slocum. The meager remains were carefully gathered up, and interred at Swan Point Cemetery in Providence.

Sarah Hart Ballou never remarried. Just twenty-four at the time of
her husband's death, she raised her two sons and later moved to New
Jersey to live with William before dying at age eighty in 1917. Yet long
after their deaths, everlasting fame was accorded to the family. With the

presentation of Ken Burns's television series *The Civil War* in 1990, the reading of an abridged version of Ballou's July 14 letter caused a flood of viewer responses, marking it as one of the most poignant and emotional facets of the entire series. Its place among the favored public documents of the Civil War has never since been in question.[2]

DAVID O. DODD—YOUNG BUT WISE IN SPIRIT

Youth is often a whimsical journey into the reality of life, developing wisdom in judgments and perspectives as the brain matures and undergoes structural changes. Reasoning and applied comprehension improve with experience and physical maturity. Youthful "simplistic" thought and perspective are usually modified by an awareness that the crux of the problem doesn't always exist with the "other" person. Rather, it often relates to one's own prejudicial beliefs and views. Wisdom in thought and deed includes astute self-appraisal. In youth an assessment of the consequences of one's actions generally tends not to be proportional to the perceived benefits sought. Spur-of-the-moment reasoning, emotionalism, and lack of real-time perspectives (i.e., How will this play in the future?) are ingredients of sometimes regrettable decisions. Maturity of the brain (a lack of fully developed cognitive controls in adolescence) plays a key role in decision making. Yet there are, throughout the ages, shining examples of reasoned perspectives at a youthful age, the most serious of which involve the certain pending death of the individual.

David O. Dodd was a precocious youth, yet he had been regarded as rather ordinary, since he was interested in girls and "adventuresome" events as a teenager. A native of Texas but in 1862 a resident of Little Rock, Arkansas, David sympathized with the South. He was only fourteen when the Civil War began and had studied at St. John's College at Little Rock. In 1862 he found employment in the telegraph office in town. Months later he went south to work in the Confederate-operated telegraph office at Monroe, Louisiana. His knowledge of Morse code made him a valuable addition to the telegraph service, and he regularly sent home a portion of his wages to help support his mother and sister, who were still living in Little Rock. Subsequently he went to Granada, Mississippi, to help his father, Andrew M. Dodd, who was serving as sutler for the Confederate 3rd Regiment Arkansas Cavalry (dismounted).

Experienced in managing his father's business while the elder was away on frequent trips to purchase supplies, David was capable and energetic. After Little Rock was occupied by Union forces in September 1863, his father sent David home in October to bring his mother and sister to Mississippi. He was thwarted in his early efforts to evacuate them to Jackson, Mississippi, and he took a job clerking in a Little Rock store while biding his time to move the family. At last, in early December, his father, Andy, unexpectedly slipped into town at night, and hurried preparations were made for all to travel to Camden, Arkansas, within the Confederate lines. By mid-December the family was safely at Camden, but his father suddenly decided to send David back to Little Rock to attend to several business ventures still pending. Being underage for military duty, he was given a Confederate pass by Brigadier General James F. Fagan. Yet, by one account, David was told by Fagan or others to gather all information possible on the Union military presence in Little Rock.

David journeyed there without incident and arrived in Little Rock on Christmas Eve 1863. Staying with his aunt, David enjoyed various holiday parties, and was even so bold as to visit the office of the Union provost marshal, where he obtained a pass to return to Camden. On the morning of December 29, David Dodd, riding a mule, passed through the Union lines without incident, and at the second and final picket post eight miles from town, he surrendered his Union pass to a private, who soon "tore it up," there being no further need for the document. David's next stop was at the home of his uncle, Washington Dodd, who lived eighteen miles from Little Rock. Here he reclaimed his revolver, which he had left on the way into town.

Yet, with the impulsiveness of youth, David decided to partially retrace his steps to reach the home of a friend who would exchange his mule for a horse. Bypassing the outer Union picket post by a back road, David that evening suddenly and unexpectedly encountered another Union picket station. Unable to produce a Union pass, he was arrested and taken to the officer on duty, Lieutenant Christian F. Stopran of the

1st Missouri Cavalry. The matter was regarded initially as a matter of routine civilian traffic by Stopran, and he told Dodd to produce something in the way of papers to prove who he was. David innocently handed over a memorandum book with random notes about his father's business affairs. Yet written in code in the back of the book was a message that David had entered, never suspecting that it might be deciphered on the spot. Stopran, however, was familiar with Morse code, and knew immediately the contents of the cryptic message: "Third Ohio Battery has four guns—brass. Three regiments [are] in the brigade commanded by [Col. John W.] Davidson. . . ." David was immediately searched; his pistol, letters, and Confederate pass were confiscated; and he was soon sent under close guard to Little Rock.

David was accused of being a Confederate spy, and on December 31 a trial by court-martial was begun, with testimony stretching over the next six days. Although he was defended by able lawyers, including the future governor of Arkansas, William M. Fishbeck, the sentence was pronounced on January 5: "death by hanging."

David O. Dodd's youth was no mitigating circumstance, announced Union brigadier general Frederick Steele, who nonetheless allegedly offered David the opportunity to save his life by revealing who had provided the information contained in the Morse code message. David refused to do so, saying, "I can die, but I can't betray a friend." He was ordered to be hanged on Friday, January 8, 1864. That morning, given the opportunity to write a final letter to his family, David confided his courage.

Military Prison, January 8, 1864, 10 A.M.

My Dear Parents and Sisters:

I was arrested as a spy, tried, and sentenced to be hung today at 3 o'clock. The time is fast approaching, but thank God I am prepared.

I will soon be out of this world of sorrow and trouble. I would like to see you all before I die, but let God's will be done, not ours. I pray God to give you strength to bear your troubles

while in this world. I hope God will receive you in Heaven—
there I will meet you.

Mother, I know it will be hard for you to give up your only
son, but you must remember it is God's will.

Good-bye. God will give you strength to bear your troubles.

I pray that we may meet in Heaven. Good-bye. God bless
you all.

Your son and brother, David O. Dodd

That afternoon David O. Dodd was wheeled up in a wagon to the square in front of St. John's College, his former school. As he stood bound in the wagon while the noose was adjusted over his head, his bravery was fully evident in front of the gathered and hushed crowd. When his executioners couldn't find a bandage to cover his eyes, David calmly said, "Look in my pocket for a handkerchief." The cloth was adjusted, the noose was straightened, and the horses were driven off. David was left dangling to die slowly by strangulation. He was seventeen, by two months.[3]

"I'll [Soon] Be in Eternity"
William S. Moore

The details are sketchy. William S. Moore of Tennessee was a twenty-five-year-old Confederate soldier, possibly of Company B, 40th Tennessee Infantry. He was married, and he and his wife, "Alcy," had young children. He had visited home in July 1863, possibly on furlough, and was traveling through northern Alabama when he was arrested and accused of being a Northern spy. The exact circumstances of his arrest and execution are unknown, but there is a poignant urgency in his last letter to his wife that transcends the ages in its message of human plight and in summoning the courage to face one's imminent dire fate. The words are terse, the thoughts simple, and the sentiment precious.

Tuscumbia, Alabama, July 23, 1863

Mrs. W. S. Moore; Dear Alcy:

It is through a great tribulation and aching heart and trembling hand . . . I take to write to you this evening and inform you of the condition I am in. Dearly and much beloved Alcy, how can I bear to pen to you this evening that I am condemned to be shot. Dear companion, this is the last letter I expect I shall ever have the chance to write to you in this world. You must do the best you can for yourself and our sweet little children. I shall never see them nor you anymore, but I want you to remember me when I am gone and not bring anyone over our little children.

You can bring them up in the way they should go. Tell my blessed father and mother to remember me when I am gone. This will be great terror to them I know, but there is no remedy for me. I must go. Farewell vain world, I am going to my long home in a few hours. Dear friends, it is impossible for me to describe my feelings at this dread and awful moment; as yet I am not satisfied to meet my God, but what few hours I have to live I shall spend in prayer and supplication to Almighty God. I feel like there is a change with me, but I want to feel more reconciled to my God, the Great I Am of Heaven and Earth. I want all my friends and relatives to live in the discharge of their duties that are enjoined upon them, and try and make their way to Heaven. I am sorry to leave you all; I love you so well; I love you dearly, but I shall never see you again.

I requested the provost [marshal] to have my body placed where my friends could get it. I want to be buried by my brother and sister. Oh, how I long to be with those in health is more than I can describe, but woe, woe is me.

Long before this you can see, I'll be in eternity. Great God, can it be possible that a poor innocent man must be killed! Oh, God, forbid that these things should be.

Dear loving wife, I want you to try and take care of all those things that are left, and apply them to yours' and the children's benefit as best you can. I want you to love them and teach them to love one another, and educate them as well as you can. Oh, dear loving wife, . . . how often I have thought of you since I left you last Thursday morning [July 16, 1863], and the tears I have shed since then are almost a fountain, and how often I have thought of my thoughts and feelings.

Dear love, when I [left] you, I felt like it would be the last time, and now I am sure it is the last time. Farewell, dear wife, remember me when I am gone. Oh, if I could be with you a little while and commune with you, what satisfaction it would be to me, Alcy. I want you to move back to the old place, and tell father I want him to see that my children do not suffer for anything to eat.

I must close my last words to you; it breaks my heart. Children, farewell; Farewell, loving wife; farewell, father and mother; farewell, brother and sister.

William S. Moore

Oh, how can I quit writing when this is the only way I can say anything to my blessed wife and sweet little children that are so near and so dear to me.

Oh, wife, take care of this letter and read it often for my sweet children that have been so good to me, and so kind to me. Oh, dearest kindly wife, I shall remember you to the last moment of my life. My heart is broken. I am sick and faint. My doom is nigh at hand.

Farewell, beloved wife and sweet little children that are so near my heart. Farewell, farewell, to Alcy Moore and family.

Wm. S. Moore
A condemned soldier,

Tuscumbia, Ala., July 23rd, 1863,

[addendum note:]

This is a copy of my Grandfather Moore's last words to my grandmother. He was a twenty-five year old soldier in the Southern

*army writing to his wife in Tennessee. Falsely accused of being a
spy for the North, he was court-martialed and shot at sunrise
the day after he wrote [this letter]. Elsie Moore Guinn,
6/19/[19]39, J. G. Moore, Moore's Modern Store, J. G. Moore,
Jr., Phone 116, Court Street, Florence, Ala.*[4]

"I KNOW THE BLOW WILL FALL WITH CRUSHING WEIGHT UPON YOU"

Lieutenant William Brown, 7th Illinois Infantry

The Battle of Corinth, Mississippi, on October 3 and 4, 1862, was one
of the fiercest "secondary" fights of the war. The bravery of the Confederate attackers in assaulting over mostly open ground to the very
walls of Battery Robinett was a remarkable event. Although the Confederates were repulsed, many of the defenders became casualties, including a young Federal officer, Lieutenant William Brown, acting
adjutant of the 7th Illinois Infantry. Brown was shot in the shoulder
while on horseback on October 3, and, in his own words, "it was not
pronounced dangerous at first." But by October 8 he informed his wife:
"I have been told by my surgeon that I could not live but a few days
longer." So weak that he couldn't write, Brown dictated a last letter to
his wife, which was recorded by a grieving friend:

> *I was shot at my post doing my duty. I have fought well and have
> earned the soldier's name and am ready now, as I must [be], to
> meet the soldier's fate. Ere this reaches you the spirit of your
> husband will have passed from earth to eternity. I know the blow
> will fall with crushing weight upon you, but trust in Him who
> knoweth all things best. He will give you rest. I have made my
> peace with my God. I have done my duty and have sacrificed my
> life in the service of my country, but hope that from heaven I may
> see the glorious "Star Spangled Banner" float in triumph
> throughout the Union. [This nation] I have loved so well; and*

now good bye, my wife and child, father and mother, brothers and
sisters. Cherish this memory—that I was engaged in the
performance of a sacred duty, and prepare to meet me in heaven.
Farewell, farewell, Your affectionate and loving husband, William
Brown, Jr.

Lieutenant William Brown Jr. died the following day, October 9, 1862.[5]

Of this fiber is our nation; and at its very core is a heritage of immeasurable emotion, sacrifice, and valor.

PART TWO

Physical Bravery

IX

EXTRAORDINARY BRAVERY, A SPECIAL VIRTUE

Physical courage was the focus in a performance standard of excellence that many both sought and admired. The willingness to risk severe injury or death by self-exposure was regarded as normal by a professional soldier, but to a civilian volunteer, the risks were often counterbalanced by a natural obligation to one's wife, children, and family. The allegiance to a nation, and usually the bond with their fellow soldiers, caused most fighting men to risk death on the battlefield. But what of combat situations beyond those of ordinary risk? Bravery as a manifestation of inherent valor seems to have been comparatively rare. Most officers and men regarded exposure in combat as incidental to their job, but gallantry over and above the required call of duty was a matter of crucial consideration.

From the recorded history of such experiences the following provide a few key insights.

LITTLE CHARLIE HARKER, BRAVEST OF THE BRAVE

Charles G. Harker was an enigma. All but written off as a penniless orphan when a youth in New Jersey, he was small in stature and looked upon as a misfit for his rather cloddish appearance. Yet that was before West Point. Harker received some very good luck when he was befriended and virtually adopted by a wealthy industrialist and U.S. congressman, Nathan T. Stratton, of Mullica Hill, New Jersey, at whose store young Harker worked as a clerk. He won Stratton's confidence and support by his tireless work ethic, and Harker's future took a strong upward turn with Stratton's election to Congress in 1851. By his benefactor's influence he obtained an appointment to the United States Military Academy in 1854. Harker blossomed with higher education, and soon became one of the most aggressively ambitious cadets at West Point. His refinement was evidenced by a newfound taste for fine wines; yet he retained his streetwise, devil-may-care attitude, revealed in a penchant for taking risks and in his soaring ambition. Mindful of his disadvantaged background, he constantly sought to prove to the world and himself that he would and could be among the best of his peers.

After graduating from West Point in 1858, Harker served on the northwestern frontier as a junior officer. When the war began he became a colonel in the 65th Ohio Volunteer Infantry, a position he accepted at age twenty-six in November 1861. His service at Shiloh earned him brigade command, and his valor at Perryville and Stones River marked him as among the most heroic and aggressive young leaders in the army. As a rising star, "Little Charlie" Harker sought to overcome his small physical stature by his aggressive battlefield demeanor. Harker was not reckless, but he saw opportunity in an encounter, a chance to do extraordinary things with a display of physical—and moral—courage.

One of Harker's key roles in the war proved to be at the Battle of Chickamauga. Here he gained a reputation as not only the youngest brigade commander in the Army of the Cumberland, but perhaps its most promising. On Sunday, September 20, 1863, Harker and his men held off repeated Confederate attacks as a part of Major General George H. Thomas's Snodgrass Hill line, which helped save the Union army from annihilation. It was important work, and in an emotional letter to his benefactor, Nathan Stratton, less than two weeks later, Charlie Harker announced that:

> *It was a momentous event. Though it is never a pleasing task to me to speak of myself, yet I can refer with just feelings of pride to the conduct of [my] little command. Since the crossing of the Tennessee River on the 3rd of Sept. until after the battle [of Chickamauga] my brigade has been honored with some important positions. . . . My brigade was the first to reconnoiter the enemy's position at the foot of Lookout Mountain. The reconnaissance was pushed up to within about seven hundred yards of the enemy's batteries, and was pronounced by my superiors to be a most brilliant affair. I was again selected to make the reconnaissance toward Gordon's Mills in the direction of Lafayette, passing over a portion of the ground which subsequently proved [to be] the great battlefield. Again my conduct was most highly complemented. In the battle of Saturday the 19th, my brigade was placed in a most perilous position, but behaved most handsomely. I had two horses shot [from] under me in the fight, but my person was not touched. On Sunday the 20th, it was the good fortune of my brigade to hold a position which must become historical [crucial] if the history of that battle is ever correctly written [the defense of Snodgrass Hill]. I will not describe it here, though the public press have in some instances referred to it, though they have not described [our actions] very correctly. For my conduct through this campaign, and especially for the part I took in Sunday's battle, I have been repeatedly assure[d]—though unsolicited by me—that my name will be most thoroughly urged for promotion. Indeed, I was shown privately a telegram to be sent to the President of the United States, from Department Head Qrs., signed by Gen'l Thomas and other gen'l. officers, asking that I might be promoted together with two or three Brig. Genl[s]. for "gallant and distinguished conduct." To be thus signalized for conduct in battle was the proudest event of my life. I desire you to keep this confidential for the present. Do*

not mention it even to my own family at present. I mention this to
you, however, as one in whom I can trust. And in case the
recommendation should not be heeded—though I cannot conceive
how the authorities at Washington can overlook such a
recommendation coming from such a source—and in case I should
fall in battle with my present rank, it will be a source of pride and
gratification to my family and friends to know that I have been so
urgently recommended for promotion.[1]

Charlie Harker was seemingly on top of the world. With the endorsement from the army's senior commanders, he was, indeed, some months later promoted to the rank of brigadier general to date from September 20, 1863, the day of his great valor at Chickamauga. Thus further inspired, Charlie Harker wouldn't let up. Indeed, he became almost reckless in his personal bravery while confronting the enemy. At Missionary Ridge on November 25, Harker stormed up the slopes ahead of his men with a battle flag in his grasp, yelling, "Rally around the flag, boys!" and flaunting the colors in the enemy's faces from a captured cannon, the "Lady Buckner."

Early in the Atlanta Campaign, a correspondent noted that four horses had recently been shot from under him in battle; two at Chickamauga, one at Missionary Ridge, and another at Resaca, where Harker was thrown to the ground and wounded in the leg by a shell fragment.

Harker's cool demeanor in the fiercest of fighting was by now the marvel of all. During the approach to Kennesaw Mountain in early June, a shell whizzed by within inches of the youthful general as he sat on his steed. The cannon shot tore away part of the horse's mane, but Harker told one of the men, "A miss is as good as a mile. Besides, here [in this regiment, the 125th Ohio Infantry] there is more timber for generals."

Harker's gallantry had earned the notice of William Tecumseh Sherman, and soon Sherman's friendship with and high regard for Harker were well known in the army. Yet Harker's disdain for the dangers of combat continued to be the talk of his men. General Oliver O. Howard regarded him with awe; "whenever anything difficult was to be done, anything that required pluck and energy, we called on Harker," he later noted. Indeed, said Howard, the only complaint he ever heard about Little Charlie was that once he got started against the enemy, he couldn't be kept back.[2]

On the morning of June 27, 1864, with a major frontal assault ordered for that day against the Cheatham Hill sector of the Confederates' Kennesaw Mountain defensive line, Harker pondered his fate. A little depressed and anxious over the desperate nature of the planned assault, Harker finished a letter home and placed his papers in order, telling a staff officer, "I shall not come out of this charge today alive." Fatalistic, he had recently told his sister, "Thousands of others must fall. Who they will be, God in his infinite wisdom alone knows."

Harker's demeanor never reflected his anxiety. When staff and field officers were given permission to dismount and lead the attack on foot, Harker determined to remain mounted. When the attack began, Harker with his brigade was in the front line, advancing against the soon-to-be infamous base of the "Dead Angle," where Rebel troops under Generals Frank Cheatham and Pat Cleburne were posted. The storm of rifle and artillery fire that greeted the attackers smothered the assault, driving the riddled ranks of Union soldiers to the ground. Harker, still on horseback, dashed forward through the midst of the 125th Ohio, yelling to the men, "Come on, boys!" A smattering of soldiers jumped up to follow him, and his aide, Captain Edward G. Whitesides, who also was mounted, dashed after Harker. Through the swirling smoke, several men saw Harker and his mount go down, sinking slowly to the ground as if by some trained equestrian stunt. Also, Whitesides and his mount were shot. Yet it was Harker who received immediate attention. Several men ran to the spot but were promptly hit. Finally, several Ohioans hastily pulled the general away and carried him off as the buglers sounded retreat. A minié ball had passed through his left arm and penetrated into his chest, inflicting a mortal wound.

Word of Charlie Harker's pending fate quickly spread at headquarters, and within minutes of his arrival at a rear-echelon hospital a large crowd of officers gathered. The words were few. At 1:00 P.M., with two chaplains by his side, Charlie Harker breathed his last and quietly expired.

The throng, including Generals David S. Stanley and Thomas J. Wood, streamed out of the tent; "all were moved to tears by the sad event," remembered an eyewitness. Even General Sherman was severely depressed by Harker's death, and wrote to the dead general's brother, "[He] was regarded as one of our best young generals, of rising fame, and his loss was deeply felt by me." Sherman was so distraught that he wrote in his report that had Harker (and Colonel Dan McCook) lived, the assault at Kennesaw Mountain likely would have succeeded.[3]

Charlie Harker, among the bravest of the brave, may have been motivated by a desire for recognition, promotion, and an enhanced reputation, with his valor further inspired by the youthful feeling of indestructibility. But Harker saw that physical bravery was not necessarily an end unto itself. There were inherent consequences of valor, some bad as well as good. Were his earlier "escapes" and close calls in battle a sign of his invincibility, or a warning?

Harker was no fool; he knew of his mortality, and had fulfilled his premonition of death, yet with remarkable honor and dash. His was the courage of the soul.

ALEXANDER S. WEBB, A SPECIAL GETTYSBURG VALOR

Alexander Stewart Webb, known as "Andy" to his family and friends, entered the army with high expectations. A military man whose forefathers had been prominent (his grandfather was General Washington's personal secretary; and his father, a noted newspaper editor who had earned appointment in 1861 as minister to Brazil), the youthful Webb suffered much frustration in his up-and-down military career despite conspicuous bravery in combat. Trained and educated at West Point, following his graduation in 1855 he was mired in lackluster assignments: three tedious years as a mathematics instructor at West Point, and nearly a year's service in the Florida swamps. At the beginning of the Civil War, Webb took a post as inspector general on Brigadier General William F. Barry's staff. Despite experiencing extensive fighting during the Virginia Peninsula Campaign of 1862, Webb earned little recognition. He remained in the background even though Barry confided to Webb's father, "I consider your son to be without his superior among the young officers of the army. I also consider that both aptitude and experience fit him to command—and command well—anything from a regiment to a division." Webb was promoted to lieutenant colonel and appointed chief of staff to the V Corps' Major General Fitz John Porter in September 1862, but shortly thereafter Porter, and Webb's friend Army of the Potomac commander George B. McClellan, were removed from their commands.

When Major General George G. Meade assumed command of the V Corps, Webb sought to prove himself again. However, after his bravery in leading Brigadier General E. B. Tyler's brigade to relieve William H. French's division at Chancellorsville, Webb received high praise but no promotion.[4]

In June 1863, Andy Webb was despondent. Nothing seemed to be going well for him. He wrote to his wife, Annie, how disgusted he was about his unpromising future, of how one of his West Point pupils, Adelbert Ames, had been made a brigadier general despite a recommendation for Webb's promotion to that same vacant post. "As for the B[rigadier] G[eneralcy] that has floated by, no hope for that," he told Annie on June 24, adding, "They sent two brigadier's appointments here today, so do not be worried, they left me out. . . . If I could live by it I might drive a clam cart around Tanneytown [New Jersey]. It would be as desirable as this." To his father, Webb admitted a few days earlier, "I am willing to retire and take a soft plank as soon as possible." He was "too closely connected with McClellan and Porter to expect any of this [Lincoln's] administration to help me."[5]

Webb's test of the soul lasted until June 28. When on the march to Gettysburg, Pennsylvania, with the V Corps, he learned that his immediate superior, General Meade, had superseded Joe Hooker as commander of the army. Incredibly, that very same day, Webb received his own appointment as a brigadier general, dating from June 23. Ironically, the deposed Hooker had signed a request for Webb's appointment on June 8 and it had been granted, contrary to the widespread rumor that only officers from Ulysses S. Grant's western army would be promoted.

Even more unexpectedly, Webb soon learned that Brigadier General Joshua T. "Paddy" Owen had been arrested on a minor charge, and by the consent of two of the army's fighting generals, John Gibbon and Winfield S. Hancock, he was to be placed in charge of Owen's unruly and often maligned "Philadelphia Brigade" of the II Corps.

Webb was now an altered man. His demeanor manifested both competence and determination. The grim responsibility of taking a new and important command virtually on the eve of battle caused Webb to narrow his perspectives. The twenty-eight-year-old newly minted brigadier was very mindful of the lax discipline that the brigade suffered from—it was known as the "straggling brigade, sixty or seventy absent daily," Webb told his wife—so he set about to firmly establish himself.

Webb's first day in command was telling. Calling the unit's officers together, he confronted them with what seemed to be radical demands. Noting their often slovenly appearance, with a lack of insignia of rank, he chided them for their unmilitary bearing and told them he would personally shoot any stragglers "like dogs." Then, when the brigade was told to wade Monocacy Creek that afternoon, there was a telling incident. Determined to regain his inadvertently lost position in the corps' line of march, Webb refused to allow the men time to take off their shoes and socks, and he made them wade the knee-deep stream without halting. With Webb himself standing in the middle of the stream until the entire brigade had passed, he heard many under-the-breath curses directed at him. One angry Irishman in the 69th Pennsylvania noted Webb's high-topped leather boots and bitterly commented: "Sure, its no wonder ye can stand there when ye are leather up to your waist."[6]

To the battle-wise if bedraggled veterans of many campaigns, Webb's demeanor smacked of "dandyism." Noting Webb's spit-and-polish staff-officer dress and his apparent inexperience, an immediate dislike of Webb spread through the Philadelphia Brigade.

Webb had only two days to fashion a reasonable semblance of order in his command prior to the furious Battle of Gettysburg, which on July 1 unexpectedly burst like an exploding bombshell upon the army. That evening, following several grueling marches, including one of thirty-five miles in fourteen hours, the Philadelphia Brigade arrived in the vicinity of Gettysburg and bivouacked along the eastern slope of Little Round Top.

Shortly after daylight the next morning, July 2, Webb's brigade was ordered to Cemetery Ridge. While en route, Webb halted his brigade of about 1,200 men and addressed the massed ranks: They would be now called on to defend their native state, Webb shouted, and each man would be expected to do his duty. He would personally shoot any man leaving the ranks—just as they could shoot him if he neglected to do his duty. The Philadelphia Brigade had a commander who would not fail, or allow his men to fail in their responsibility, he asserted. With these stern words ringing in their ears, Webb's men marched off to Cemetery Ridge, and military immortality.[7]

That afternoon Webb may have gathered what was in store for him when a sudden crisis erupted. Webb's brigade had been posted along the lower "shank" portion of Meade's "fishhook" line at Gettysburg. Cemetery Ridge—a low, sparsely treed, rocky ridge extending south from the town cemetery—was the center segment. Webb held about a two-hundred-yard front amid the nearly half-mile length of Gibbon's division, with a prominent clump of umbrella-shaped trees standing along the skyline near the ridge's crown at Webb's center. The ground was too rocky to entrench; besides, the men were without tools. With little natural cover, Webb had for protection in his near front only a farmer's rail fence and stone wall, two to three feet high, that ran helter-skelter along the ridge. Clearly, since the ridge was low, even ill-defined in places, it lacked good military strength.[8]

The vulnerability of Webb's position was clearly demonstrated on the afternoon of July 2 when a lone Confederate brigade, that of Brigadier General A. R. Wright, attacked obliquely across the Emmitsburg Road and moved swiftly up the slopes of Cemetery Ridge just south of the clump of trees. Wright's Georgians quickly overran a Rhode Island battery posted along Webb's flank, and pushed to within a few yards of the ridge's crest. Called on by corps commander Hancock to counterattack, Webb led two of his regiments, the 106th and 72nd Pennsylvania, in a furious charge. Their rush overwhelmed the Confederates, who were caught in a severe crossfire, and high praise was heaped on Webb and his men for their gallant fighting.

Although his horse had been shot, Webb was already basking in the glory of what he termed "a brilliant affair." As he later admitted, however, "we did not know how much more severely we were to suffer." Indeed, the attack by Wright's lone brigade had demonstrated that the Union Cemetery Ridge line was vulnerable, and might be taken if sufficient force was used. Mindful of this was General Robert E. Lee, whose plans for July 3 directly involved Webb and his men. Unknown to Andy Webb, Lee had targeted the prominent clump of trees at the Philadelphia Brigade's position on Cemetery Ridge as the very objective to strike with a massive infantry assault.

Webb spent much of that morning chatting with his officers and waiting. The oppressive heat made many seek shade, but it was so quiet following two days of grim combat that most endeavored to relax.[9]

Jarring everyone to their senses, about 1:10 P.M. a lone signal gun fired from Seminary Ridge, a mile across the mostly cleared valley from Cemetery Ridge. Immediately, a heavy barrage of Confederate artillery opened from 142 cannon (forty batteries) and began pummeling the Union lines across the way. "The air above and around us was filled with bursting shells," wrote division commander General John Gibbon. Indeed, Andy Webb found the cannonade awesome. "It was terrible," he later wrote, for "I have been through many battles, in all sorts of places, under all fires, but never have I heard such cannonading." When General Gibbon, who had been eating lunch at his headquarters behind the lines, jumped to his feet and ran over the crest of Cemetery Ridge, he saw "the most infernal pandemonium it has ever been my fortune to look upon."

Amid the guns of Lieutenant Alonzo Cushing's Battery A, 4th U.S. Artillery, Gibbon found Andy Webb seated on the ground near a cannon, acting "as coolly as though he had no interest in the scene." As the cannonade was replied to by the Union guns, and intense firing continued for more than an hour, Webb was seen standing amid the din, leaning on his sword and smoking a cigar. Yells from several of his men to take cover went unheeded. Webb stood like a statue, watching for the movements of the enemy, wrote an eyewitness.[10]

Undoubtedly, Webb was as frightened as many of his men, but his courage swelled amid a heightened sense of duty. "My men did not know me," he confided to his wife a few days later. "It was necessary to establish myself. They were to be made to feel that I ordered no man to go where I would not go myself." In fact, Webb felt he must prove himself worthy of his new star. He simply made up his mind that he would die before betraying the trust the government had placed in him.[11]

At shortly past 3:00 P.M. the Confederate plans became fully apparent. Into the bright sunlight from the woods along Seminary Ridge swept brigade after brigade of troops in butternut and gray uniforms. Pickett's, Pettigrew's, and Pender's Divisions of the Confederate Army of Northern Virginia, nearly 10,550 strong, surged forth in three main lines and began marching directly for Cemetery Ridge. They faced across the mile-wide valley about 6,200 Federals along the targeted portion of Cemetery Ridge. Webb, whose brigade before the cannonade had numbered 953 (down from 1,200 on July 2), was already convinced that his position was the focal point. From observing that the Rebel fire had been concentrated on his position, Webb later told his wife: "I knew then that we [our brigade] were to have a fierce attack."[12]

Webb had much to think of in a short span. Two companies of the 106th Pennsylvania were out as skirmishers along the Emmitsburg Road, and he sent word for them to hold on as long as possible. His main line was irregular, with two regiments, the 69th and 71st Pennsylvania, along the low stone wall in front. Since a step in the wall jutted at a right angle back toward the crest, support was distant on their immediate right flank. Because most of the 106th Pennsylvania had been sent the previous evening to help defend Culp's Hill, only a single regiment, the 72nd Pennsylvania, was available as a brigade reserve. It was now posted just behind the crest of the ridge. Lieutenant Alonzo Cushing's six-gun battery of U.S. Regular artillery held the open ground behind the stone wall, about midway back to the crest.

The Confederate lines were shifting by the oblique and rapidly concentrating in Webb's front. Cushing, who had already suffered a grievous wound, limped down to Webb's position amid the 69th Pennsylvania and obtained permission to wheel a couple of his cannon down to the stone wall. Soon two three-inch rifles were rolled forward and loaded with double charges of canister for close-range combat; one gunner even added a stray bayonet at the last second.[13]

Webb noted that the enemy pressed onward with measured step. It was magnificent; it was terrible, he said. The cruel blasts of artillery fire and volleys of musketry caused the gray lines to shudder and shake like a rag doll in the grip of a big dog. Amid the swirl of thick smoke, the myriad Confederate flags dipped and waved, but moved ever forward. The noise was deafening, and the scene defied description. There was little time to think. Webb stood in the midst of it all and watched the dizzying scene with sharp-eyed focus. Because of the heavy small-arms fire and artillery blasts, the Confederate brigade formations soon dissolved into one solid mass from fifteen to thirty men deep, crowding forward toward his sector. Above their ranks waved about a dozen red Confederate battle flags patterned on the St. Andrew's cross of Scotland. There were perhaps three thousand Rebels directly in Webb's front. Under the urging of their officers, a gradual, gathering movement began adjacent to the angle in the low stone wall. For the first time the wild, eerie Rebel yell rose above the din of battle, and the gray ranks surged forward.

Amid Webb's regiments all was chaos. The 69th Pennsylvania began giving way along its right flank, near Cushing's two guns. "We could see their faces, and hear their officers," wrote an excited Union rifleman. "It was almost too much for human nature to stand. [We] began to leave . . . , not because the enemy was upon us, but because it seemed impossible to stay." Back into the clump of trees ran many of the 69th's fleeing men. To their right, the 71st also began to break up. Cushing died of his wounds, his guns were silenced, and it seemed that disaster was imminent.[14]

Webb, furious that his line was giving way, ran to the 72nd Pennsylvania just behind the crest of the ridge and attempted to bring the regiment forward. Frightened men from the front line were breaking through the 72nd's ranks, and Webb angrily flailed at a passing artilleryman with his sword. The 72nd began slowly edging forward, then suddenly stopped. Despite Webb's repeated urgent shouts, the men refused to go farther, and only continued firing into the enemy in front.

Webb was appalled. Noticing the hesitation of the enemy when confronted by the 72nd's looming line, he saw that a rapid counter-charge would likely win the day. Yet in the deafening noise, smoke, and confusion, no one seemed to hear his shouted orders. Webb ran to a color-bearer and tried to grasp the flag to carry it forward, but the man in his excitement misunderstood and wrestled with the general for its possession. Entreaty, gestures with his sword, personal example—nothing seemed to work for Andy Webb. The 72nd remained stationary along the crest, suffering heavy casualties. Webb now felt all but "disgraced," he later wrote.[15]

Indeed, victory seemed to be slipping away. Precisely at that moment, Confederate Brigadier General Lewis Armistead, familiarly known as "Old Lo" to his men, pushed through the milling throng of gray soldiers. With his old black slouch hat on the tip of his sword, Armistead crossed the low stone wall and shouted to his men, "Give 'em the cold steel." Behind Armistead, a mass of gray poured over the wall and surged forward toward Cushing's abandoned midground guns, their red battle flags waving in seeming triumph.[16]

Andy Webb, seething with anger and humiliated by his inability to get the 72nd Pennsylvania to advance, promptly made his way toward the 69th Pennsylvania, still doggedly fighting amid the clump of trees. Despite the thousands of rifle muskets blazing about him—as he admitted to his wife a few days later—he *walked* to the embattled 69th, passing obliquely across the path of Armistead's advancing ranks.[17]

In one of the more improbable scenes of the entire war, Armistead and Webb, opposite commanders upon which the entire battle now turned, passed within a few feet of one another, each partially obscured by the blinding smoke, but both seemingly living a charmed life. "To die in such a fight is nothing," Webb later explained to his father. "But God protected me. I firmly believe that He does protect individuals." His thoughts at the time were crucial: "No general ever had more to depend upon his individual exertions than I had. Had Pickett broken through my lines this army would have been routed."[18]

His attitude resolute and his wits collected, Andy Webb continued to walk—rapidly, to be sure—back to the remnant of the 69th Pennsylvania near the clump of trees. Here he stationed himself a few paces in front of his men and directed their fire, both to the front and rear. "At this point I was just 39 paces from thousands of Rebs," he later noted. "Their officers desired to have me shot, and yet they only got one little wound on the inside of my right thigh." Struck a glancing blow by what he said was a ball from a Mississippi rifle, Webb was more fortunate than his counterpart, Lo Armistead.[19]

Having jumped the wall with about 150 of his men and now about forty feet in Webb's rear amid Cushing's cannon, Armistead went down with a mortal wound, his uplifted sword and hat striking one of Cushing's guns as he fell. With their leader down, the impetus of the Confederate attack seemed to dwindle. Many gray-clad riflemen began to fall back to seek cover. Yet they still outnumbered Webb's men, and their control of the Angle continued, with more than a third of the stone wall and rail fence remaining in Confederate hands.[20]

Webb was everywhere, one of his admiring soldiers later wrote, but there was little more he could do pending the arrival of reinforcements. On Webb's left flank, the brigade under Colonel Norman J. Hall had been forced back by the breakthrough at the clump of trees. Yet, spontaneously and almost instinctively, some of Hall's regiments began to face in Webb's direction. Despite the lack of organization and amid the great confusion, by personal exertion Hall and a few officers got the head of the retiring column moving northward, toward Webb. Soon they crowded amid the 69th Pennsylvania at the clump of trees. To Webb the appearance of Hall was a godsend. Hall sent few men but a good many flags, reported Webb, and "it looked like strong reinforcements." With two of Brigadier General George J. Stannard's Vermont regiments firing into the attackers' exposed flank, the Confederate lines again began to shake violently. Webb, bolstered by what he saw, now yelled out, "Boys, the enemy are ours," and led a rush of men from the clump of trees.

Along the crest of the ridge to his right, at the urging of General Gibbon's aide-de-camp, Lieutenant Frank Haskell, the 72nd Pennsylvania finally began moving forward toward the stone wall. A great, rushing crowd of men ran among the gray ranks and began fighting hand to hand, with officers using their pistols, and the soldiers wielding bayonets and clubbed muskets.[21]

In the melee, Webb passed over two downed Confederate flags without bothering to stop and pick them up. Cushing's guns were swiftly overrun and recaptured, and in moments that seemed part of a fleeting dream, Confederates by the hundreds threw up their hands or fled in disorder. It was over that fast. The struggle ended amid Union shouts of triumph. Webb suddenly found that his prisoners outnumbered his own men: "more than double my number," he later wrote. Once the confusion died down, a Confederate colonel noticed the scanty number of Webb's soldiers and guffawed in disbelief. Webb took it as a high compliment.[22]

Too emotionally wrought and stunned after this vicious combat to realize its enormous impact, Webb could at first only talk about "the fearful fight" in moderate terms and of "pretty good fighting" by his men. Despite the trouble with the 72nd along the crest, and his inability to make a decisive charge until the appearance of Hall's men, Webb soon began to realize what had occurred. It had been the high point of the crucial Battle of Gettysburg. He had been at the very crisis point of the battle, with the fate of the army in his hands, and had performed commendably, with both physical courage and composure. He had acted the part up to and even beyond his every ambition. "We have whipped them everywhere, and they are off," he declared to his wife on July 5. "Gone, run, whipped. God be praised."[23]

Webb wandered the smoldering battlefield shortly after the action. He meticulously counted 42 dead Confederates within "the Angle," and paced off the distance between his position with the 69th and the spot where Armistead fell: less than forty feet. His brigade, he soon discovered, had been fearfully cut up. Of the 953 officers and men present before the charge, the Philadelphia Brigade had taken 494 casualties, including the loss of 42 officers. Yet they had earned his full praise: "no men ever fought better than my own," he boasted to his wife several days later. "[I have] a real fighting brigade which has learned to obey me implicitly." Of particular pride, only 13 men were absent from the brigade that fateful day, instead of the usual 60 or 70.[24]

Now that he was a well-established general, Webb confided to his wife that he could not go back to being a captain or major in the regular army. "[I must] find some civil pursuit when this war shall be over. I must make reputation enough to be fit for a good place, even president of a railroad." Soon called to division command in the II Corps, and later brevetted major general for war service, Webb continued to be watched as among the most highly regarded of the army's young generals.[25]

Yet there were dark days ahead for Andy Webb. Despite promising his wife that he would not expose himself unnecessarily in battle, Webb was shot and nearly killed at the Battle of Spotsylvania on May 12, 1864. While attacking the "Bloody Angle," Webb, on horseback, was hit with a minié ball that entered the corner of his right eye, passed along the skull, and exited behind his ear. Miraculously, he survived this terrible wound, but he was absent from the army for eight months while he slowly recovered.

When he finally returned to duty in January 1865, General Meade made him his chief of staff, and after resigning from the regular army as a lieutenant colonel in 1870, Webb became president of the College of the City of New York, a post he retained for thirty-three years prior to his death on February 12, 1911.

Andy Webb never tired of reliving his Civil War past, for the war had been a bold lesson in life. "If I have changed, it must be because I have been through a great deal," Webb had noted a few days after Gettysburg. Indeed, remarkably, at a time when he had sorely despaired of remaining in the army, his life had turned full circle in the brief flicker of a moment. Present at the climax of the climax, and perhaps the central moment of the nation's history, he had stood the test well: when it counted the most, he had acted with courage and honor. Awarded the Medal of Honor in 1891 for his "distinguished personal gallantry" at Gettysburg, Webb had earned the enduring gratitude of the nation, if not the enormous fame that was accorded to his opposite number at Gettysburg, Lewis Armistead. Aware that if had he been killed that fateful day at Gettysburg, he would have been remembered as a martyr and national hero, Webb knew that fame was only superficial. What counted the most was peace of the soul, of having fulfilled God's life-purpose with courage and perspective.[26]

Major William Ellis—a Hero's Pain

Pain is perhaps the most feared word in our language. Pain is the essence of the most horrid of life's experiences. Physical pain involves suffering extreme discomfort from bodily harm, perhaps to the point of obliteration of all other stimuli. Pain in its most heightened intensity may result in unconsciousness, a practical relief from unbearable distress. Yet the pain threshold varies from person to person, as evidenced from confronting a dentist's drill or playing injured in a sporting event. That some individuals have been able to rise above extreme pain and perform effectively is food for thought. Is it courage of the mind, or endurance of the body? Is there a method, or is it a matter of will? To tough it out may involve a matter of seconds, minutes, or hours. But protracted endurance of extreme pain is a matter of dire experience, and in the case of a few individuals, it involves the height of courage, both physical and mental.

William Ellis was the sort of man who would be successful in most endeavors; he was smart, energetic, and committed. A youthful Union officer from the Buffalo, New York, area who had risen rapidly from second lieutenant to major for valor in combat, he was known for his dashing appearance and furious-paced riding of his horse about camp. His boldness was especially evident at the Battle of Spotsylvania, Virginia, on May 12, 1864. Ordered with his regiment, the 49th New York Infantry, to attack the infamous "Mule-Shoe Salient," Major Ellis was among his men, shouting encouragement and doing all in his power to get them over the defiant earthworks. Fighting was hand to hand at the very parapet walls, and Ellis, said an eyewitness, excited everyone's admiration with his conspicuous bravery. He was everywhere amid the swirling smoke and intense confusion, pushing, shoving, flailing with his sword, and boosting men over the rails. He drew the attention of the enemy. One Confederate soldier, in his haste to fire, didn't remove his ramrod. His rifle-musket was aimed at Ellis, only a few paces away, and the piercing whirr of the ramrod as it skewered the air was lost in the deafening noise. The ramrod struck Ellis end-on squarely in the left arm, sliced through the arm into his torso, and struck a rib. With the ramrod protruding from his body like some grotesque elongated metal thorn, Ellis was dragged from the scene in intense pain. When the ramrod was removed and the wound was examined by surgeon George T. Stevens, it was discovered that the ramrod-projectile had missed the bone in the arm, but had severely torn and bruised his left side below the heart. Dr. Stevens was worried that it might have injured the heart, but despite Ellis's great agony while in the hospital at Fredericksburg, his wound seemed to heal. Soon his strength returned, and he was discharged in early July, after about seven weeks' convalescence. Instead of going home on furlough, Ellis opted to return to duty, and was given an assignment on the staff of Major General David A. Russell, commanding the 1st Division of the VI Corps. As inspector general, Ellis was responsible for checking on the condition of each regiment in the division. This was an active-duty assignment that required extensive travel by horseback to and from the various camps. When other circumstances necessitated his duty as provost marshal, Ellis performed this task as well. For a full month, Ellis served on active duty, complaining little, but at times suffering in obvious pain.

On the morning of August 4, Dr. Stevens was summoned to Major General Russell's headquarters. There he found his former patient, Major William Ellis, dead. Russell was distraught, and wanted an immediate autopsy. Stevens went to work, and soon discovered what he had not known following the initial wounding. The ramrod had struck the rib cage with such force that a splinter "as sharp as a needle" had broken off. This gradually worked its way forward through the torso, "piercing and irritating the internal organs," so that "abscesses had formed and broken in the spleen," and "finally the splinter had pierced the lung" and killed him. Stevens and the others couldn't believe it. Ellis had endured what they supposed others could not, and continued to do hard, active duty. Given a hero's funeral in which the entire division participated, Ellis was later laid to rest in New York, the victim of a bizarre wound and fate, but one of the nation's most profound if unheralded heroes: a man whose courage extended far beyond the ordinary through the threshold of pain to a level that few could even imagine.[27]

X

"THE SUN SHINES BRIGHTLY; I SEE IT FOR THE LAST TIME"

The naval war was almost an afterthought to many who daily read of the endless casualties from battle after battle in Virginia and Tennessee. Yet the naval service for both Union and Confederate sailors was anything but devoid of courage. From raging storms at sea to the fearsome shell bursts of a naval engagement, the call for valor was profound.

Despite the monotony of blockade duty off the Southern coast, the role of the U.S. Navy in winning the war was great. From stifling importation of munitions and commerce from abroad, to seizing and controlling the South's major river systems, the Federal navy, which grew from forty-two to about seven hundred warships during the course of the war, was dominant. Yet the scope of the war was expanded and amplified by the often daring seafaring men of the Confederacy, who raided Union ocean commerce worldwide and kept a supply of products flowing through the blockade by means of their swift blockade runners.

In an era of vastly changing sea warfare, featuring armored warships, steam propulsion, and terrible, effective new weapons such as sea mines, submarines, and more accurate, longer-range naval guns, the call for heroism was great. To know the navy's heroism on both sides was to know the full measure of gallantry.

A MATTER OF PERSPECTIVE

John Yates Beall seemed at first glance but an ordinary man. Only five feet eight inches tall, the blue-eyed, brown-haired Confederate navy master resembled a bantam-sized businessman more than one of the most ardent, daredevil sea raiders; his demeanor left no doubt about his intense spirit and valor. The seventh child of a prominent and wealthy Jefferson County, Virginia, family, Beall attended the University of Virginia for three years, studying law, and was known for his gentlemanly refinement. Only twenty-six when the war began, Beall started out as a captain in the 2nd Virginia Infantry but took a wound in the chest in late 1861. Incapacitated for extensive field service, he turned his efforts to the navy. When convalescing from his wound, Beall came to the attention of Confederate navy secretary Stephen R. Mallory when he expressed interest in releasing Confederate prisoners held at Johnson's Island, Ohio, on Lake Erie.

Following an 1863 interlude as a will-of-the-wisp leader of a military unit raiding shipping and targets of opportunity on the lower Potomac, Beall was captured and imprisoned at Fort McHenry, Maryland. Although at first treated as a pirate, he was redesignated a prisoner of war when Confederate authorities threatened retaliation. Paroled, then exchanged in May 1864, Beall was more than ever committed to the intrigue and excitement of Northern adventures. He wrote a proposal to the secretary of war for special service along the boundary of Canada and the United States with a band of Confederates that would terrorize the Great Lakes region. Sent to join Confederate operative Jacob Thompson in Canada, Beall was shot and wounded while attempting to pass Union sentries en route. Making his way to Cascade, Iowa, where friends of his brother concealed him for about three months and nursed him back to health, Beall finally arrived in Windsor, Ontario, in early September 1864.

A plot was then under way to capture the USS *Michigan,* a 163-foot-long, 685-ton iron-hulled warship mounting fourteen guns that was assigned to protect Lake Erie, and was the only U.S. warship permitted on the Great Lakes under the Ashburton Treaty with Canada. The *Michigan* regularly was anchored near the Johnson's Island Prison, at Sandusky, and a special Confederate operative, Captain Charles H. Cole, an escaped prisoner of war living in Canada who had once served with Nathan Bedford Forrest's cavalry, was sent with four thousand dollars in gold to establish a rapport with the officers and crew.

Cole easily ingratiated himself, posing as a wealthy oilman from Pennsylvania, and planned to attend a lavish "wine drinking" party on board the *Michigan* on the night of September 19, 1864. Cole would attempt to drug some of the wine, incapacitating the ship's officers. He would then fire a signal rocket from the boat, telling a Confederate boarding party, waiting on a commandeered steamer, to proceed and overwhelm the unprepared deckhands of the *Michigan.* Once in control of the warship, the Confederates, led by John Y. Beall's boarding party, would man the guns and demand the surrender of Johnson's Island, enabling the release of the estimated three thousand Confederate officers being held there.

Beall's role was among the most daring. He would lead the working party of about thirty Confederates, mostly ex-soldiers, who would first capture a passenger steamer regularly plying the lake and use it to approach and board the *Michigan* following Cole's signal. Beall seemed confident of success, and on the morning of September 19 boarded the 221-ton side-wheeler *Philo Parsons* at Sandwich, on the Canadian shore near Detroit. At Malden (Amherstburg) another party of about twenty men carrying a trunk boarded the vessel, and the *Philo Parsons* set off for its normal route to the Lake Erie islands. After leaving Kelleys Island, Beall approached the acting master of the ship, Mate D. C. Nichols, and, displaying a revolver, commandeered the steamer in the name of the Confederacy. The old trunk was then opened, and Beall's passenger-crew armed themselves with the revolvers and hatchets it contained. A few shots were fired when an excited engineer attempted to escape, but at about 5:00 P.M. the *Philo Parsons* was guided under the watchful eyes of the Confederates toward the entrance to Sandusky Bay.

When Beall discovered that the steamer didn't have enough wood fuel to run seven or eight hours, as planned, he ordered a return to Middle Bass Island. Here the *Philo Parsons* was resupplied with fuel, and the regular passengers were put ashore after giving their paroles. While it was refueling, another small steamer, the *Island Queen,* docked and was seized by the Confederates. They towed it into the lake, opened its seacocks, and set it adrift; the *Island Queen* eventually foundered in nine feet of water on a reef near Pelee Island.

About 8:00 P.M. Beall and his Confederates steamed off with the commandeered crew of the *Philo Parsons* for Sandusky and Johnson's Island. They arrived off Sandusky Bay in full darkness, and the captive steersman warned Beall of the narrow channel, saying it was dangerous to proceed at night—they'd likely run aground. Beall had anxiously been scouring the sky all evening for Captain Cole's signal flare. There was nothing. Now there were rumblings among his crew that considering the absence of the arranged signal, the Yankees had been alerted to an attack.

Beall was on the spot. Options about what to do raged like a firestorm in his mind. Beall paced the deck, wrestling with his emotions and his sense of duty. Finally, he decided he could wait no longer—they would take the risk and run into the harbor and attack the *Michigan.* It was now after midnight, and word of what was about to happen spread like wildfire among his crew.

Captain John C. Carter, USN, captain of the USS *Michigan,* was, in the words of Confederate agent Charles H. Cole, an unpolished man, an old navy sea dog who had been shunted aside in the modern navy, and resented his treatment. Carter had been shocked on September 17 to receive a telegram from the provost marshal's office in Detroit, warning him that a Rebel deserter had just appeared and disclosed a plot to capture the *Michigan.* Further information was forthcoming the following day, and Captain Carter was told on the morning of the nineteenth that some of the *Michigan*'s officers had been tampered with by the alleged businessman Cole, who was a Rebel agent. The Confederates would seize the *Philo Parsons,* the informant noted, and would attempt to overwhelm the *Michigan* by surprise. Captain Carter was duly prepared, and that night at the wine-drinking party he had Cole arrested as a Confederate spy. On deck, his guns were loaded, and the crew was put on alert.

By this hour, John Y. Beall was incensed. Instead of proceeding into Sandusky Harbor, he was confronted with a mutiny. Sixteen of his crew signed and presented him with a petition saying that the expedition could not possibly be a success under the current circumstances, and they declined to proceed any further. Beall angrily called off the foray and headed the *Philo Parsons* for the Detroit River. He and his crew went ashore at Sandwich, and within hours the conspirators scattered throughout Canada.

Beall never knew how close he and the others had come to being blown out of the water by the trained guns of the *Michigan,* but his good fortune that night was later matched by the misfortune of being identified while scrutinizing the suspension bridge over the Niagara River in New York. Arrested by a New York police detective on December 16, 1864, he was held on charges of espionage and actions in violation of the laws of war. Beall's trial began February 10, 1865, and it was soon apparent that the odds were against him. His capture by force of arms of the *Philo Parsons* was deemed to be without lawful authority, and it was stated that he had further acted as a spy in Ohio, and also as such at the suspension bridge, while further serving as a guerrilla in trying to wreck a train near Buffalo. Convicted following a three-day trial by a military court, he was sentenced to be hanged.

Beall put up a fight, claiming he was acting under the orders of the Confederate government as a duly commissioned naval officer. His plea to the Confederate commissioner of exchange, written February 21, three days before his scheduled execution, claimed that "they [Federal authorities] know I acted under orders. I appeal to my government to use its utmost efforts to protect me, and if unable to prevent my murder, to vindicate my reputation. I can only declare that I was no spy or guerrilla, and am a true Confederate."

A furor among supporters and even sympathetic Northern congress-men and senators (ninety-one congressmen and six senators signed a petition for clemency) quickly placed the issue in the lap of President Abraham Lincoln. Yet Lincoln, aware of the great publicity in the news-papers about the case, demurred, returning the matter to the hands of Major General John Dix, commanding the Department of the East. Dix was the staunch politician-general who on the eve of the Civil War had ordered: "If anyone attempts to haul down the American flag, shoot him on the spot!" Dix was adamant. In approving the death sentence, he wrote that any action to prevent Beall's execution would be an outrage to civilization and humanity. There was "not a gleam of hope" that he would change his mind, Dix firmly announced.

One last visit by dignitaries to President Lincoln on the evening of February 23 proved unproductive. Lincoln displayed a telegram from General Dix stating that Beall's execution was necessary for the security of the area. A recent Confederate plot to burn the city of New York was fresh in Dix's mind, and neither he nor the president would encourage the prospect of more violence there.

John Y. Beall faced death on the morning of February 24 with compo-sure. His request to have a photograph taken was complied with. Beall looked into the camera with dignity and yet a firm, icy stare, as if his character were being tested. Having already met with his mother, who had journeyed from Virginia six days earlier, Beall, an Episcopalian, re-ceived the last sacrament. When called for in his cell on Governor's Is-land, New York, shortly before noon, he greeted his executioner and several officials calmly. He was at their service and knew their purpose, he said, so they should do their work quickly. He said that his part was simply a question of muscular power: "I think I can bear it," he re-marked.

With arms pinioned, a military cape across his shoulders, and a black cap on his head, Beall strode up the hill with the gallows in view. "The sun shines brightly," he thoughtfully remarked, "and I see it for the last time." The order of execution was read by the post adjutant, and

Beall's head was placed in the noose. Asked if he had anything to say, Beall spoke loudly: "I protest against this execution of the sentence. It is absolute murder—brutal murder. I die in the defense and service of my country."

The cap was drawn over his eyes, and following his whispered words, "I beg you to make haste," Beall heard the provost marshal draw his sword.

At thirteen minutes past one o'clock, John Y. Beall was dangling in the air. There was a convulsive movement of the right leg, a shrugging of the shoulders, and a few twitches of the hand. Twenty minutes later he was taken down. An army doctor stated that his neck had been broken instantly by the fall.

An observer noticed that there were tears flowing down the cheeks of many Union soldiers who had been paraded to witness the event. Terrorist or patriot, the result had been the same.[1]

"I Will Succeed"
Lieutenant William B. Cushing, USN

William Barker Cushing was not a man to be trifled with. A navy lieutenant in 1864, he had been dismissed from the Naval Academy in March 1861 following a series of practical jokes. Restored to the navy when the war began, Cushing had served as an acting master's mate and a midshipman before jumping to lieutenant in 1862.

By 1864, Cushing, only twenty-one years old, had already suffered through the agony of losing his much-admired older brother, Alonzo ("Allie"), who had been at the epicenter of Pickett's Charge at Gettysburg with his Union artillery battery. Allie had earned a hero's status for his fighting along the stone wall at the Angle. "I'll give 'em one more shot," he had shouted to Brigadier General Alexander S. Webb, then discharged his three-inch rifle loaded with multiple charges of canister into the onrushing Rebels' faces. An instant later, Lieutenant Alonzo Cushing had gone down, killed by a bullet that entered through his open mouth, burrowed into his throat, and exited out the back of his head.

Brother Will had been devastated by the news. He once wrote that he loved Allie "better than I do my own life." If his brother was killed, he had reasoned, he would "become a fiend." Prior to the loss of Allie, Will Cushing had already earned a reputation for daredevil bravery. In one action, he led a commando-style raid into the Cape Fear River near Wilmington, North Carolina, capturing Rebel mail and obtaining vital intelligence. His renewed determination and aggressiveness following the events at Gettysburg were soon evident; indeed, Will Cushing suddenly became the talk of the North.

In mid-1864 the major problem for the Union commanders at Albemarle Sound, North Carolina, was the presence of the Confederate ironclad ram *Albemarle,* a 158-foot-long blockade-smashing warship that seemed impervious to injury from the flotilla of Yankee vessels offshore. In mid-April 1864 the *Albemarle* had helped the Confederates capture the important river port of Plymouth, North Carolina, sinking a Union vessel and damaging another after their shots ricocheted harmlessly off the ironclad's heavy armor. Will Cushing's close friend Lieutenant Commander Charles W. Flusser was killed by a rebounding shell that exploded on the vessel from which he had just fired it. The loss of Plymouth, with nearly two thousand prisoners, twenty-five guns, and immense stores, was a severe blow to the Union cause, and Will Cushing vowed to avenge his friend's death.

A few months later he had the opportunity. The navy, desperate to put the *Albemarle* out of action, decided to assign Cushing to this special project. Cushing's bravery in conducting raids along the coast of the Carolinas, and his commitment to avenging the deaths of Allie and Charley Flusser, were well known.

Lieutenant Cushing accepted the assignment with a will. His steely nerve was evident when he devised plans to approach the *Albemarle* at night, using small boats, each with a spar torpedo (a mine fixed at the end of a long wooden spar). These would be lowered by a long boom below the ram's waterline, then exploded beneath the ship to sink her at her berth in the Roanoke River near Plymouth.

Cushing traveled to Brooklyn, New York, to obtain the proper craft and selected two thirty-foot-long wooden boats, both steam launches being built for picket duty with the blockade. Each was fitted with a twelve-pound howitzer on the forward deck and rigged at the bow for the spar torpedo, which would be the primary weapon. Considered dangerous to use and uncertain in operation, Cushing's torpedo device was highly risky. He barely had time to test a torpedo in the Hudson River before starting with his boats for North Carolina.

En route, one boat was lost to Confederate militia when it mistakenly put in to the Virginia shore for repairs on its engine. Relying thereafter solely on *Picket Boat No. 1,* Cushing made plans for the night of October 26, 1864, but the raid was aborted after the launch ran aground near the mouth of the Roanoke River.

The following night was cloudy and gusty, with occasional misty rain. Cushing now revised his plan. He would tow a boatload of thirteen naval volunteers behind the launch in a small cutter. This would provide a boarding party that might capture the enemy picket guard, said to be aboard the half-submerged Union ship *Southfield,* sunk in midriver during the April fight with the *Albemarle.*

Since Cushing's expedition was looked upon as a suicide mission by nearly all the officers and men who knew of the secret plans, Cushing warned the volunteers selected that it was a dangerous mission from which few might return. To a man, they agreed to continue. While in New York to obtain his boats, Cushing had visited home and told his mother in general terms of the dangerous foray he was planning against the *Albemarle.* She couldn't understand how so few with small wooden boats could hope to do what many with big warships had failed to accomplish. "I will succeed," he told her calmly, "or you will not have any Will Cushing." Together they prayed, reciting together the Lord's Prayer, and she added, "God, have mercy on my son!"

Mercy was far from Will Cushing's mind on the night of October 27, 1864. Departing about 8:30 P.M., his launch with fifteen men aboard crept slowly up the Roanoke River with its muffled engine chugging. By 2:30 A.M. Cushing's launch with the cutter in tow approached the dark, bulky form of the sunken *Southfield,* a mile below Plymouth.

The plan was to set the cutter adrift here and for the cutter's men to capture the enemy pickets aboard the sunken vessel. But in the inky darkness the Confederates failed to notice the launch and cutter as they glided by only twenty yards away.

Thinking quickly, Cushing now determined to proceed with both craft to the *Albemarle,* which was tied to the shore a mile ahead. Perhaps they now might attempt to surprise, board, and capture intact the dreaded enemy ram. Arriving undiscovered in the vicinity of the *Albemarle* shortly thereafter, Cushing steered for a wharf visible just below the ship's looming hulk. They were within yards when a dog barked loudly. A drowsy Confederate sentry on the *Albemarle* was immediately alerted and shouted a challenge, "Who goes there?" Cushing knew his plan of quietly boarding was foiled, and he cast off the towed cutter, yelling for them to go back and capture the pickets on the *Southfield.* Cushing then sent his steam launch full speed ahead for the *Albemarle.* Suddenly, he saw that the ram was protected by a "pen of logs"—a barrier of chained logs set about thirty feet off her side to protect against just such an attack. Amid the sharp rattle of alarm bells and whizzing musket shots, Cushing's *Picket Boat No. 1* sped away into the darkness.

The crisis was profound. What to do? Lives, careers, and perhaps the nation's future were at stake. Cushing never hesitated. Swinging hard about, he determined to ram his open launch at full speed over the logs to get within the barrier and then detonate his torpedo. He would never escape, he knew, but he had his duty to do. The boat sped ahead, engines churning, just as a huge bonfire, prepared for such an emergency, blazed suddenly from ashore. A fusillade of musketry ripped through Cushing's craft. One bullet tore into the sole of his left shoe. Another ripped through his sleeve. A shotgun blast tore open the back of his frock coat. Will Cushing never wavered. Guided by the light, he rammed his speeding launch into the log barrier, and with a splintering crunch the boat slid to a halt, its bow resting awkwardly atop the logs.

The chaos was terrible; amid angry shouts aboard the *Albemarle,* gunfire, and the shuddering of the boat, confusion was everywhere. Hurriedly, Cushing had the boom lowered, and the torpedo sank beneath the water's surface. Yet he saw only imminent disaster. His boat had come to rest within ten feet of the glowering muzzle of one of the *Albemarle*'s eight-inch cannon. Shouted orders from aboard the ram warned him it was about to fire. To explode his torpedo, Cushing had to carefully and slowly pull the firing lanyard so as not to break the slender cord. He pulled, and everything went swirling.

At the same instant, the *Albemarle*'s eight-inch gun fired, and the pressure from the blast seemed to flatten the boat "like a pasteboard box." The heavy charge passed over the launch and slammed into the river behind, but simultaneously the torpedo exploded with a roar. A towering geyser of water that shook both ram and launch engulfed both boats. The *Albemarle* shuddered and settled lower in the water. An instant later, Cushing felt blood running from his hand. Another bullet had grazed him. Cries from the ram of "Surrender!" echoed in his ears. "Never, I'll be damned first," yelled Cushing reflexively. Throwing off his coat, sword, and revolver, he dived into the river, even as he shouted to his men to save themselves.

The river was cold, and Cushing swam arduously into the current, avoiding a small boat that put out from the wharf loaded with Rebel soldiers searching for survivors. Exhausted, he finally collapsed upon the muddy shore, half in and half out of the water. When he awoke it was nearly daylight, and Will Cushing discovered he was at the edge of a swamp adjacent to the town of Plymouth. Laboriously, he crawled for yards across an open spot, avoiding the eye of a nearby sentry. In the swamp he encountered a black man from whom he learned the *Albemarle* was on the bottom of the Roanoke River. Encouraged and revitalized by the news, he pushed onward, eventually discovering a picket post of seven Rebel soldiers along a muddy stream. Nearby was a small square-prowed skiff they had used to reach the remote spot. Carefully waiting until they moved away to eat, Cushing swam to the boat and quietly set it adrift. After floating behind it for thirty yards around a bend, he was soon aboard, paddling for the mouth of the Roanoke River. This he reached after dark, and while Albemarle Sound would normally be much too rough for the flimsy skiff, this night the waters were miraculously calm.

SAMUEL W. WOLCOTT,
7th Connecticut Infantry.
He had it easy—a noncombatant assignment in the rear—yet Wolcott longed for combat duty. He wanted to do his part and hold his head high with his comrades from Salisbury, Conn. It cost him his life when he insisted on being transferred to the front and was shot in battle.
Courtesy of U.S. Army Military History Institute

HORACE B. ENSWORTH,
81st New York Infantry.
Following a boast to his father in 1861 that "we are tougher than pigtail lighting," and "if we could get a chance at a Southerner, we would suck his blood," Ensworth learned the hard realities of war. Compelled to make repeated frontal assaults in Grant's Overland Campaign of 1864, he reflected: "I believe . . . that they are not going to leave a man [alive], for that old Grant has to charge from here to Richmond, and charging is played out with me. I never will make another one [again] . . ." *Courtesy of Don Wisnoski/U.S. Army Military History Institute*

**DAVID W. NORTON,
staff of Maj. Gen. John
M. Palmer.**
Among the physically bravest
of the brave, Norton (shown
here in a captain's uniform)
rose to the rank of major in
the Union army, and an
exalted position on a fighting
general's staff. Yet his psyche
was that of a jilted man.
Rejected in love, he set out to
win glory and prove his worth
on the field of battle. During
the Atlanta Campaign he was
shot and instantly killed while
at the side of his exposed
general. *Author's collection*

**THORNTON BROADHEAD,
1st Michigan Cavalry.**
A Harvard-educated lawyer whose great
determination was the admiration of all,
Colonel Broadhead took what he knew
to be a mortal wound at Second
Manassas. His final deathbed letter to his
wife reflected intense emotion about "the
crushing weight" that would soon fall on
her, and yet a keen patriotism beyond
the love for life itself.
Courtesy of Blue & Gray Magazine,
Columbus, Ohio

SULLIVAN BALLOU,
2nd Rhode Island Infantry.
The emotionally inspired, presentiment-of-death letter written by Major
Ballou prior to the Battle of First Bull Run was made famous by filmmaker
Ken Burns in his Civil War series. Ballou's comments to his wife were
written with a keen perspective of human mortality, and yet these remarks
were conditional; Ballou wrote the letter believing he would survive the
battle, and it was placed amid his belongings "just in case."
Author's collection

DAVID O. DODD,
Arkansas civilian,
Confederate spy.

A mere youth of seventeen when he was hanged at Little Rock, he was offered an opportunity to save his life by revealing the source of his information. Dodd refused, and during a mishap at the hanging, he calmly produced his handkerchief for use as a blindfold when none had been brought. Fate was unkind; the gallows failed and rather than quickly dying of a broken neck, Dodd was strangled by the noose. *Photo from "The True Story of David Owen Dodd," a 1929 pamphlet of United Daughters of the Confederacy*

CHARLES G. HARKER,
U.S.V., brigade commander.

An exceptionally brave man, Harker was an orphan of small size known as "Little Charlie," but was determined to prove his large stature in life. Almost reckless in his physical exposure, he took grave chances in combat to win both glory and the battle. Harker was mortally wounded in the assault on Kennesaw Mountain, June 27, 1864, causing General Sherman to mourn that he had lost one of his best officers. *Courtesy of William Simms Collection/U.S. Army Military History Institute*

**WILLIAM ELLIS,
49th New York Infantry.**
His remarkable story illustrates how even severe physical pain can be surmounted by intense bravery of the soul. Grievously wounded by a fired rifle ramrod that penetrated his side during the "Bloody Angle" fighting at Spotsylvania in May 1864, Major Ellis returned to duty in July and served in a mounted capacity as inspector general. On August 4 he collapsed and died. From the autopsy it was learned the ramrod had broken off a splinter from the rib cage, which for months had worked its way internally, creating abscesses, until finally it penetrated the lung. *Courtesy of Roger Hunt Collection/U.S. Army Military History Institute*

ALEXANDER S. WEBB, U.S.V.,
chief of staff to General Meade.
So distraught as to consider resigning in June 1863—many of his pupils at West Point had been made generals while he languished as a lieutenant colonel—Webb won his general's star only a few days before the famous Gettysburg battle. Cast by chance into perhaps the most critical role during Pickett's Charge on July 3, he defended the famous angle at the clump of trees on Cemetery Ridge and won everlasting glory, including the Medal of Honor. *Author's collection*

JOHN YATES BEALL,
Confederate navy captain
and special agent.
Look into the eyes of a thirty-two-year-old man knowingly about to die. Beall, convicted of being a guerrilla and spy by the federal government, had requested that his picture be taken prior to his execution. With only a few hours remaining in his life, Beall stares intently into the camera. The man's courage was well demonstrated that day, Feb. 24, 1865, when he acted with calmness and fortitude before being hanged at 1 P.M. on Governor's Island, N.Y. *David Rankin Barbee Papers, Box 16, Folder 820, Spl. Collections Div., Georgetown University Library, Washington, D.C.*

LEWIS HANBACK, 27th Illinois Infantry.
An earnest volunteer who anticipated war's harsh reality, Hanback wrote to his
wife after his first battle (Belmont, Mo.) in 1861: "Leaving you . . . was by far
the hardest blow. I am not sorry the sacrifice was made. . . . I could not bear
the idea to have to stay at home while the country is . . . [facing] the enemy.
When this war shall cease . . . if I am safe, I can return home conscious of the
fact that I have . . . perform[ed] my duty. If I shall fall, . . . yet I shall not have
died in vain. My last moments shall be given to my country; my last thoughts
shall be given to you." *Courtesy of U.S. Army Military History Institute*

JULIUS GARESCHE,
U.S.V., chief of staff to
Gen. William S. Rosecrans.
A Cuban and graduate of West Point,
Garesche was well-known in the regular
army for his religious devotion and great
competence. During a grisly incident at
Stones River, Dec. 31, 1862, Garesche
was riding in the company of General
Rosecrans when a Confederate Hotchkiss
shell decapitated the unsuspecting staff
officer. As another staff officer later noted,
Garesche had been calm and cool that
morning and had read his Bible. His fate
was one that he accepted.
Author's collection

JOHN BELL HOOD,
Confederate general.
Hood's physical bravery was
evident from his years as a regular
army officer fighting Indians on
the frontier. Yet his lack of moral
courage and a want of character
contributed to his own and the
South's ultimate defeat. *Courtesy of*
U.S. Army Military History Institute

ALBERT SIDNEY JOHNSTON,
Confederate commander at Shiloh.
Sidney Johnston's courage in fighting the battle of Shiloh, despite his chief subordinate Beauregard's recommendation of retreat on the very eve of combat, reflects his great determination and sense of purpose. A leader who died too early in the war to fully credit with greatness, Johnston, nonetheless, displayed the high character requisite for a superb commander. He was unwilling to blame others, and said: "The test of merit . . . in my profession is success; it is a hard rule but I believe it is right." *Courtesy of National Archives*

PIERRE G. T. BEAUREGARD,
Confederate commander.

Beauregard was one of the South's most famous early commanders. Yet his record failed to match the expectations of military brilliance. His woeful performance at Shiloh included flaws in planning, organizing, and directing the surprise attack. Further, on the eve of the battle he lost his nerve and suggested a retreat, revealing a want of moral courage. Other events during the war contributed to his record as a commander with an inflated reputation. *Courtesy of* Blue & Gray Magazine, *Columbus, Ohio*

ULYSSES S. GRANT, Union military commander-in-chief. "Sam" Grant was much of an enigma in the aftermath of his career. Despite failing throughout much of his life—in his early prewar career and even later as U.S. president—he nonetheless accomplished great tasks. His command competence during the Civil War rested largely on his dogged determination, ability to remain cool in a crisis, and effective use of overwhelming material resources. At the heart of the matter was his bravery of the soul; to try to do that which is possible, even if not probable. *Courtesy of* Blue & Gray Magazine, *Columbus, Ohio*

ROBERT E. LEE, commander, Army of Northern Virginia. Lee's great competence was early recognized. After agonizing over leaving the U.S. Army to fight for his native Virginia, Lee played a key role in the war with ability, dignity, and honor. Yet his great character was perhaps his greatest gift. Rather than blame others for failures, he accepted such as a matter of his own responsibility—which could not be delegated. A larger-than-life legend and Southern icon, Lee survived the war's dire combat as an ultimate warrior. *Courtesy of* Blue & Gray Magazine, *Columbus, Ohio*

GEORGE H. THOMAS, U.S.V.,
Union commander at Nashville.
Among the greatest heroes of the war, George H. Thomas displayed enormous
moral courage in fighting as a Southerner loyal to the Union against family and
friends, and in managing the critical situation at Nashville in Dec. 1864.
Besieged by Hood's ragtag but dangerous army during inclement weather,
Thomas refused to attack until he was certain of victory. His delay of nearly
two weeks almost cost him his career, yet it resulted in the greatest large-scale
victory of the war. *Author's collection*

ABRAHAM LINCOLN,
president of the United States.
Beyond the man's honesty, humility, and great character were the perspectives of a leader committed to an ultimate task—that of winning. People were the means, and also part of the problem. Until the proper combinations were secured, Lincoln continued to make changes without regard to personal considerations, reflecting great moral courage. *Courtesy of* Blue & Gray Magazine, *Columbus, Ohio*

JEFFERSON DAVIS, president of the Confederate States of America.
Davis's stoic pride and great prejudice were an enormous factor in the war. Unwilling to change commanders when compelling evidence suggested it was the proper course of action, Davis maintained a stubborn insistence that resulted in far too many disasters of his own making. In contrast to his counterpart's methods in Washington, D.C., Davis's conduct of the war is clear evidence of the want of a deeper moral courage. *Courtesy of* Blue & Gray Magazine, *Columbus, Ohio*

PATRICK R. CLEBURNE, Confederate major general.
An outstanding tactician and perhaps the best fighting general in the Confederacy, Cleburne displayed enormous moral courage in proposing a plan in January 1864 to enlist slaves as a part of the combat army. His sincere efforts to do what he believed was right at the cost of political expediency cost him severely throughout his career. His competence largely unrewarded by the administration and his senior commanders, Cleburne died in a forlorn charge at the Battle of Franklin, Nov. 30, 1864, an ultimate victim. *Courtesy of* Blue & Gray Magazine, *Columbus, Ohio*

MARIA LOUISA FLEET,
Confederate mother.

Perhaps the circumstance requiring the greatest bravery of all was that of a long-enduring ordeal. In the aftermath of the war, when all was ruin and squalid conditions threatened even survival, this devoted Confederate mother kept it all in perspective. Her commitment to her family amid the worst of conditions revealed her grit, and the fortitude she evidenced in coping with the daily difficulties ennoble her as a woman to be honored as a true heroine of the war. *Photo from* Green Mount: A Virginia Plantation Family During the Civil War, *Betsey Fleet and John D. P. Fuller, eds.*

Your Friend

ASA M. WESTON,
50th Ohio Infantry.
The grim visage of battle is clearly evident in this photo taken in 1865, following arduous combat at Atlanta, Franklin, and Nashville. Weston's "fire and ice" stare reflects this veteran's grit, yet also a "somehow I survived" perspective. *Author's collection*

Cushing kept paddling, and guided by starlight, he continuously moved out to sea for two hours, making a total of ten straight hours without stopping. Aware that his strength was rapidly failing, he hoped desperately to reach the fleet or find a patrolling Union gunboat. At last, after 10:00 P.M., the dark hulk of the *Valley City* loomed in front, and Cushing yelled out, "Ship ahoy!" before collapsing in the bottom of his boat.

He was brought aboard and identified, then provided with brandy and some food. All but given up for dead or captured, Cushing swiftly learned that he was a hero. Word of his recovery at sea quickly spread, and within hours he was aboard the commander's flagship giving his report. He learned that only one other crew member had escaped to the fleet; most of his comrades in the launch had been captured by the enemy. Amazingly, he had persevered through all the bullets, explosions, and adversity to survive almost unscathed. A brief telegram to his mother confirmed that he was "all right" and would be rewarded. Indeed, soon he was feted as a celebrity. Rockets were fired in his honor, and everywhere he went there were loud cheers.

Most important of all to his mind, the *Albemarle* was out of the war. A few days later the Union fleet steamed into the Roanoke River and recaptured the town of Plymouth, now devoid of the seemingly invincible ram for its vital riverborne defense. Among the captured booty at and near Plymouth the navy found the partly submerged *Albemarle* resting on the muddy river bottom with a gaping six-foot hole in her hull from Cushing's torpedo.

Within a few days of his important feat, Cushing was sent north, where he received accolades in the papers and commendations from top officials, including Navy Secretary Gideon Welles. Most important of all, President Abraham Lincoln asked Congress to pass a vote of thanks to Cushing for his "important, gallant, and perilous achievement." Wrote Lincoln in his endorsement: "[The destruction of the *Albemarle* is] an important event touching our future naval and military operations, and [is] to the credit of this young officer, and the few brave comrades who assisted in this successful and daring undertaking."

Promoted to lieutenant commander, granted award money that eventually exceeded fifty thousand dollars, and honored by the resolution of Congress, Will Cushing had earned instant celebrity status. Thereafter, his new nickname, "Albemarle" Cushing, honored his outstanding valor. Indeed, wherever the popular hero went he was feted and congratulated.

Yet, Will's fortunes soon changed. Although Cushing was given good seafaring assignments by the navy and again promoted, after the war he was eventually relegated to a desk job because of failing health. He married in December 1870, and a year later witnessed the birth of a daughter, but his life was increasingly racked with pain, perhaps caused by prostate cancer.

Shortly after his thirty-second birthday it was evident that Will Cushing's remaining days were few. His mother and his wife, Kate, were with him on December 17, 1874, when together they recited the Lord's Prayer before he quietly died. The last word on his lips was "Amen." It was perhaps a fitting eulogy to a man whose short life had been so long in courage.[2]

XI

—

"RALLY 'ROUN DE FLAG, BOYS"
The 13th U.S. Colored Troops at Nashville

They had a magnificent regimental flag. It was vibrant blue with a bla-zoned eagle and shield, marked "Thirteenth Regiment U.S. Colored Infantry," with letters heralding: "Presented by the colored ladies of Murfreesboro." Only little more than a year old and still understrength, the regiment had served on railroad guard duty in Tennessee, and was without significant combat experience. Further reduced to 556 men and 20 officers by sickness and discharges, the 13th USCT, like many of its sister black regiments, was composed mostly of former slaves rounded up from the "contraband" camps around Nashville and middle Ten-nessee. They could serve as enlisted men, but not as officers; it was still a white man's task to lead and command.[1]

There was, in fact, little to distinguish this black unit from the oth-ers; its senior officers were combat-tested former line officers of German extraction in Illinois and Missouri regiments. Perhaps it was the matter of discipline that early marked this regiment for notice. Its lieutenant colonel, the exacting Theodore Trauernicht, who had served in the 2nd Missouri Infantry before organization of the 13th USCT in September 1863, was so upset over the lack of drill and discipline in his small unit that he petitioned the department to make up its mind whether his unit was to be laborers or fighting men.

In keeping with early concepts of their utilization, most black troops were little more than glorified laborers, serving secondarily as soldiers while constructing forts, repairing railroads, and serving on a variety of military labor details. Trauernicht was so chagrined by this that in October 1863 he complained that they were virtually isolated in an outpost on the Nashville and Northwestern Railroad thirty miles west of Nashville. Here his understrength and incomplete unit was struggling to be of some military significance. Because of a lack of white officers, the black non-commissioned officers were compelled to act as commissioned officers, complained Trauernicht. Moreover, since there weren't enough men to both serve as guards and furnish laborers, the 13th was liable to be gobbled up by roving Confederates, in which case the black "officers" might be treated by the enemy as "an irregular body and hung as spies." "Give me a full regiment," he pleaded, and they could do some good.[2]

The authorities seemed unrelenting, however. The 13th remained on construction duty until the middle of May 1864, when the work was finished and the unit was dispersed on guard duty along the railroad. Part of the regiment witnessed the shelling and burning of Johnsonville, Tennessee, by Nathan Bedford Forrest's guns as they fired from across the Mississippi River in early November. Yet the 13th was hastily recalled and summoned to Nashville in the wake of Hood's invasion of Tennessee later that month. Suddenly called upon to be soldiers in deed, the 13th USCT rushed to prepare for active combat duty, but after being refitted and reclothed, the troops found themselves again laboring—this time on Nashville's extensive entrenchments. Finally, the opportunity to wield rifles rather than shovels occurred on December 13 during a brief skirmish near the Rains house. Here during a reconnaissance the 13th Regiment sustained its first combat losses, one man killed and four wounded. The excitement of that combat had hardly passed when word came that the army would assault the Rebels' positions around Nashville on the morning of the fifteenth.[3]

Again the 13th was relegated to a lackluster role, remaining in the line of fortifications that day while General George H. Thomas's veteran troops drove back Hood's Confederates. Even on the morning of December 16, when they were sent in pursuit of the withdrawing enemy, the regiment found few Rebels remaining in its front. Its colonel, John A. Hottenstein, seemed nonplussed when told his regiment would be posted in reserve with its assigned brigade. It again appeared others would do the basic fighting. The men of the 13th USCT lay on the ground behind the frontline regiments, enduring an occasional incoming shell with growing indifference.

Suddenly, early that afternoon word came that an attack was about to be made on the enemy's works in their front on Overton Hill. There was a momentary swirl of excitement, and minutes later Hottenstein received an order to advance. Yet, the 13th seemed once more relegated to a secondary status. The column under Colonel Sidney Post, consisting of white troops, would make the primary assault, while the black brigade of Colonel Charles R. Thompson (to which the 13th was assigned) would serve as their support. Moreover, Colonel Thompson had posted two other units, the 12th and 100th USCT, along his front line. The 13th would thus advance behind the others, past a dense thicket in an old open cornfield, then hopefully be in position as reserves to move up during the final push over the enemy's imposing breastworks.[4]

The attack on Overton Hill, which began about 3:00 P.M., was an assault into hell itself. With a misty rain falling and the leaden skies emitting a pall of gloom, Thompson's black troops trudged forward into the open fields. Mud mired their every footstep, and ahead, shell fire raked the ranks of the 12th USCT; one bursting shell took out an entire file of men.

Directly in the 12th's front loomed an imposing thicket of tangled trees, briars, and bushes. By prior instruction, the 12th was told to detour around this all but impassable obstruction, even as the other units halted beyond the thicket to allow the 12th to rejoin. Yet the whole line now was under intensifying shell fire. With the 12th's soldiers moving at the double-quick in an attempt to catch up, the men of the 100th USCT were noticeably nervous while standing under the heavy fire. Then, seeing many of the soldiers of the 12th running, they thought perhaps a charge had been ordered. Suddenly, some of the 100th's inexperienced men began dashing ahead. Brigade commander Thompson was with the regiment, and seeing the confusion, he thought that perhaps greater disorder would occur if he attempted to stop them. Impulsively, Thompson loudly shouted for the men to charge. With a yell the ragged line of blacks sprang forward.

They quickly got to the base of Overton Hill, but here found their way blocked by Union Colonel Sidney Post's men, who were just ahead, struggling up the hillside from their position on the right. The 12th and 100th Regiments began swerving to the left to avoid Post. But already their badly fragmented and strung-out ranks were in disarray. The result was a disaster.[5]

Entrenched in the fieldworks on Overton Hill were two veteran Confederate brigades of General Stephen D. Lee's Corps, who were just then being reinforced by two brigades from Pat Cleburne's old division. Together, the combined gray ranks poured an incessant fire of musketry into the approaching blue ranks. Added to the fire of Stanford's Mississippi Battery, whose blasts of canister tore gaping holes in the struggling black lines, the withering firestorm forced the Union troops to take cover. A few staggered onward but they were soon tangled in the interlaced branches of downed trees, felled to hinder an attack. Post's troops, on the right, were at first pinned down, then fired into by the Confederates from an enfilading angle and forced back.

Thompson's men were equally devastated. Amid shouts of "Fall back! Fall back!" men began running wildly to the rear. Others were seen milling about, uncertain what to do. The lines of troops were by now intermixed, and many soldiers were seen crawling away to escape the terrible fire.

It was soon obvious that the attack had failed. Colonel Sidney Post was down with a severe wound in the side, and both his main attack lines and supports were fragmented, the Union men streaming to the rear in disarray.[6]

Suddenly there was much more to behold.

Forward from behind the scattering ranks moved Thompson's reserves, the 13th USCT. They were but a single regiment, 556 men and 20 officers, still surging forward heedless of the wild, desperate men streaming past in flight. The billowing smoke and dreary mist had helped obscure their approach to the Confederate works, but now they abruptly loomed in front, flags unfurled and officers waving their swords.

Colonel John Hottenstein here saw that it was full disaster they were facing. His untried black soldiers gasped in shock at the fearsome spectacle in front, even as the fugitives from ahead ran screaming through their ranks. "It was not calculated to give much courage to men who never before had undergone an ordeal by fire," winced Hottenstein. Yet the men of the 13th marched steadily on. Directly across the face of the salient angle moved the compact mass of blue uniforms, shoving and forcing their way through the downed timber. By now the firing had nearly ended along other sections of the line. Hastily, the 13th reformed in the brush beneath the breastworks, then again rushed at the Rebel lines with a loud yell.

The charging men were a single regiment in the open against a multibrigade front protected by earthworks. It was unfair, and the ordeal was painful. A concentrated sheet of fire leaped from the Rebel works. Shotgunlike blasts of canister tore into their flanks at point-blank range. Beneath the gushing smoke the flailed black lines reacted like lightning-jolted straw. Torn kepis and blood-spattered body parts were flung skyward. Whole rows of men went down in a heap, and the waving flags abruptly disappeared.

Yet the survivors never stopped. They kept going forward. Into the concentrated cone of fire ran the yelling men, their many groans and shrieks drowned out by the enormous roar. Wide-eyed in disbelief, Union infantrymen trapped on the slopes beneath the works watched in stark horror. An astonished Ohioan had never seen such a grim yet remarkable sight. These men who were recently slaves kept charging onward although they were being slaughtered by the dozens. Right up to the works they ran, their bayonets dripping with the misty rain.

Two sergeants had the colors, and one jumped on top of the breast-works, furiously shaking his flag in the enemy's faces. He was instantly riddled with bullets. Both color-bearers were killed within moments, and their flags dropped to the ground. Still the 13th's men fought on.

Confederate Brigadier General James T. Holtzclaw could hardly believe what he saw. Five separate color-bearers, one after the other, seized a fallen flag and attempted to plant it on his works. Each was promptly shot down. Urged on by their white officers, the remnants of the 13th repeatedly surged against the breastworks. "They came only to die," wrote the stunned Holtzclaw. General Holtzclaw was so impressed by the valor of these black soldiers that he formally cited their bravery in his battle report, an almost unheard-of concession for a Southern commander. "Their brave officers" repeatedly attempted to lead their men "to certain death," the Rebel general marveled, and he noted the bravery of three Yankee officers who were observed to fall in advance while urging their men forward.

It was all in vain. The survivors "had to fall back," wrote the 13th's grim commander. It was not for want of courage, he candidly reported; it was just impossible to take the works with such a small force.

An officer rescued the regiment's national flag as the 13th streamed to the rear in the wildest disorder. The blood and gore remaining in the wake of its retreat convinced nearly all that the 13th USCT had tried its utmost. Of the 576 present in the regiment, 221 were casualties.[7]

Holtzclaw's men wanted to pursue, and some of his soldiers sprang over the works, but their commander feared a counterattack and recalled them. An Alabama lieutenant, before he returned, ran over to the 13th's regimental flag and brought it in as a trophy. The lettering on the blood-spattered banner was still readable: "Presented by the colored ladies of Murfreesboro." Thereafter, the forlorn charge by the black regiment was the talk of the men who were there. "I never saw more heroic conduct shown on the field of battle than was exhibited by this body of men so recently slaves," commented a veteran Ohio officer. When a wounded black soldier was brought to the field hospital, an assistant surgeon noted the man's three wounds and remarked, "They went for you, didn't they?" "Yas," came the reply. "I jes shouted, rally 'roun de flag, boys, and dey heard me." Later the surgeon rode over the battlefield where the fallen blacks were found closest to the breastworks, their faces toward the foe. "Don't tell me negroes won't fight!" he wrote in a letter home. "I know better." It was perhaps a fitting tribute to the 13th Regiment USCT in its maiden battle. They had, indeed, come "only to die." The ladies of Murfreesboro could well be proud of their brave regiment.[8]

IN TODAY'S PERSPECTIVE

The question of race as a matter of competence, and hence courage, had long been pondered by many in an era of prejudicial comparative values. At the time of the Civil War, many Southerners viewed blacks as "inferiors" based upon their long-standing servitude and radical cultural anomalies. The absurdity of that position was never questioned by the Old South's society, which denied formal education, the means of equality, to blacks, who in 1860 numbered about 34.5 percent of the South's total population (versus only about 2 percent for the Northern states). The often seen dehumanization of blacks was predicated on a long-standing bias that proclaimed cultural and "racial" superiority for a white civilization in full control.

Courage was one of the character traits that many whites in the South laid claim to in both maintaining the long-established societal order and waging a war. Southern invincibility was said to be predicated on courage, determination, and manly honor. As characterized by the famed "Virginia mystique"—Virginians were said to be bred of a superior cavalier heritage as the planter descendants of Norman aristocrats who had ruled England for centuries—the myth of Southern superiority was given substantial credence by some citizens at the beginning of the war. Virginia cavaliers possessed gentlemanly martial skills such as riding, shooting, and outdoorsmanship. The chivalrous virtues of manliness were akin to the character of one of King Arthur's Knights of the Round Table in the mind of many white Southerners.

Furthermore, many whites in the Old South believed that the European "Yankee" immigrants who had settled in New England were of inferior Saxon ancestry. Allegedly coming from the lower socioeconomic classes that had long been dominated by their Norman rivals, the Saxon descendants were said to be burdened by an emotional inferiority that denied them the confidence to effectively confront Southerners.

This ideology fueled Southerners' belief in their superior martial skills, which would ensure victory in the war. On the eve of the Battle of Gettysburg, one ardent Southerner assessed the results thus far and concluded: "[We are now] dictating to the [local Pennsylvania] inhabitants as masters. I do believe in it [Southern prowess] now more than ever before. There is an innate difference between a Yankee and Southerner. [This] I have ever believed, but the exalted superiority of one race has never struck me so forcibly as now."

This opinion was deflated following the Rebel defeat suffered at Gettysburg, and the course of the war convincingly demonstrated the myth of Southern superiority. Indeed, the conception of greater Southern courage and ability was clearly proved false. Courage and the will to win had paled in the face of overwhelming numbers, resources, and technology. In an emerging era of modern war, with more lethal weapons and effective communications and transportation capabilities, the reliance of the South on personal prowess was both outdated and invalid.[9]

The basic elements common to all mankind, courage and ability, had been balanced on the battlefield.

XII

A WOMAN'S ORDEAL: COPING ON THE HOME FRONT

Courage, as a reflection of the degree of difficulty to be coped with, often relates to knowledge of what one is facing—the relative certainty of disaster or the hope, no matter how flickering, of relief from adversity. The anguish of waiting in an ordeal, of not knowing, of hoping against hope, of keeping mental control when one's heart and soul are bursting with apprehension and grief, involves distress of infinite proportions.

This often cruelest of Civil War ordeals for the soldiers' families was accentuated by the lack of communications technology that, today, we take for granted. Immediate notification of disaster or any important news is facilitated today by cell phone, electronic transmission, and the multiple media. In the 1860s there were only telegrams and letters, both of which usually involved considerable delay. The agony of waiting for personalized word, especially given general news of a battle or injuries sustained by specific units, generated profound distress. Most often, those greatly affected were the women: wives and mothers, whose husbands and sons were the initial victims of the war but not the ultimate sufferers. In death the individual soldier found the peace of the grave. Those of his family who survived knew prolonged suffering—of the nagging ache of nevermore, and of love and companionship forever lost.

WON'T YOU COME HOME, BILL MORSE?

Lucy Morse was a highly emotional woman. Her status as a mother and homemaker in Smyrna, Michigan, was intensified when her husband, William H. Morse, enlisted at age twenty-four in Company C of the 3rd Michigan Volunteer Infantry on June 10, 1861. Aware in July that Will had survived the highly publicized carnage reported in the newspaper of First Bull Run, she confided in a letter:

> [I] received your letter last night, and never was a letter received with more joy than yours. It has been three weeks today since I received a letter from you, and you may be assured that a letter has been anxiously looked for since the battle. Dear Will, you do not, cannot, know how thankful I am that you are safe. I was almost crazy before I heard from you for fear that you had shared the fate of many a brave soldier. Oh, it seems cruel that so much blood must be shed. . . . Oh, Will, I wish you could be at home now. It seems so odd to have to plan for myself, but you must write what you think is best for me to do. Will, our little curly head [infant son] is well and grows every day.

Told by her husband that many of the 3rd Michigan's soldiers were homesick or afraid, but he was "neither," that he had been in two fights, those of Blackburn's Ford and Bull Run, "and I don't think I had any more fear of being killed than I would [if I had been] at home," Lucy was encouraged to bear up. "Be a good girl and don't be scared about me," he reassured her. "Kiss Bub [his son] for me, and tell him his papa is a soldier fighting for the constitution and the [nation's] laws."

Will's Bull Run letter noted that he had "seen many brave men fall by the cannon and musket, and I could pass by them without scarcely looking at them," yet Lucy remained apprehensive. When a new campaign began the following spring she was nearly shorn of her senses. Reports surfaced in the local newspaper that the 3rd Michigan had been savaged at the bloody Battle of Fair Oaks, May 31, 1862. Worse yet, her husband, Will, was listed among those wounded!

"It is with trembling hand and an aching heart that I pen these few lines to you," wrote the stunned Lucy on June 12, 1862.

The sad news that you were wounded reached us, and you cannot imagine my feelings as I contemplate the possibility of your being mortally wounded. Oh, God, the thought is agonizing. Oh, I hope that it may prove a false report, or if it is so, that it is a slight one [wound]. Oh, dearest husband, if it is true you must endeavor to get a discharge. I know they will give you one. . . . Oh, get a discharge if it is a possible thing, and come home where you can have careful care. Do not, you must not, go to the hospital, where there will be no gentle loving hand to administer to your wants. Tomorrow is mail day, and Oh, I hope that it will bring better news. I will try to compose myself until I know for certain. Will tomorrow ever come!

Friday afternoon [June 13, 1862]; I hasten to answer your long and anxiously looked for letter, which I received about noon. Oh, dear William, you cannot think how my heart bounded with hope when I saw your well known writing. Oh, my husband, you do not know what a relief your letter was to me, for although it was the bearer of sad news [about the wound in his knee], I had feared that it might be worse. I cannot complain. I am so thankful that it is as well as it is [and] that you were not killed. Oh, I can bear the thought of your being wounded if you are spared to me. I could bear to see you a cripple for life, but I could not bear the thought of your being taken from me. Oh, Willy, it would kill me if you should die and leave me. But hope is strong in my bosom. I think that you can get your discharge, and just as soon as able to

ride, you must come home where anxious hearts are waiting. . . .
You don't know how unwilling I am to trust you to any other care
but my own. Keep very quiet and bear it patiently. I know it will
be trying to you to have to keep still, [as] you were always so
stirring. But you must remember the anxious heart that hangs on
your recovery. Keep up good courage, dearest, and I will trust all
will be well. . . . I feel thankful you are spared to me. Oh, Willy,
dear Willy, you do not know how much I love you. It seems as if
my very heart was bound up in you. There is not another on earth
that could love you more than I do.

Neither love nor the soul-bearing emotions of Lucy Morse proved to be the final arbiter. Private William H. Morse was sent to the military hospital at Philadelphia, where on August 8, 1862, he died of an infection. Her hope had become but a final, sad requiem. Her fate, and her husband's, were the inherent, stark tragedy of war.[1]

BILL SHAFTER'S SISTER, ANN

Often results of everlasting consequence are locked in nebulous decisions that initially seemed less than monumental. Such is the reality of life. But in wartime, personal danger magnifies the consequences. When Job Aldrich, a prosperous merchant from Galesburg, Michigan, was recruited by his brother-in-law, Bill Shafter, there was little thought of ordeal and hardship.

Bill Shafter had a big problem on his hands in December 1863. As the lieutenant colonel of the 19th Michigan Volunteer Infantry, he was offered the opportunity to be promoted to full colonel and given command of a new black regiment, which was very appealing to the twenty-nine-year-old former teacher. Yet he had to organize and staff this new regiment of volunteers within nine days.

The men didn't seem to be the problem; they might be obtained from the multitude of blacks gathered at Nashville. Most were former slaves and were eager to join the Union army to fight for their freedom, and even get paid for doing it! As members of the 17th Regiment U.S. Colored Troops, they were to be commanded by white officers per the regulations of the day. Most of the 17th's officers, whom Shafter recruited, were combat-experienced junior officers and former noncoms who had served in other regiments and were happy to be promoted in their new assignments.

An exception was Job Aldrich, who ran a profitable hardware store in Galesburg. With his wife, the former Ann Shafter, who was Bill Shafter's only sister, he had three young children, the most recent a baby aged six months. Since Job was thirty-five and a successful businessman, there really was little reason to leave Galesburg, except for this sudden opportunity. Brother-in-law Shafter desperately needed officers for his new regiment and promised Job a commission as a lieutenant and an assignment as adjutant of the 17th. Job had to decide almost immediately, since the organization had to be completed by December 21, 1863; it was then December 19. It was a chance to see the war before it was too late. Job later wrote that he had only two days to decide, but being patriotic and wanting to help, he agreed.

Commissioned as a lieutenant on December 21, 1863, Job Aldrich spent most of the next year on duty with the 17th. Life was relatively good; the regiment had been assigned light garrison duty in Tennessee, and Aldrich was granted several leaves of absence by Colonel Shafter to return to Michigan and look after his family and business. Then, when a vacancy occurred for commander of Company G, Shafter had Job promoted to captain in October 1864.

With the approach of John Bell Hood's Confederate Army of Tennessee to Nashville in early December, the 17th Regiment U.S. Colored Troops was assigned to a fighting role. Indeed, when Major General George Thomas's plans were complete for the attack on Hood's army on December 15, the 17th Regiment was given the assignment of attacking the extreme Confederate left flank, along the Murfreesboro Pike near the Rains House.

Aware that they would be experiencing their initial combat the following morning, on the night of the fourteenth the men of the 17th USCT were quite apprehensive. Captain Job Aldrich wrote a brief letter to his wife back in Michigan, telling her that he had a strange premonition about the coming battle. In fact, he feared he might be killed, and gave his valuables and this letter to Hattie Shafter, Bill's wife, who had been visiting Nashville and stayed to support her husband in the budding crisis. Job's letter closed with the remark: "The clock strikes one, good night. At 5 the dance of death begins around Nashville. Who shall be partners in the dance? God only knows. The echo alone answers who? Farewell, Job."

There was really little need for this letter, surmised Bill Shafter, for Job had just been given a new assignment—a desk job—and would not have to go into action with the regiment, but Job insisted. He had led his company for three months, and was not about to desert the men on the eve of their first combat, when his presence would count the most. Thus Job was in line on the morning of December 15, when the 17th marched off into battle.

Advancing westward at about 10:00 A.M., from the Murfreesboro Pike, the 17th, as a part of Colonel Thomas J. Morgan's brigade, overran some lightly defended Confederate trenches and proceeded onward toward its objective, the last of the forward line of enemy works. The previous evening, Colonel Morgan had scouted the area from a distance and had seen what he believed was a curtain of logs supported by rifle pits that extended south to protect the flank of the enemy's northward-facing earthworks. As Shafter and his men dashed forward into a patch of timber to get beyond these rifle pits, suddenly they came to an abrupt halt. In this patch of timber perpendicularly lay the railroad bed of the Nashville and Chattanooga line. Here the railroad ran through a twenty-foot-deep cut that had been blasted into a ledge of solid rock. The walls of the cut were steep, and Shafter's men were now caught in a deadly trap. Unable to escape right or left because of the sudden, intense fire opened on them, they began milling in confusion. Shafter looked in the direction of the supposed curtain of logs that Colonel Tom Morgan had noticed. He saw instead a crude but strong lunette—an open-sided fort that had been constructed by the Confederates of Brigadier General Hiram B. Granbury's Brigade—that held four cannon.

These cannon, suddenly trained on Shafter and his men, now sprayed deadly blasts of canister into the bewildered Union ranks only thirty yards distant. Granbury's men had carefully watched the approach of Shafter and his men toward their right rear. Realizing that the Yankees couldn't see the lunette through the timber, they had patiently held their fire until the enemy was trapped beneath their guns. Their artillery blasts, together with the musketry of Granbury's men, bowled over the hapless bluecoats like so many tenpins. In a panic, many of Shafter's men jumped into the cut. It was a serious mistake. Brigadier General Daniel C. Govan's supporting infantry brigade of the Rebel army now swung across the mouth of the cut and fired repeated volleys into the milling crowd of Yankees, who had no place to hide. The encounter came close to being a massacre. The survivors among Shafter's officers and men ran for their lives back across the fields. In less than ten minutes Shafter's command had lost 110 men and 7 officers. After the winded men stumbled to a halt along the Murfreesboro Pike, it was learned that Captain Job Aldrich was missing. Bill Shafter looked in vain, and finally learned from one of his men that Aldrich had been seen to fall at the railroad cut and was presumed dead.

The battle continued, and after the Rebel troops retreated, Bill Shafter had a chance to go to the battleground early the next morning. He was the first to search for and find Job. Job lay on his face. There was a gaping hole in his head from a canister ball; but at least he had died instantly. The Confederates had ransacked the body and removed all his clothes. Bill Shafter hastily wrapped the body and had it sent to Nashville before going off again into battle.

After the two-day battle ended and Shafter had a moment, he wrote a tender letter to his sister, Job's wife, who would be waiting anxiously for information—knowing from a hasty telegram only that her husband had been killed.

Bill's anguish was profound. He pondered what to say to a loved one in the family who had so abruptly lost her husband—especially when Bill's recruitment had enticed Job to join the army. Bill Shafter struggled with his thoughts, and penned an emotional, compassionate note. His words echo through the years, reflecting the agony and inequity of battlefield deaths for wars past and present.

Nashville, Tenn. Dec. 19th 1864

My Dear Sis: For the first time since the fight of the 15th inst. I have had time and opportunity to write you. It is useless to attempt by words to soothe your sorrow, and though you are the sorest afflicted, believe me when I say that you have shed no bitterer tears than I when I found poor Job. He was as dear to me as either of my own brothers. It was an awful battle, Sis, and we are of the many who are called to mourn. Job seemed to have a presentiment that he should die, and the night before the fight [he] wrote you a letter, the most affecting I ever read. He left it with Hattie to send [to] you if anything happened. Hattie will bring it to you in a day or two with the rest of his things. I hope his boys will remember the last words of their father.

Job never knew what hurt him. He did not suffer an instant. May my last end be like his! He died for his country, of which there can be nothing more glorious. He left all his money and valuables in camp. Hattie has them.

The circumstances were these. We were ordered to drive the enemy out of a piece of woods and take the battery on the other side. We drove them from the woods, but there was just in front of the battery a deep cut at least twenty feet deep. We went to that and had to stop. Job was killed there. We had to leave him. I was on the right side of the regt., and did not know he was killed till we had fallen back, or I should have seen him off [the field].

We got the ground [back] in the morning and I was the first to find him. He lay on his face. The Rebs had taken all his clothes, everything. I had him taken up and sent to town. I had to go on myself for another fight.

Hattie will be home in a day or two. I will get Job's things all fixed up without a bit of trouble to you. Be of good heart, Sis. I feel for you from the bottom of my heart. I will write soon again. Love to all,

Your affectionate brother, Bill

*The good die first, while those whose hearts are dry as summer
dust burn to the socket.*

As might be expected, Job's widow, Ann Shafter Aldrich, was devastated by the cruel blow of losing her husband. It was Christmas evening when Hattie arrived from Nashville with Job's letter and a few of his belongings. It was a tragic and sad Christmas. Yet, as many heroic American women have done, she chose to take the high road, so to speak. Rather than drown in sorrow and anguish, she looked at the many good qualities of her life: her children, the comfortable lifestyle Job had provided for her, and the loving memories of their time together.

A few weeks later she wrote to family members about some of her thoughts, and enclosed copies of Bill's December 19 and Job's last letter: said Ann, "Financially, we shall have (if we get the insurance of Job's life, which we doubtless shall) about $1,800 in money with a pension of $20.00 per month and a good home, for all of which I can thank Job's watchful, provident care every hour of my life. . . . I send you these copies of letters now in my possession, knowing that you will highly prize them as mementos of the loved & lost. Hattie, brother William's wife, arrived here Christmas night, Sunday, bringing Job's effects and the letters prized more highly than all."

For Ann Aldrich it was a meager consolation, but the government granted her a monthly pension of twenty-three dollars, and her family was well provided for by family and friends. Bill Shafter became her financial guardian and later was a leading figure in the army during the Indian wars before commanding during the Spanish-American War the force that captured Santiago de Cuba. Although controversial for his many personal feuds and rough demeanor, Bill Shafter was belatedly awarded the Medal of Honor for Civil War bravery. Later he became known as "Pecos Bill" for a hard-driving overland journey to the Pecos River in 1875.

Ann Shafter Aldrich, like countless other war widows, bore up well under the challenge of adversity and loneliness. Only twenty-six when Job was killed, she eventually remarried and lived a full, productive life prior to her death in 1889.[2]

Ann Aldrich's story is both remarkable and unremarkable. She bore a heavy cross in life. A woman burdened with sorrow, she personified both dignity and courage. She met her ordeal with the fortitude so characteristic of the American spirit. All but forgotten, she resurfaces today as a reminder of the quiet heroism that characterized those years of trial and travail, being a noble example of what helped make this nation the greatest on earth.

XIII

OF AGONY EXTENDED
AND ENDURED

Thomas Hart Benton seemed to be a rather typical young soldier. Along with his close friend, Sam McCown, he had gone off to war with the spirit of adventure and patriotism. A sergeant based upon his community standing—his father, Thomas Sr., was a respected hardware merchant in Richmond, Indiana—he had enlisted at age twenty in Company B, 19th Indiana Volunteer Infantry, on July 29, 1861. Benton looked forward to doing military duty and seeing the sights, saying after a routine six months' army service, "I wish this war was over so that I could come home, but I do not want to come [home] until everything is settled. If I was there I could do nothing in these dull times." Candidly, he confided, "If I were at home it would be a source of great annoyance to me. To know that almost all of the young men of my age were rallying under the flag, and I safe at home."[1]

Despite eagerly anticipating active service, the 19th Indiana had mostly remained on occupation duty near Fredericksburg, Virginia, during the spring and summer of 1862. Along with Sergeant Sam Mc-Cown, Tom Benton had fattened up on buckwheat pancakes; then, when honored as a color sergeant, he had visited the Capitol in order to present to Congress a captured enemy flag. Although patriotism was keen in his mind, he gave thought to the rigors of combat, saying that if captured in action he would attempt to write a double letter, the second one invisible to the naked eye, being overwritten with water and sugar, which would become visible by holding it near a heated stove. Yet the weeks dragged by, and nothing but rumors were afloat as the 19th Indiana maintained its position opposite Fredericksburg. In early July, Tom Benton wrote in despair, "I don't think our regt. will ever be in a battle." Anticipating that McClellan's Peninsula Campaign would capture Richmond, Sergeant Benton gloomily predicted that "after the fall of the enemy's capital the war will be over."[2]

Finally, in July 1862, the active war involved Pope's army, including Brigadier General Rufus King's brigade (then under Brigadier General John Gibbon). Gibbon outfitted the men with the distinctive old army style "Hardee pattern" hats, and soon thereafter they were known as the Black Hat Brigade. Benton's morale was heightened, and he told his parents that "nothing short of death will stop us" from getting to Richmond. "Every night when I lay down I expect to be wakened by the long roll and marched out to meet the enemy," he continued. Soon their brigade was on the march, and when passing the recent battlefield of Cedar Mountain on August 14, Sergeant Benton found time to view its gruesome carnage. Trees more than a foot in diameter were cut off and shattered, dead horses were strewn about, and the hastily fashioned graves of men had arms and feet grotesquely sticking out of the ground. The papers had written that the Union forces were victorious, he noted. "But one half [of what they report] is not true." The enemy had a decided advantage of position, he considered, and "we lost as many or more men than they did." War's stark reality was more than any newspaper account could depict, he clearly saw.[3]

Fourteen days later, Sergeant Tom Benton and his friend Sam Mc-Cown were in the midst of a battle, near the old battlefield at Bull Run.

It was the 19th Indiana's initial fight. Benton was in the forefront of the fighting against Stonewall Jackson's celebrated troops on August 28. He had advanced along with the rest of the regiment in an open field on the Brawner farm near Gainesville, Virginia, only to encounter the 4th Virginia Infantry of the Stonewall Brigade. In a close-order, stand-up, ranks-to-ranks shoot-out at about seventy-five yards, Benton's 19th Indiana was badly mauled. Posted on the regiment's extreme left, Company B fought with Springfield rifle-muskets amid piles of dead and wounded, not giving ground until Rebel artillery was brought up to enfilade its line.[4]

In the fearful firefight the "Richmond City Guards," Company B, took terrible losses. Shockingly, Tom Benton's close friend Sam Mc-Cown was seen to fall. Then Sergeant Benton was hit; a minié ball ripped into his thigh, but he continued loading and shooting. When Second Lieutenant Samuel Hindman was shot in the leg, Benton helped carry him over the adjacent hill and out of danger. The lieutenant, noting Benton's wound, wanted him to stay with him and seek medical attention. But Tom Benton said no, he was going back to fight as long as he could stand.

Returning to the battle, Sergeant Benton was mindful of the prospect of his death; he had written only a few weeks earlier: "Today we are well and doing well; tomorrow a bullet may end our career in double quick time. Yet life is no more uncertain here than at home." This fatalistic attitude about death had been evident when his sister suddenly died in early 1862. Benton then had expressed shock and sorrow, mentioning that while he had hoped to see her again "before she left this sinful world," it was "ordered otherwise."

When a second bullet found Benton, slicing through his lungs, he was observed to drop heavily. A comrade was about to rush to his side and help him, but instead was ordered by an officer to close up the line. Benton painfully crawled to an apple tree in Brawner's nearby orchard, and as the 19th Indiana staggered backward in the face of oncoming enemy reinforcements, a last look at Sergeant Benton revealed he was certain to be captured and was undoubtedly mortally wounded.[5]

September 2, 1862, was a day that Thomas Benton Sr. would remember for the rest of his life. That day, amid rampant reports of the terrible Union defeat at Second Manassas on August 30, the hardware merchant learned of the fight near Gainesville, at Brawner's farm, on August 28. A list published in the local newspaper, the *Richmond [Indiana] Palladium,* showed "McCown of Richmond, wounded; Benton, of Richmond, wounded in the breast." The shock had hardly worn off when Benton Sr. boarded the train for an abrupt trip to Washington, D.C., where the 19th had retreated following three days of fighting. By Wednesday morning he was amid the confusion and turmoil of a city crowded with defeated soldiers and rampant despair. Benton Sr. visited army hospital after army hospital—ten in two days. But he couldn't learn anything about his son Thomas or his fate, or of Sam McCown. His plight was fully evident in a grieving letter to his wife on Friday, September 5:

> *Thomas was left on the battlefield and is thought to be dead, and Sam was badly wounded and fell in[to] the hands of the Rebels. I have also heard they were both in the Rebel hospital beyond Manassas. The balance of the 19th Regiment is only six miles from here, but it is impossible to get a pass to go over the river, neither for love or money. Hence I cannot see them. . . . I shall return home Monday [September 8], or start home at that time. I have made up mind that my poor boy is dead, and in some ditch on the battlefield. From all the circumstances it seems like hoping against hope [that he is still alive]. Lieutenant Samuel Hindman (Co. B) is here wounded through the leg. He said Thomas was wounded in the thigh before he was [hit], but helped to carry him in the rear. . . . Young Hyatt told me he saw him fall, and . . . when he looked again, he [saw] Thomas had crawled to an apple tree, and was sitting with his back against it, and the enemy was then so near to them they had to fall back and leave the wounded in the hands of the enemy. He said in falling back, Sam was wounded*

and they left [him] also. Tell Mr. McCown I have some hopes of
his son [being alive], but none of mine. Dear wife, try to be
resigned to the will of the Lord, and not let it worry you too much.[6]

To compound the misery, a letter arrived about that time from an old friend in Washington, R. O. Dormer, who had sought information about Sergeant Benton; he was certainly killed in battle, read the short note, written September 2. The fatal shot was the one through the lungs, according to his comrades. "He was likely buried by the Secessionists, as they still hold that portion of the battlefield. I have written to the colonel to know what chance [there] will be in recovering his body." These words burned like fire through the very soul of the aggrieved parents.[7]

It seemed to be a miracle. Sergeant Thomas Hart Benton was *alive*! He was in a makeshift hospital on Twelfth Street in Washington, D.C. The surprise was enormous. Before leaving for home, Benton Sr. had discovered his son's presence by accident; R. O. Dormer, the friend who had written the note on September 2, had learned of Benton's survival and hastened to inform the father before he departed for Indiana.

It was an emotional reunion; his son had been given up for dead, and he was now alive! Moreover, Thomas Jr. was doing very well with his chest wound. The doctors seemed encouraged, and Thomas Sr., after spending several days with his son, felt confident enough to return home on September 10.

Joyously, Sergeant Benton was able to write home on Sept. 11, telling his parents "my wound is getting along finely, so Dr. Stephenson says. It is still quite painful, and still continues running." He was more worried about the expense of his disability, having to pay for washing the sheets and shirts, which were constantly being changed. It was but a minor, almost laughable circumstance considering all that the family had been through. Even with the good news, there was a sadness to consider. Ironically, Tom Jr.'s good friend Sam McCown had died on the battlefield on August 28, and the grief that seemed to have been the

Benton family's special burden was now transferred to their neighbors, the McCowns.[8]

The word came furtively, silently—almost like a candle that burns lower, to go dark suddenly, without a flicker. On Thursday night, Sept. 11, the day Sergeant Benton wrote to his parents, he seemed to breathe heavily. The wound in his lungs was painful, but on Friday he was much better. Saturday was difficult; the doctor spent much of the day with him, dressing his wounds three or four times. The sergeant seemed to sleep most of the time, occasionally shouting out in his dreams, as if he were giving orders to his men on the field of battle. Sunday morning, Sept. 14, Dr. Stephenson felt the end was near. He told the young sergeant that he feared the injuries would soon prove fatal. Tom Benton's answer was only, "Well." By one o'clock that afternoon he was thirsty, and asked for a drink. The army nurse tried to hold the tumbler, but Benton wanted to do it himself. He grasped the container, drank heartily, and moments later quietly died.

They later opened his wallet; there was a twenty-dollar bill.[9] And also the unrecorded price of courage.*

The death of a family member involves a personal grief that reaches to the heart of our existence. How could an all-wise and just God allow the demise of one so precious to our very own life? The pain is especially sharp when the lost loved one was younger, even a youth whose future seemed to be endowed with the bright promise of success and happiness—is this fair or even conscionable? The stricken survivors often wonder, what remains other than the cherished memory; how can I cope with such a great loss?

Solace is found largely by the bravery of the soul. The basic courage of our existence warns that there are to be crosses to bear and burdens to

---

* Thomas Hart Benton's legacy would well endure in the regiment and brigade he had so faithfully served. They were to become the Army of the Potomac's famous "Iron Brigade."

endure in making the journey of life. We are not alone in facing death; it is an experience that all face sooner or later. Not that we relish or anticipate such, but we can learn from our experiences, no matter how painful or difficult.

The essence of knowing and loving a dead son, daughter, or family member involves an awareness that we were privileged to share life's experience to a significant degree with the deceased. We know the good and bad, and with the personal loss comes eventually an acceptance of the result: not because the value of his or her life is diminished by time, but because beyond the emotion is a sense of God's purpose in creating that very person. Each and every person's contribution to humanity is perhaps best explained by the fact that other lives were touched by his or her existence. Be it great or small, the common good is apparent upon mature reflection, even in dire situations.

Many moan, "Why did this have to happen?" or, "If only such had occurred, his life might have been saved." Yet, perhaps it is more relevant to consider what we need to do to best exemplify the spirit of the deceased in carrying on the noble virtues of life. To the extent that we can, we summon courage to continue to exist, to do and perceive. We know relatively little about life's ultimate value, but we know that, be it a matter of religious or practical experience, we must try to do our best. By climbing that next hill of life, we exhibit a courage worthy of those who are gone from us. As they strove, so we, too, quest for a higher reward, as exemplified by valor in the effort. As surely as the real enemy of mankind is fear, we have a greater means, love, both present and remembered, to show the way ahead.

XIV

OF VALOR LESS THAN GLORY

It was almost unmentionable. Soldiering, it was assumed, meant fighting, as inspired by the manly virtues of bold adventure and toughness in demeanor. Sickness, the antithesis of martial ardor, at first wasn't much regarded or anticipated. If the perceived courage needed to grapple hand to hand with the enemy was self-evident in the panoply of close-range weaponry brought to camp by many of the volunteers in 1861—bowie knives and revolvers—the prospect of wasting away in the squalor of an army hospital seemed antipatriotic and even demoralizing.

The perception, however, rapidly changed. The day-to-day practical existence of army life was the reality, and coping with the mundane, the boredom, and the ugly circumstances was among the foremost and most common experiences of every soldier. The need to face the prospect of severe illness and even an ignominious death from disease often led to the mental denial that caused so many to recoil from the sick. They had come to fight opposing soldiers; but the greater enemy, the one they must constantly grapple with in unsanitary camps while often ingesting putrid food and contaminated water, was the ill health so prevalent everywhere. The invincibility of youth quickly faded when one was stricken with fever, fatigue, pain, and mental anguish. It seemed unsoldierlike, unmanly, and even disgusting. Yet illness was always lurking with unprecedented fury. Coping with thousands of sick, many of whom were contagious, was not only a nightmare for the medical authorities, it was mentally the most damaging threat to the well-being of the entire army. Those that best understood the threat knew its intense demand for courage.

Confederate Captain James Vance, soldiering in western Virginia with the 37th Virginia Infantry in August 1861, witnessed what he considered a gross outrage: the hypocrisy of local citizen "patriots" rushing to the distant battlefield of Manassas while ignoring the dire needs of the sick near home. Wrote Captain Vance angrily,

> *I never [witnessed] such utter neglect of sick men in my life—men rolling about in their dirty clothes, not a change of clothes nor anyone to bathe their aching bones. Men were detailed [to do so], but the physicians failed to make them do it. If they could get whiskey to drink, [then] the sick might go to the old scratch. . . . I understand we have some 800 or 1,000 sick at McDowell and Monterey, and yet the patriots and heroes who are so deeply interested in the welfare of the* poor soldier *are rushing on to Manassas—the Waterloo, the Crimea of the Southern Confederacy, . . . offering their service gratis to Pres. Davis, to wait upon the sick and the wounded who fell gallantly fighting for his country. Yes, that it would immortalize them forever.*
>
> *But posterity is not such a fool as to hand down to other generations their names as heroes and patriots and [it] will spot them as cowards and rogues. Yes, [they] went there by the hundreds after the battle was over to rifle the dead [and] take home trophies. Why did they not give all they found to the soldier, or the Confederacy? No, [they] must take it home to be handed down from generation to generation as trophies captured by their brave*

and illustrious sires and grand sires. If anyone can see patriotism
and kindness in such deeds of valor, *'tis more than I can [see].*

Now, if Manassas was away off like this place is [Pocahontas
County, Virginia], I would not think so hard of them. But . . .
[it] is accessible to all the cities and towns most in e[astern] Va.,
where the wounded could be taken over railroads with ease, and
there waited upon by the inhabitants. But the sick and dying of the
unfortunate command of the late Genl. [Richard] Garnett, don't
deserve the attention and respect that the wounded who gallantly
fell at M[anassas].

Now I contend that those who have been prostrated by disease
in the service of their country in this unfortunate region are as
much entitled to the sympathy and respect of the South as those
who fell at M[anassas]. But thus goes the world in war as in
peace—all for show. The big bugs getting all the credit, and the
poor unfortunate dogs none.

Not a man has come to the aid of the sick at M[anassas] save
the parson. *All get a free pass over the [rail]road who come here*
(an imposition on the Confederacy), yet not a one of them has
offered his services to wait on the sick, stay a day or so, and go
back. And, when asked where [have] you been?—"Been to see the
poor soldiers." Now a sick man with [a] fever is just as much [in]
danger of dying as the wounded man—if anything more so. . . .
My blood has been stirred up.[1]

Vance's outrage was conditioned by the reality that he knew was soldiering. All was not guts and glory, at least in the popular sense. Death
was more prevalent in the hospital than on the battlefield. This hard lesson in existence was by the midwar years ingrained in the mind of
many. Corporal John S. B. Matson of the 120th Ohio Infantry, in the
midst of the Vicksburg Campaign, found that his views had matured
commensurate with his experience as a soldier:

I do not wish you to, nor anyone I respect, to be put to the trials
of . . . this kind, for it is rough and a man must have a

*constitution to bear it. I am more afraid of fever than bullets, for
if a man gets down sick with fever on this damnable [Mississippi]
river he is almost as sure to die as though a bullet was put through
his vitals. And if boating along this river will put down the
Hell-long rebellion, we are certainly doing our share toward it.
There are now over 600 unfit for duty, and still [they] keep us
fooling along the river. Sometimes I think it is to run us into the
ground as fast as possible. If that is the intention, well are they
succeeding. I have not been very well since we left Memphis, but I
am so [able] as to be about. I do not report to the surgeon, for I
think it don't amount to much.*[2]

To Sergeant Lewis Hanback of the 27th Illinois Infantry, it was excruciating watching the demise of a close friend and fellow soldier,
Richard Megginson, over a four-week span. He had been sick with
measles, then when feeling better had been stricken with pneumonia.
Said Sergeant Hanback in reflection:

*Poor Dick, gone down to the grave at an early age in life; [at]
springtime when bright hopes filled the mind. [His] hopes of the
future years, bright anticipation of happiness and prosperity—once
living, breathing realities—are now dead, gone down into the
tomb of darkness forever. [Yet] his life is not one to be shunned,
but rather patterned after. In the dark hours of the country's
troubles . . . like a true patriot he went to her rescue; went to soon
die—not on the battlefield amid its carnage—but upon a soldier's
cot, to lay and waste away under a blighting disease. Yet it will not
detract from his honor and fair name that disease struck him
down. . . . He died for his country and her glory. . . . Friends will
strew flowers over his grave, and [after the war] some white haired
man will relate his history, and bid the stranger tread lightly past
his grave.*[3]

By the end of the war, the soldiers' perspectives on sickness seemed
less idealistic. In many cases they accentuated the despair of enduring

modern warfare with all its rigors and hardships. Especially amid the rapidly failing war effort of the South, the need for courage in confronting illness, want of subsistence and equipment, and the prospect of only more military despair reduced some to questioning what all the agony was leading to. Lieutenant Joseph G. Younger of the 53rd Virginia Infantry had survived Pickett's Charge at Gettysburg as a part of Armistead's Brigade, but a year later he was mentally worn out and despairing about even surviving. There was no sympathy in the army anymore for anyone, it seemed. The war had ruined the health and minds of so many, it seemed inevitable that life was reduced to its lowest common denominator:

> *I am quite sick and have been for some time. I do not think I shall be able to finish this epistle on account of my head swimming so bad; it seems to me the paper is turning 'round all the time. Cousin, it is so bad to be away off here sick, where no feminine hand is to feel of one's pulse, nor any kind and affectionate sister, mother, relative, or friend to watch one as he lays and suffers upon the ground. Soldiers here become used to so many sufferings that they have no sympathy for one that is sick, so long as they can keep well. If one die[s] it makes no difference with them, so [long as] the unfortunate one is no relative of theirs. If one gets killed in battle it is the same case. This, indeed, is a hard time. People are bound to become better, or I think they will be cut off and perish all over the land.*[4]

The terrible tragedy of it all was the unrelenting scything of the youth of America in both body and mind. The lessons learned about life had been so severe as to alter the essence and demeanor of a generation. The nation's innocence had gone with the winds of war, and the tariff had been the death of 620,000 Americans—about one-quarter of the soldiers enlisted, and 2 percent of the entire population of thirty-one million.

Ironically, once the historians and statisticians sorted it out, the fatalities on the battlefield (about 205,000) paled in comparison with those from disease. More than two-thirds of Civil War deaths were not battle induced (a total of about 415,000), nearly all from sickness.[5]

Who could have conceived this? Who might have understood? Ingrained in these statistics was the personal horror of those illnesses. The extreme suffering belied the courage inherent in coping with such a catastrophe. For every soldier who, instead of fighting the enemy, lay prone in a cot or on the ground enduring from moment to moment, hour to hour, the ongoing pain of sickness, it was an agony of courage in the most morbid sense.

Yet, if there was no glory in dying of disease, there remained the awareness of effort in the purpose—of venturing one's life for the common good. To do and die thus was also an indelible contribution to the cause in which they had joined. If not glorious, it gave meaning to the mettle of mankind—to face with courage the future and expend all in the process.

Perhaps it was valor in an ultimate sense: to risk all, without reward, for a worthy ideal.

XV

THE WORKINGS OF THE MIND

Truth be told, there were myriad small but courageous events almost daily in a Civil War soldier's life. Situations involving the nature of his duty, conformity to the code of military law, interrelationships with others—superiors, equals, and subordinates—required constantly making small decisions. With those choices came the need for courage in perspective and deed, or else surrender to the pressures of the moment.

One of America's great war heroes and important public figures, John McCain, in his book *Why Courage Matters,* reflected that the day-to-day, less-than-physically dangerous events that require fortitude in coping with are evidence of virtuousness, but do not necessarily exemplify courage. Courage he defines as "acts that risk life or limb or other very serious personal injuries for the sake of others, or to uphold a virtue." John McCain should well know; he sets a standard of excellence in courage, both in deed and thought, that all might emulate.[1]

Yet, there are little crises of thought and deed that require the commitment of a form of courage; the consequences are not life threatening or severely dangerous, but they are of vital importance to us as individuals. Coping with fear—be it of bodily harm or the risk of personal stature, financial means, or one's well-being—is often a daily occurrence. Thus we invoke frequently a modest courage in conducting our lives via the decisions we make. Grand courage—the kind that, according to John McCain, inspires us to reach beyond goodness to greatness—is not always required.

Although great courage might be needed by relatively few of us in dire circumstances, this is cause for understanding the standard of daily courage that promotes a larger valor when needed. The righteous convictions of the soul, of steadfast morality, dignity, and honor that pervade our consciousness, inspire virtue in our daily lives. We feel better when we reason and act with valor according to life's higher principles—especially when there is so much in the world to threaten our favorable status quo.

ANGER AS A MATTER OF COURAGE

In the Civil War, amid the managed mayhem that always seemed on the brink of unconscionable violence, anger was an emotion that easily bubbled to the surface. In an environment where one witnessed many inhumane wrongs and was continually told what to do, the rigors of the military were conducive to anger. It manifested itself in many forms, from outright physical action against the enemy, or perhaps internal resistance to or disregard of orders, to sullen acquiescence. But once created, the essence of despair, fury, and outrage usually remained, to be dealt with personally in due time. Coping effectively with one's emotions was sometimes the key to well-being and survival in a variety of difficult circumstances. The need for courage in thought often translated into giving meaningful expression to the remedy of a person's perceived difficulties.

To vent one's anger in a practical yet discreet manner usually meant complaining—to someone who might be sympathetic, or at least objective.

In many cases comments in letters home served as a catharsis, letting one express anger without endangering one's status. Was this a form of reasoned courage—or the easy way out?

To address the issue was, at least, taking some type of action. Carrying the issue to an extreme might not be courageous but foolhardy. One needed to be careful about how much "courage" to employ. As the circumstances varied, so, too, did the expected results.

A soldier's mind-set usually involved his relationship with the enemy as well as with his comrades and commanders. Of obvious concern were the outrages, both real and reported, perpetrated by the enemy. The initial motive of fighting for a cause was often augmented by witnessing the atrocities of the enemy. To many this made matters personal. The sense of outrage in the face of inequity and wrongdoing was often profound. It frequently translated into inspiring courage rooted in hatred of the enemy, who were the visible source of so much misery and hardship.

Private William H. H. Winston of Company G, 11th Virginia Infantry, had long noted the suffering of his native land. Two years of devastating warfare in Virginia had brought to many of that state's veteran soldiers a yearning for retribution. Virginia's ravaged farms, despoiled crops, and slaughtered livestock were mute testimony to the vicious war being waged by the enemy. Aware that a chance to retaliate against their opponents' homeland was in the offing, many of Robert E. Lee's Virginians looked forward to the invasion of Maryland and Pennsylvania in the summer of 1863. Twenty-three-year-old Private "Willy" Winston anticipated venting his long pent-up anger. Writing on June 13 he noted: "Most everybody is anxious to go into Pennsylvania, and if we do go, I am going to destroy everything that I can, unless it is positively against orders—which I am afraid it will be."

Ironically, three weeks later, for Willy Winston the courage of his convictions required not destroying Northern property, but taking part along with his brother Charley in the famous Pickett's Charge as a member of Kemper's Brigade. Both Willy and Charley were among the casualties; Charley was wounded but returned to duty in December, and Willy was captured. For nearly the remainder of the war, while a prisoner of war at Point Lookout, Maryland, Private Winston could ponder his expressed intent to pillage the enemy's farms and property in Pennsylvania.[2]

Anger directed at his own officers served to motivate a commitment to courage in First Sergeant John S. Harris of the 11th Massachusetts Volunteer Infantry. Having enlisted as first sergeant in June 1861 and experienced First Bull Run, where the regiment suffered many casualties, including officers, Harris anticipated his rapid promotion to lieutenant. Shocked and disappointed by the promotion of others his junior, he became bitter that his professed popularity with the men of his company was thwarted by the ranking officers of the 11th Massachusetts. His spirit of outrage had already resulted in his arrest for alleged insubordination, and in January 1862 the army's idle status caused him to reflect upon his future course of action. Harris informed his brother:

> *I am under arrest in quarters and I expect to be court-martialed. But the most they can do with me is to reduce me to the ranks [as a private]. . . . I will try [to] live long enough to get square with them all. If I could be promoted by the vote of the company I should have been [a] lieutenant long ago. But I have to be appointed by the colonel [William Blaisdell], and there are two or three [officers] working against me all the time. But it is a long road that doesn't turn. . . . The opinion here is that there will be a general forward movement soon. . . . But God knows I don't care how soon, for I am tired of being in hell. If I have come out here to die I don't care how soon, but I will show them that I won't show the white feather [i.e., cowardice], and I think my life will be spared to see some of these selfish officers die, so that I can smile over their dead bodies. I don't think you would know me [now], as I have become as cross as hell.*

Keeping to the course and planning for the future were the measured responses considered by Harris for the anger-induced crisis he faced. His courage reflected his resolve and determination, no matter what the consequences.

True to Sergeant Harris's prophecy, the 11th's lieutenant colonel was killed at Second Bull Run only a few days after Harris was finally promoted to second lieutenant. Also, Colonel William Blaisdell was killed in June 1864 at Petersburg, Virginia. Yet, Harris didn't live to see that event. On May 3, 1863, at the Battle of Chancellorsville, First Lieutenant John S. Harris was killed in action.[3]

DEVIL-MAY-CARE COURAGE

If motives of revenge fired the ardor of some individuals on both sides, obscuring fear and inspiring courage in combat, there also was almost the mental opposite—a rather devil-may-care sneering at danger by some of those most exposed. The mind-set that led one to expose one's person deliberately may have been rooted, ironically, in psychological survival. To scoff at the presence of danger was to invoke a fatalistic sense that survival on the battlefield was beyond anyone's control. But was this a true form of courage? By seemingly flaunting a disregard for danger and surviving, one's worst fears were kept in check, at least on the surface. Perhaps this was false bravado, keeping rampant fear in control by acting bravely. Be it a resort to luck, religious conviction, or sheer fatalism, boldness in the face of death was a psychological perspective that contradicted practical wisdom. It was, in a certain sense, saying, "The bullet hasn't been made that will kill me." Although very few took such a stance, some individuals through their continued carelessness or recklessness were the talk of their comrades.

The spirit infusing such behavior was revealed by a rifleman on the skirmish line during the siege of Chattanooga in 1863. An astonished Union sergeant who took dinner forward to the skirmish line found most of the men behind large trees, randomly shooting at the opposite enemy skirmishers, and "having some fun" in it. Wrote the sergeant, "They would stand there and tell each other where they shot—whether too high, too low, or too far to the right or left. If it had been me, I would have left it to their own judgment and perhaps they would not have hit [the mark] so often."[4]

Another happy-go-lucky rifleman, a private in the battle-hardened 2nd New Hampshire Infantry, found it amusing to shoot at the Rebel infantry attacking at Gettysburg on July 2 in the Sherfy Peach Orchard sector just as if they were so many approaching ducks. A former hunter in the coastal marshes, the private wrote to a friend that he ought to have been there for a chance at some "grays," that is, graybacks—Confederate soldiers. "I had a good chance to try my skill and got so I could fetch one nearly every time [I shot]. I don't think I wasted as many shots as I have before now on grays [ducks] at home."[5]

"Sucking It Up"

Courage great or small manifested itself in many forms. "Sucking it up" is an expression of resolve: to endure the worst, yet persevere in one's duty or task. Men such as Sergeant Russell T. Knight of the 6th Iowa Infantry found war's experience a severe "trial" and contrary to their original conceptions. After enduring the ordeal at Shiloh—"I didn't expect to [survive] by the way the bullets passed by at my head," he wrote—Sergeant Knight prayed that he might get out of the war. Yet he knew a greater good would come only from his continued effort in fighting, to which he was now committed. "I would like to be with [my family]," he pined in a letter to his brother, "but my country calls me away, and for that, and only that, would I be away from them." Knight's modest courage, of enduring the difficult and even the hideous to fulfill an essential duty, didn't result in glory or even a fruitful career, yet it cost him his life. Little more than ninety days after writing these sentiments, Russell Knight died of "inflammation of the bowels." He was an obscure soldier, and soon all but forgotten, however, today his words resonate with duty, honor, and country, and the personal sacrifice so prevalent and yet precious to the history of this nation.[6]

Shiloh had been the scene of another soldier's subtle courage—of fulfilling his duty when all about him was chaos and hellfire. Trapped at Shiloh in the famous Hornets' Nest, Sergeant Martin V. Miller of Company E, 7th Illinois Infantry found that there seemed no escape from the incoming bullets and shells. He watched with horror as his relative, Henry Miller, "was struck by two spent balls, one on the foot and one between the shoulders. [As] he [was] then laying down on his face, another ball struck on the [cross-the-chest] belt of his cartridge box and glanced off. It struck with sufficient force to render him almost helpless, and in this condition he was carried off the field." Martin continued: "He had been gone but a few moments—we had been lying together—when a man behind me raised up to shoot, and was shot and fell on me. And at the same time the man on my left got a ball in the left shoulder, making three wounded right by me in less than five minutes, and I thought sure the next bullet was mine."[7] Sergeant Miller kept his wits about him and "sucked it up," not by rash acts of valor in fighting, but by steadfastly doing the duty of a soldier, maintaining self-control and letting the events take their course and play out to their fullest. Today the attribute is perhaps more familiarly associated in sports with "playing hurt," or overcoming imminent adversity by sheer resolve, but it is a form of courage, the extent of which only the individual may understand.[7]

COPING WITH A PREMONITION OF DEATH

Among the most difficult circumstances requiring courage of thought were the occasional premonitions of death that bedeviled some individuals. The prospect of dying was self-evident to most soldiers in combat. But what of the absolute belief, by some random concept, that death was imminent? It was an awesomely devastating, mind-numbing thought. To anticipate by intuitive forewarning was in essence to confront the absolute end. The mystery of life and death was put in profound perspective. What lay ahead was in some unaccountable measure suddenly clear in the most negative sense imaginable. Finality in a physical realm was apparently at hand, and if the mind could thus comprehend, how might the total person react? The playing-out of one's emotions and behavior under such dire stress sometimes proved as fascinating as the thought itself.

First Sergeant Hiram Talbert Holt of the 38th Alabama Infantry Regiment was a prolific writer, sometimes writing two or three letters a day to his beloved wife, Carrie. Holt was a former school teacher, and writing came easily to him. Being emotional, he often told Carrie about the petty army hardships he encountered, and revealed his innermost thoughts. Although the 38th Alabama had escaped from Fort Pillow prior to the fort's loss, Holt learned in mid-1862 of the battle death of two close friends in Virginia. The fact that death had struck so close to him quickly made its impact. Yet Carrie was unprepared for the letter she received in late June, while he was stationed near Mobile:

> *Carrie, I am so torn to pieces with double sorrow that it seems like it will kill me. John reported dying and Jim dead! . . . Carrie, I think how I would feel this morning were you no more. It nearly kills me. . . . Hasten in your love to give [the widows] what comfort you can, [as] you may need it yourself. I feel very strange of late, I know not why. It may all be superstition, but somehow I feel a presentiment that I shall be killed the next or first battle I get into. It may be that my mind is out of order a little, but it is a fact that cannot be denied, that men do sometimes have presentiments of this kind. . . . I could say much more that to me is strange, but to you it would be both unpleasant and foolish—as [is] what I've already said. But you will pardon [me], it is all I know . . . and my gloomy mood is fit only for me.*[8]

Sergeant Holt was so convinced that his battlefield demise was coming that he had already prepared a six-page letter to be kept by a comrade and delivered to Carrie upon his death. Yet Holt seemed mistaken in his rampant, morbid fears. Campaigning with the Confederate Army of Tennessee from the Tullahoma Campaign in 1863 through the bloodbath at Chickamauga and the debacle at Chattanooga, Holt survived many hard-fought actions that others of his company did not. He courageously kept performing his duty, and his mood seemed almost ebullient when he wrote to Carrie on February 17, 1864.

A week later, Holt was on picket duty near Dalton, Georgia, when a flurry of shots exchanged between outposts resulted in his mortal wounding. Within hours Holt was dead, killed in a brief skirmish that had no significant military impact. The widowed Carrie could but ponder the grim letter she had received nearly two years earlier—was it a premonition fulfilled, or merely a random chance of fate?

Private Asbury Fouts, at age nineteen, had been at home in Iowa when he enlisted in October 1864 in the veteran 9th Iowa Volunteer Infantry, then at Atlanta preparing for the March to the Sea. Fouts had been routed through Nashville when on his way to the regiment, but while there in early December he suddenly found himself caught up in the turmoil of Confederate General Hood's invasion of Tennessee. Men returning from leave of absence or new recruits were pressed into emergency service amid the crisis at Nashville. With Hood attempting to besiege the city, Fouts was placed in a makeshift brigade and took part in a reconnaissance along the Murfreesboro Pike on December 13. Here as they waited to advance against the Confederate skirmish line on the Rains farm, a nearby soldier suddenly turned and said, "Boys, this is the last time I will have of speaking to you." Pointing to the enemy line, he continued: "There are the Rebels, they will kill me," and he handed his revolver to a friend to send home. Fouts was shaken by the incident, but more so when a few minutes later as they advanced, the soldier "was shot through the neck and killed instantly." Only ten casualties were suffered that day in Fouts's unit, and he could but later marvel that God had acted to warn the unfortunate soldier of his pending fate.[9]

Sergeant George W. Tallman, Company E, 20th Iowa Infantry, was literally shaking. His apprehension was great that he would soon be killed in his first battle, leaving a widowed young wife and an infant child to the mercies of the world. Accordingly, as the Battle of Prairie Grove, Arkansas, approached, he wrote an emotional letter to his father-in-law, not daring to mention his apprehension to his wife.

> *Whatever may be . . . it is best to be prepared for the worst. With the many who must go down in the blast of battle, I may be numbered. I desire to arrange some little matters which ought to be*

in better shape in case I should be killed. You know with what
means and in what condition I leave my wife. The money in your
hands I would have her use as she sees fit, but . . . should she not
need it for herself, it [might] be accumulating and made available
for the education of our child. . . . I leave the whole matter in your
hands, believing you to be an honorable Christian gentleman who
would shrink from doing injustice to the dead or living. . . . I
implore you to steady her spirit, and not treat her hardly, for
I know she means right in every act.

Sergeant Tallman did, indeed, face death days later at the Battle of Prairie Grove. Yet he wasn't injured, or even touched by the many bullets that claimed forty-six of his companions in the regiment, including two dead in his own company.

Tallman was so relieved by his escape that he even anticipated with relish going into the next fight against "the miserable, faithless hordes of Rebels who were . . . in arms here on the Arkansas River." The Army of the Frontier "is marching on [to victory]," he proclaimed, and Tallman experienced a successful army career, becoming a lieutenant in the 73rd USCT Regiment prior to being discharged unscathed in 1865.[10] Like changes in the weather, the workings of the mind weren't always predictable, not even the anxiety-induced intuition that seemed to proclaim the worst of fates.

PUTTING YOUR FAITH IN GOD

For many soldiers the mystery of life and death was put into manageable perspective largely by religious faith.

There was no easy explanation for death or serious injury in combat, or for the equally dreaded fatal sicknesses that stealthily crept like a blanket of darkness over the lives of so many. The great mystery of who would perish and when, and for what reason death selected certain individuals to the exclusion of others, was one of the most poignant and emotional of concerns to many. There really was little that made sense in the selection process—from the death of innocent civilian women and children, to the escape in battle of the greatest rogue and sinful individual.

What bothered most was that reason could not predict survival, death, or injury by standards of human conduct and/or morality. It was beyond mankind's reckoning; hence it must be God's mysterious providence. For the courage needed to cope with such questions, many turned directly to God and religion. During the most trying of circumstances, finding solace in the will of God was the only answer that made sense.

Captain Alfred J. Sofield of the 149th Pennsylvania Infantry, one of the famous "Bucktail" units, had left his wife, Helen, and three young children behind in Tioga County, Pennsylvania, when he joined the military in 1861. A former justice and county official at Wellsboro, Pennsylvania, Sofield was a highly regarded and effective administrator, one who was known for his levelheaded competence. It seemed highly unusual for Sofield to emotionalize in a letter to his wife, as he did on June 3, 1863, when he admitted: "I have the blues worse than ever. To be reminded [by a letter from home] that I was so necessary to your happiness, and feeling far short of my duty as a husband as I have been for the past twelve years, and how indulgent and forgiving you have been, causes me to feel sad, indeed. . . . If I am permitted to join you again after getting out of this war, I will try to atone for past errors."[11]

Aware that important events were pending—"it is supposed that the Rebels contemplate assuming the offensive and their late operations indicate a movement by them into Maryland and Pennsylvania"—Sofield told Helen that they soon would likely have a big fight with the enemy. Indeed, twenty-eight days after writing this letter, Captain Sofield was in the midst of horrific combat along Seminary Ridge at Gettysburg. While leading his Bucktails in a charge against the railroad cut along the Chambersburg Pike, Sofield went down with a mortal wound.

His wife, Helen, soon learned of his fate and was devastated by grief. Instead of coming home to rekindle their love and care for his family, her husband was consigned to a shallow grave in an obscure field, nevermore to caress his wife or play with the children. An impassioned letter to one of Albert's fellow officers seeking solace brought a tender reply: "You speak of your deep sorrows. I wish I could shoulder part of them. 'Tis best for every heart to know its own bitterness, . . . [but] let me be a brother to you, as I was to him; I will feel that I am honored." Another friend, her cousin George Jones, reflected upon Helen's need to trust in God:

> *Dear cousin, there is a care exercised over us by Our Heavenly Father that we fail perhaps to realize until we, through affliction, or misfortune, are brought to turn our minds or thoughts to things beyond this world. We can then trace God's goodness to us through all our past life. Though we were perhaps unconscious from where or how that care has been exercised over us, still we must acknowledge God's care through all the past. It is said that all things work together for good to those that love God. Although you have been bereaved of a husband and your parents have long since been taken away, and we may utterly fail to see any Providence in these things, yet we are led more fully to realize the truth that there is a high power where we hope to gather strength, and to more fully trust in God. We will pray that God will be a father to your fatherless children, and the widow's God in bringing you through all your affliction, and providing a way for your comfortable support.*[12]

Helen Sofield was like thousands of other American women; if consumed by grief, her courage inspired by many past memories was profound. Aged thirty-two when Alfred died, she never remarried, and bolstered by her staunch Episcopal faith, she saw to the education and later success of her children. In 1864 she made plans to visit Gettysburg to see for herself the site where Alfred fought and also his grave. Later she moved to Berkeley, California, and she lived until 1902, the recipient of an army pension of twenty dollars per month.[13]

J. P. Graves of Warren County, Mississippi, had been too young to go to war in 1861. Forced to bide his time despite his ardent desire to join in this splendid adventure, the teenaged Graves was finally, in the spring of 1864, allowed to enlist in a local artillery unit, Swett's Battery, then on duty with the Confederate Army of Tennessee at Dalton, Georgia. In honor of the occasion he composed a song:

> "Ho for liberty, freedom, or death, for that's the watchword. . . .
> Farewell to the scenes of my childhood, to my mother, who's praying for me. . . .
> Farewell to the home and hearth, where my sisters are weeping for me. . . .
> Adieu to the church where Christians are, For the soldiers each will pray.
> But the bible and chaplain go with us, And Jehovah our God is our stay."

Graves's introduction to the army was severe. Assigned to the hard-fighting division of Major General Patrick Cleburne, Swett's Battery took heavy losses in the Atlanta Campaign. At the Battle of Pickett's Mill, May 27, 1864, J. P. was wounded in the head by a bullet that tore a two-inch gash in his scalp. "I did not know what soldiering was like when I came out here, but I know now." He pleaded: "I am tired of fighting now, and am willing to come home since I got my wound." Yet Graves was in for more heavy combat. At the vicious Battle of Jonesboro, September 1, Swett's Battery was overrun by the enemy while defending the critical salient angle in Cleburne's line. Graves later wrote with stark candor of what he had endured:

> About two o'clock the enemy was seen to be massing their whole army in our [front]. Our battery commenced playing on them. Then the enemy brought up four batteries and commenced playing on our battery. We kept up the fight [and] artillery duel until all of our limbers to the guns were shot down. [During] all that time the enemy was massing in a hollow about three hundred yards in our front. Then they commenced charging. The first charge they were hurled back and shattered like leaves in a whirlwind. But they went back under the cover of the hill and formed again. They

came again, but were repulsed with the same result. All the time
our battery was pouring double charges of canister into their ranks.
By this time their reserve lines had got up, and they came again
with overwhelming numbers. Our men were driven back with the
loss of half of Govan's Brigade and Swett's and Key's Batteries. We
never left our guns until the enemy were on our breastworks. Some
of our men clubbed muskets with the enemy. We lost seventeen
men out of our battery; they were all wounded or captured. When
I ran, I thought the Yankees would put about fifty bullet holes
through my back. But as it happened, not a one touched me. I
know that nothing saved me but the prayers of my mother. The
Yankees were mounting our works when Graves Tennant and
myself left. Both of us came out safe. Captain [Charles] Swett
came down to the battery the day before yesterday and made a long
speech to us, saying that we had the thanks of Generals Hood,
Hardee, and Cleburne for gallantry showed on the field. Captain
Swett complimented us very highly and said he considered every
man of us a hero.

Graves's view that only the prayers of his mother had saved him
from destruction reflected his strong religious upbringing. A mere youth
who at first had worried about his sister taking good care of his chickens
and puppy at home, J. P. after six months in the army had so often "seen
the elephant" that the only sustaining influence in combat was his faith
in God. Accordingly, Graves later wrote that despite the reports that
Richmond had fallen and other troops were refusing to attack the Yankees, "that can never be said of the Army of Tennessee!" He, like his
comrades, would summon the courage to fight to the end against "double numbers," and rely on God's guidance. Shielded, so he insisted, by
God's mercy, Private J. P. Graves survived the war and was paroled at
Greensboro, North Carolina, April 26, 1865.[14]

Julius P. Garesche was a Cuban. After graduating near the top of his
class from the U.S. Military Academy at West Point in 1841, he served
continuously in the United States Regular Army, becoming lieutenant
colonel and chief of staff to Major General William S. Rosecrans in

1862. Garesche was not only extremely competent, but highly religious, and on the morning of December 31, 1862, he was found reading his Bible by another staff officer. Garesche was calm and cool, remembered Major Frank Bond, despite the prospect of battle that day at Stones River, near Murfreesboro, Tennessee. Bond and the others of Rosecrans's staff were riding with their general across the battlefield that afternoon when, as Bond later informed Garesche's son:

> *General Rosecrans and Col. Garesche were riding together, then came Major [Holly] Skinner and myself, then the other members of the Staff, and after them a few orderlies and an escort company. While riding across a cotton-field, we came within range of two or three batteries of Rebel artillery, posted upon an elevation on the opposite side of Stones River. The commanding officer of the battery, seeing a general officer with staff within easy range, brought his guns to bear on us, and for a short time we were under a very heavy artillery fire. Among the guns in the battery, were some rifled cannon, carrying what is known as the "Hotchkiss Shell," having a conical solid head. The solid part of one of these Hotchkiss Shells struck your father squarely on the temple, carrying away all that part of his head above the chin. For an instant I did not realize what had occurred, as the body preserved its equilibrium in the saddle while the horse continued in motion at rather a fast walk, but it very shortly leaned towards the left, taking the horse out of the line, and then fell from the saddle to the ground. I immediately looked for the Sergeant of Orderlies, whose place was on the side of the column near to where I was riding, but he had also been shot in the thigh, probably by one of the bullets [fragments] from the same shell when it exploded. I then called an orderly, pointed out the body, and told him to see that it was cared for, so that it could be found after the battle, and then rode alongside of Gen. Rosecrans and told him what had occurred; that Col. Garesche was killed. The Gen. was at the time so much engrossed in watching the movements of the enemy that he was not aware that his chief of staff had been struck. . . .*

*A few days afterwards, the body was disinterred; I was present
at the time, and helped to identify it, by the blanket in which it
had been wrapped, and by his chin and goatee, the balance of his
face having been carried away by the shot. The remains were then
sent to Nashville. . . . I shall never forget the shock and impressions
made upon me by your father's death, and the sight of his
apparently headless body maintaining its poise in the saddle for a
few seconds after he was killed.*

*I knew Col. Garesche but slightly . . . [but] I well know the
regard and esteem in which he was held by his commanding
officer, Gen. Rosecrans, as well as by all others of his staff. . . .
That the fortunes of war should have removed from so responsible
a position a soldier so capable and so useful as was Col. Julius P.
Garesche, is one of those mysterious events occasionally occurring,
that lead one to almost doubt the wisdom of an over-ruling
Providence.*[15]

To Sergeant Jesse Waltner, Company K, 49th Ohio Infantry, the
prospect of charging up Missionary Ridge at Chattanooga on November
25, 1863, seemed daunting. Together with the other troops of Brigadier
General August Willich's brigade, the 49th would be in the forefront of
the spontaneous, unplanned assault. Waltner was shaken, for there were
"twenty-five pieces of artillery playing on us all the time we were advancing up the hill." A few days later he told a friend back home: "You had
better think Jesse thought he would never reach the top, but by some
kind providence I was spared to reach the top. I have no one to thank but
God for the preservation of my life through this battle."

Amazingly to Sergeant Waltner:

*"When we reached the top, the Rebs broke and ran, but not until
we mounted their rifle pits. They stood and fought us till they
could reach us with their bayonets. But Missionary Ridge was
what we started for, and we were bound to have it, and we got it.
But many a brave soldier there sacrificed his life in taking that
stronghold. We captured all their artillery, numbering 60 pieces,*

*and took three thousand prisoners. Our company had three
wounded. The regt. lost in killed and wounded 42, [plus] three
officers."*

God had mercifully spared his life and limb, concluded Waltner, and
he would remember that favor for the rest of his life. Indeed, Sergeant
Jesse Waltner was mustered out of the army in November 1865, never
having doubted the courage, inspired by God, that enabled his survival.[16]

The victory of light over darkness in the lives of many, despite their
worldly ordeals and grief, related to their trust in God. It was God who
inspired the courage to continue, to meet adversity or danger with fortitude and hope. The resilience of mankind to cope well with both triumph and disaster looms among the best of human qualities. To an
amazing degree, the Civil War soldier and his family, both North and
South, gave witness to the timelessness of life's noble virtue in attempting to face with courage all that we meet in our journey to eternity.

XVI

OUR CONSCIOUSNESS PREVAILS

How we assess "fairness" is typically a matter of interpretation. The ability to weigh the pros and cons in making our judgments is usually influenced by a rationale that varies with each individual. Obviously, differences of opinion are quite ordinary in a diverse environment of varying cultures, beliefs, educations, and intellects. Yet the established, basic core of fundamental values involving life and death is remarkably consistent throughout the world. Usually, the high value of life is a matter of both common sense and widespread popular practice. Despite modern terrorists' disregard for life, the vast majority of the world seek to coexist in peace.

The recklessness of terrorists in perpetrating suicide bombings is contrary to the teachings of history. Mankind must live and let live to achieve security and well-being within highly sought-after ideal standards of existence. It is where a change in the behavior of "others" is mandated that conflict arises. What is best for one, or for all, varies by interpretation. Freedom to act is counterbalanced by the effect of one's acts on others. Our actions create reactions that sometimes result in contrary actions. Instead of peace, harmony, and a common perspective, there exist discord, chaos, and often violence.

Much of this disorder arises from altering views, not altered standards. The basic and logical commandment of mankind "to love one another" is easily distorted by programmed endeavor, often involving political objectives. What is evident upon closer scrutiny is that a war for political purposes is detached from the normalcy of beneficial interpersonal relationships. A direct order to kill another in combat is regarded as valid in political purpose and hence appropriate, even if counterbalanced by a natural law of morality. The courage to do, or not to do, in mortal conflict rests upon the shifting sands of what is deemed decent. What is right may years later be wrong, or vice versa.

In the Civil War, taking a life in the line of duty was often regarded practically. The objective of beating the enemy, winning the war, and ending the awful ordeal of combat was served by physically obliterating the enemy's soldiery. Private Isaac Miller, 93rd Ohio Volunteer Infantry, considered what happened at the Battle of Franklin on November 30, 1864, and offered these thoughts: "[The 175th Ohio Volunteer Infantry] was in the fight. They [the Union army] had what they call arbaties [abatis] in front of the works—that is brush and sharp pointed stakes so that a man can't hardly get through them. . . . The Rebels charged up to them and couldn't get over, and they hollered to the boys to cease firing—they would surrender. But the 175th was a new regiment, and [this was] the first fight they had been in, so they just kept firing away at them and wouldn't let them surrender. So much the better. All they kill we won't have to fight or feed anymore."[1]

Corporal John S. B. Matson of the 120th Ohio Volunteer Infantry found that at Arkansas Post in January 1863 he could kill a Rebel soldier and be pleased about it. "I loaded and looked, and saw a curl of smoke, and as he raised to fire, I fired and there was no [more] [gun] smoke coming from that place. If my ball killed [him] I have no regrets, for I never took more deliberate aim at a woodpecker." After the fighting ended, Matson "had the curiosity to go in where I saw the smoke curl, and found a Reb shot in the forehead. He had a bad wound, but [it] didn't look as though it hurt him much. He had dropped a very nice Enfield rifle, which I captured and have yet."[2]

Callousness was often a by-product of the earnest business of fighting and killing. It was a method of psychological survival for many. But the larger purpose of enduring combat—winning the war—provided the real impetus. As Corporal Amos Kibbee of the 4th Illinois Cavalry wrote after fighting at Shiloh: "I have seen blood enough spilt, yet I can hardly content myself to be a noncombatant in the present impending battle. I think you will hardly demonstrate [call] this 'bloodthirstiness,' but a desire for a speedy peace which can only be accomplished through the enemy's utter and complete overthrow. To accomplish this I am willing; yes, anxious to brave the leaden storm once more."[3]

Purpose was paramount in the minds of many soldiers. It explained why one officer, Assistant Surgeon Jesse W. Brock of the 66th Ohio Infantry, could write home saying, "Let your young men pitch in & show their grit—[there is] nothing like it when you once get used to it. The thing [war] has lost its novelty to me. I make it a business now."[4]

The business of war involved a basic, well-profiled personal courage, both physical and that of the soul. A vivid acknowledgment of the intense spirit of warfare by both sides at Port Hudson, Louisiana, in June 1863 was written by a grizzled veteran of the 114th New York Infantry, Private Erastus Gregory, who noted that "the men are fighting with a will on both sides . . . , fighting like tigers today." Amid the grisly scenes of an assault on the enemy breastworks, Gregory observed that "a musket ball hits a man on the head, and he is carried from the field in an expiring condition; another has his leg or arm shot off by a cannon ball or grape shot, while another is shot in the breast in such a manner that you can see right inside him." Nonetheless, wrote Gregory, it was "not very often that one word of complaint is heard from these brave men, so eager are they to save their country from ruin."

Indeed, if bravery was a much-needed virtue, at times it seemed that fear itself led to an unforeseen, perverse justice. Private Gregory wrote of Rebel shells falling in profusion on June 2, but said they "have done us no hurt yet, except to scare us pretty bad. One man in Co. K probably being a little more scared than some of the rest, started to get out of the way [run away]. But his gun went off. The ball passed through his foot in such a manner that it had to be cut off. But during the surgical operations he suddenly passed into eternity."

To men such as Gregory, there was virtue in braving the perils of the battlefield with courage:

> [W]e have taken the job to put down this unholy rebellion, and
> with the help of almighty God we will see that it is done . . . if it
> takes ten years to do it. I dare not come home and tell my neighbor
> that I gave in [with] my voice to have peace on any terms after the
> Rebels had killed over 200,000 of [our] brave boys. . . . We are
> having a terrible fight here to get this port [Hudson], but nothing
> daunted, we press forward with a will, not forgetting to ask the
> blessing of almighty God. [Thus] we do not fear anything that can
> be devised by Southern Rebels or Northern traitors. . . . All I want
> is to bring them to terms, unconditional surrender, and then with
> as much joy as the father at the return of the prodigal [son], I will
> receive them back and call them brother again.[5]

Gregory's intense feelings reflected the typical grit of many veteran Union soldiers in soldiering on "to save the country." Yet that grit failed to save him. The day after finishing his letter, he was sitting by a tree reading his Bible when shot through the head by a sharpshooter and instantly killed.

Despite brave words and resoluteness, seeing the gruesome sights of wanton destruction throughout the war zone, and enduring the atrocities of the battlefield, often created feelings of helplessness. It also produced in some a desire for vengeance, and they reacted to the horror by inflicting as much pain and damage on the enemy as possible. Indeed, revenge was often a consideration in the behavior of individuals who had a greater than usual personal stake in the war. A brother of Private Barnard Fuller, 36th Massachusetts Infantry, had been killed in the war, and another had been captured. Said Fuller after laying low several gray-clad soldiers at Petersburg, where the Rebs had "shot a button off my cap": "I am satisfied I have done as much to the Johnnies as they [have] done to them [his brothers]."[6]

It was hard to overcome feelings of outrage, such as that experienced by Colonel William R. Shafter of the 17th U.S. Colored Troops when he found one of his dead officers stripped on the battlefield of Nashville in December 1864. Captain Gideon Ayers, said a wounded black soldier who lay nearby and had viewed the scene, "did not die for an hour or two [after he was wounded]. The Rebs stripped him while yet alive, and [he was] begging them not to hurt him so."[7]

A negative-based motivation wasn't always related to another's death or the vile sights of the battlefield. Deep-seated anger drove some when they enlisted early in the war. Private Cecil Fogg of the 36th Ohio Infantry wrote in August 1863 how he had volunteered "not so much [because of] patriotism, as it was [due to] hatred of the South and a desire to help end slavery."[8]

Hatred of the enemy was expressed repeatedly in letters home, especially early in the war by those whose experience in warfare was limited. Much of the indignation stemmed from newspaper or secondhand accounts of atrocities, and inspired a ruthlessness that as the war continued often became modified by personal honor and the larger perspective of duty. Generally, a practical understanding of the impersonal nature of modern warfare had occurred by 1865. Private Fuller of the 36th Massachusetts, despite having lost a brother in the Wilderness fighting, commented in January 1865 on the "civil" nature of the enemy in their front at Petersburg. "We [as opposing soldiers] are so near together [in the trenches] we tell each other what time of day or night it is. We don't fire on them, and they don't [shoot] at us. It is only murder to kill a man on picket." Also, Corporal Amos Kibbee of the 4th Illinois Cavalry reflected that despite the rampant feelings when in combat of "utter forgetfulness of everything but a desire to destroy the enemy in the quickest way possible," he "had never seen a soldier offer the least indignity to a dead or wounded enemy." It was against their code of personal honor to do so, he surmised, for "no truly brave man would do such. Only cowards are capable of it—inhumanity to a suffering friend or foe." Private Erastus Gregory, who was killed at Port Hudson, considered that although the men of his regiment feared nothing in combating the enemy and were ruthless in fighting, it was "not that I have any hatred toward them in any other way than to hate their actions."[9]

The impersonal task of winning for the cause often dominated one's thoughts while in combat, transcending in one's mind the personal motives contemplated beforehand. Thus in the heat of battle many would fight with intense aggression and kill enemy soldiers without hesitation. Yet in the aftermath, a sense of propriety, of finding some human dignity, led many to reconsider their behavior. Confederate Private Henry Webb of the 50th Virginia Infantry found himself confronted at the Battle of the Wilderness, May 5, 1864, by Private Jacob Smiley of the 1st New York Sharpshooters. Smiley had shot one of Webb's comrades, only a few feet distant, when Webb raised his rifle musket and fired at Smiley. The big minié ball struck Smiley in the chest and he went down with a mortal wound. Webb rushed past; then, after the firing halted, he had an opportunity to return to view Smiley's body. Here he saw that the Yankee's pockets had already been rifled, but he found and took a small memorandum book that contained family pictures and was inscribed with Smiley's name. When captured at Spotsylvania a week later, Webb was sent to Point Lookout Prison, Maryland, with the battlefield souvenirs still in his possession.

He thought about the circumstances, and began to consider the awful trauma of it all. The victim could just as easily have been himself rather than Smiley, Webb realized, and he considered the anguish that his death would cause within his own family. He realized from reading Smiley's memorandum book that the dead soldier had been drafted, an apparently reluctant soldier caught up in the strife. His compassion was profound. Webb managed to obtain pen and paper and found the moral courage to write to the mother of the man he had killed:

> *Mrs. Smiley, Madam, In the providence of God I deprived you of your husband [son]. I hope you will not blame me for making you this announcement. It seems from his journal that he was not out as [a] volunteer, but was drafted, and as such I heartily sympathize*

with you. He acted the part of a brave man. The moment before I
fired on him, he shot down one of my comrades only about 20 steps
from me. After the firing had ceased I had occasion to pass by
him. I found someone had emptied his pockets, and I found his
memorandum book containing pictures probably of your
family. . . . May God in his mercy close this horrible strife between
the two sections at no distant day. Henry Webb.

Following an emotional reply from Mrs. Smiley, Webb again wrote her about his sentiments. "I deeply sympathize with you in all your bereavements, and sincerely hope your son is better off, also [I] wish you much joy and comfort in this life."[10]

Webb's awkwardness in addressing a woman who in his mind had every reason to hate him masked the profound sense of moral responsibility he felt in explaining that the battlefield incident was not the result of personal rancor or ruthlessness, but rather of the grim and impersonal vicissitudes of a "horrible" war. Webb's act exemplified the sense of morality that enabled a Christian soldier to cleanse his conscience to the extent of his capability. By giving vent to his thoughts and personal remorse, Webb apparently found peace of mind, and in a subtle way expressed high moral courage by attempting to abate the mental suffering of an enemy—a fellow human being.

XVII

DOING WHAT IS RIGHT

Stoicism, characterized by the ability to be mentally strong to the point of unlimited toughness or implacability, was venerated even in ancient times. Indeed, being able to act completely on the basis of virtue, rather than of emotions—such as fear, hate, or envy—was suggested as the basis of true happiness. Being detached from such detrimental emotions, all of which impeded efficacy in thought and deed, was said to be the key. If what you believed (your judgments) could be reappraised and adjusted on the basis of reason and understanding (versus false values such as self-esteem and pride), one might possibly achieve full self-control.

Virtue remains at the center of stoicism. Defeats and misfortunes in life are superficial; the real value is inner happiness with oneself. Being immune to misfortune, by realizing that there are aspects of life you can control but much that you cannot, requires mental discipline. To find dignity in one's own behavior while under great stress, such as in combat, is perhaps an ultimate survival mechanism. Today, understanding our thoughts and actions promotes in a military context a detached professionalism that excludes anger and other strong emotions. Rather than hating and dehumanizing the enemy or a terrorist, one copes better with the threat by understanding that such emotions beget the very behavior that characterizes the often fanatic enemy. This variation of the precept "Two wrongs don't make a right" locates the true source of enemy misbehavior in ignorance and a lack of perspective. To remain above the enemy's low level of thought and deed and to act with professionalism are the duty of the modern soldier in coping with war and terror, both physical and psychological.[1]

During the Civil War, however, the thought process was often predicated on raw emotion, with often unpredictable results.

John D. Compton was an admitted "tough" and a rather headstrong youth when, at age nineteen, he enlisted as a private in Company G of the 105th Ohio Volunteer Infantry in August 1862. His rural background, meager education, and fondness for alcohol foretold a rough-and-tumble army career. When on a foraging expedition in the Tennessee countryside near Murfreesboro on January 21, 1863, Compton and a few others of his regiment were captured by Confederate cavalry. Soon paroled, he was returned to the vicinity of Murfreesboro and at first kept in the custody of provost guards pending his exchange. Yet Compton was unhappy. Believing that because their exchange was delayed it was only fair that he be given a furlough—men from other units had received permission to go home, he said—Compton was angry about the inequity. He anticipated that the 105th's officers would swiftly "put us back in the ranks" because the prisoner exchange cartel "was broken," and "I expect every day that they will say so [to go out with the regiment for a fight]. If they do, old Hall [Colonel Albert S. Hall, commander of the 105th Ohio] will get the first charge from my gun if he goes in front [of me]," Compton confided in a letter to his brother. "Don't tell or say this to everyone, for it might get out . . . and it might go hard with me. But I will do as I say if I get a good chance, for I should have been [sent] home if it had not been for him, and I always pay my debts. [Thus] I guess he will get his [just] pay, for the boys all owe the same debt [and] I guess some of them will pay the debt." (Colonel Albert S. Hall died at Murfreesboro on July 10, 1863.) Compton thought the "damned Northern shoulder straps [officers]" were always conspiring against the men, and he was going to see to it that "there will be some of the straps catch hell," particularly as he "was a very good shot with the gun they gave me."[2]

Like "fragging" (the Vietnam War term for killing an overly strict or unpopular officer with a fragmentation grenade), intentionally if surreptitiously shooting a detested Civil War officer by his own troops was considered just by many aggrieved soldiers. Rather than murder, it was regarded by some as fair retaliation for wrongs endured, and an available remedy for the otherwise helpless enlisted man in dealing with superior authority.

To an impassioned Irishman, Private John Downes of the 35th Iowa Infantry, the orders of the "damned Codfish officers" of his regiment prompted him to assert in a letter home his pent-up fury. After the men were told to send all privately owned pistols home or else they would be seized by the government [so as to prevent accidents], Private Downes was indignant. "Now I think that damned hard," he wrote. "The boys have paid for their revolvers, and they ought to be allowed to keep them. The Codfish [a metaphor for a rough, undesirable officer] have done this mean trick. . . . The[se] shoulder straps [officers] had better not put on too many airs, or by God, some of them will get shot. They have been playing [us for] the fool long enough [and] I am getting tired of these little ticey-ass Codfish officers." Infuriated by the thought that "this Codfish plan of taking the sidearms from the soldiers" would weaken their battlefield prowess, Downes, who had never been in battle, raged that "it gives the Rebels a decided advantage over us on the field of battle, because they go armed to the teeth, and us, we'll have nothing but our muskets to fight with. . . . God damn the Codfish! They will ruin us," he bitterly predicted. Perhaps on their own "the soldiers would kill a few thousand Codfish officers," he warned.[3]

Actions taken against one's own comrades straddled the line between right and wrong. If two wrongs didn't make a right, the discreet utilization of any means at hand to accomplish a desired objective did serve for some as a practical catharsis. The outright display of collective courage was not unusual in the sometimes tenuous relationships between officers and their men. A riot broke out among enlisted men of a volunteer unit in March 1862 after they objected to an overly strict captain of the 18th U.S. Infantry tying up several drunken soldiers in what seemed to be an inhumane manner. Each guilty soldier was bound around the wrists by a rope, which was then pulled tight over a tree limb and secured; the victim was barely able to touch the ground with his toes. The resulting hour or two of "stretching" was known to severely hobble the miscreants and was an old regular army "remedy" long in use. Yet it was strongly resented by the neighboring 9th Ohio Infantry, whose soldiers attempted to take matters into their own hands. A crowd of infantrymen from the 9th Ohio descended upon the scene, cut the ropes, and freed the men. When several regular officers tried to stop them they were knocked down. More irate volunteers soon appeared and gathered around the 18th U.S. Infantry's separate guard tent. Emboldened by their success, the mob chased away the regular army sentinels and freed the prisoners, all the while "hooting and cursing" at the 18th's officers. Perhaps two hundred or more men had gathered by now, and the colonel of the 18th was summoned. One irate volunteer threw a log at his head, precipitating a general brawl among guards, officers, and the mob. The handful of regular officers and soldiers present were assaulted, one lieutenant having his sword taken and broken in two, and the 18th's major was knocked unconscious. Finally, the entire regular regiment had to be called under arms, formed with fixed bayonets, and ordered to charge the rioters before order was restored.[4]

In another incident, when mutiny was threatened by the men of the 1st and 2nd U.S. Sharpshooters because of the prolonged denial of promised Sharps breech-loading rifles (a condition of their enlistment, said the men), their officers attempted to retaliate by ordering extra duty and severe marches carrying fully packed knapsacks. Soon a full-blown protest was in progress. Although the crisis was resolved when Colonel Hiram Berdan posted documentation that their Sharps rifles were being manufactured and would soon be delivered, the rebelliousness of the soldiers was not taken lightly. Resignations were sought, and the turmoil involving both U.S. Sharpshooter regiments was particularly troublesome.[5]

Coping with righteous indignation was only one difficulty in the broad spectrum of the military's crucial personnel relationships. Aware that controversial or unpopular orders might provoke consequences likely to be focused on individuals, many in authority routinely fretted about the implications of their orders in dealing with others who might react unfavorably. Lieutenant Anthony Burton of the 5th Ohio Battery was considerably distressed during the siege of Vicksburg when his orderly sergeant, Walter Trotter, who was temporarily left in charge of the camp, was intimidated by the men. "Trotter is a first rate fellow and [is] willing as can be at all times, but [he] did not like to take hold and make the boys do as he said," complained Burton. "He is too sensitive and is afraid the boys would think he was putting on airs and going beyond his authority. A number of times he has come to me quite discouraged because the boys talk about him, and even the [subordinate] sergeants grumble. Why, I tell him, so long as I sustain him it is no matter what anybody thinks, and I will see they don't give him any impudence. But popularity is dear to Walter, and he can't see it quite in that light. A man to be a perfect orderly sergeant should be deaf and blind to everything but his duty."[6]

The ability to manage and control one's subordinates went beyond rank; it often went to the heart of self-confidence and what was later known as "guts"—the moral fiber involving one's self-respect. The courage to do what was right, despite regulations or protocol, pervaded soldiers' relationships. Sometimes it might mean taking the easy way out.

Lieutenant Calvin Shedd of the 7th New Hampshire Infantry found three of his sentries sleeping on duty in November 1862 and pondered the consequences of arresting them. Wrote Lieutenant Shedd:

> *When I was [officer of the] guard three weeks ago, I visited a*
> *picket post in the morning & found all three of the sentinels asleep.*
> *They were boys & new recruits, & I had not the heart to put the*

*ball & chain on them. But I gave them a good lecture, & told
them to go & sin no more. If I had put them in the guard house,
as most officers would have been glad of the chance to have done,
they would have been court-martialed, punished severely, lost their
self respect, & proved their ruin. My conscience tells me I have
done right, but it would not do for Col. Put[nam] to know it, for
then I should catch it, & be broken. . . . This soldiering, or war, is
the meanest business in the world.*[7]

Doing what was right in one's mind was frequently a difficult and nebulous undertaking, often involving the contrast between regulations, propriety, and equity. Strength of character was not readily discernible at first glance; one did not wear courage like a badge of rank. The mind was the arbiter in a realm of usually imperfect understanding. What ultimately proved crucial was the result—the way any controversial decision played out.

Consistently making a "good" decision, even if for the wrong reason, was a matter that few fully understood or could adequately explain. In the full aftermath of decisions, right versus wrong was usually apparent. Hindsight enabled wisdom in perspective.

Less scrutinized were the whys and wherefores of critical decisions. Decisions that resulted in a "right" were easily rationalized. Yet the technical explanation often obscured the choice's true basis, which was perhaps rooted in one's moral fiber. "Luck" might be a primary factor, but reality was usually couched in more definable terms. No matter how difficult, making key decisions required having the courage of one's convictions or else an intuitive reliance on another's data or opinions. When the lives of many hung in the balance, decision making was a matter of profound implication.

COPING WITH THE MORAL ENIGMA—U. S. GRANT

Major General Ulysses S. Grant epitomized the practical commander. He knew from long experience that the essence of success was often as basic as being resolute. An aggressive, determined fighter, "Sam" Grant was a proactive military leader with an inborn dislike of being placed on the defensive. His mental acuity, easy grasp of critical circumstances, and administrative capacity had by 1863 impressed even his severest critics. Above all else it was his mental toughness that personified strength as a leading general. Indeed, he was a man to manage events rather than be managed by them.

Certainly, at Chattanooga in mid-November 1863 he was the man of the hour. Grant was again on the verge of a make-or-break opportunity that would largely determine the outcome of his career. Called upon as the "Victor of Vicksburg" to rescue the besieged Army of the Cumberland at Chattanooga following their crushing September defeat at Chickamauga, Grant was Abraham Lincoln's choice to control the war and win a decisive victory in the West. Rosecrans's army not only had been soundly beaten by the Confederates at Chickamauga but was penned up and nearly starving in Chattanooga. The Confederates had cut off virtually all supplies to the city.

When Rosecrans was replaced by George H. Thomas and Grant was put in overall department command, the nation looked to Grant for a redeeming victory. There was an enormous amount at stake, observed one of Grant's subordinates, Colonel Emerson Opdycke. "Grant has immense responsibilities on him. Should he fail here, his past reputation will be dimmed, and he [will] be shelved again. But if he succeeds now, he will be in the flood tide of success at the death of the rebellion, and will stand peerless in the annals of American generals."[8]

Matters had proceeded relatively well following Grant's arrival in Chattanooga on October 23. The "cracker line" [new supply route] was raised by the Union attack at and occupation of Brown's Ferry on the Tennessee River, and supplies were again flowing freely into the besieged city. William Tecumseh Sherman, commanding Grant's former troops, the Army of the Tennessee, had brought his veterans to the relief of Chattanooga, arriving in the vicinity in mid-November following an overland march from the Mississippi Valley. Joe Hooker's troops, two corps hurriedly sent from the Army of the Potomac, were also present.

Since he greatly outnumbered the besiegers, Grant planned to attack the Confederate army under Braxton Bragg during the third week in November.

Encouragingly, on the twenty-fourth Hooker's troops outfought and chased the enemy off nearby Lookout Mountain, setting the stage for the main attack by Sherman's troops against North Missionary Ridge, planned for November 25. Relying on Sherman to break the end of Bragg's line and envelop its northern flank meant Hooker's troops could simultaneously sweep through the Chattanooga Valley and roll up Bragg's southern flank. Caught in a pincers, Bragg's army would be forced to flee, even while confronted in front of Chattanooga by Thomas's passive army. Thomas's men would serve mostly as a decoy, merely threatening a frontal assault while Sherman and Hooker did the real work.

Yet November 25 did not go according to plan for the Union commander. Grant spent much of the day on Orchard Knob, witnessing from a distance the protracted attack by Sherman against General Pat Cleburne's Confederates on Tunnel Hill along North Misssionary Ridge. By early afternoon it was evident to Grant that Sherman was having severe difficulty. His piecemeal attacks had repeatedly been repulsed by the aggressive Cleburne, forcing Sherman by 3:00 P.M. to call off the attacks and withdraw his troops. Soon thereafter, Sherman's thirty thousand troops (only ten thousand of whom had been engaged) went into bivouac.

Grant remained oblivious of this fact. Believing Sherman had only temporarily halted his assaults, Grant sought to relieve some of "the pressure" on Sherman so that his main thrust might succeed. Observing through field glasses Rebel troops moving along Missionary Ridge toward the north, Grant believed the enemy was heavily reinforcing that sector. He knew that Hooker had been delayed in the Chattanooga Valley by burned bridges and was unable to rapidly effect the opposite end of the pincers movement.

Seeing the remnants of Sherman's troops falling back down North Missionary Ridge's slopes in disarray, Grant realized that his master plan was in severe trouble. Mindful of November's short daylight hours, Grant believed he had to do something to help Sherman. The only remaining viable option was to use George H. Thomas's troops, whom he considered unreliable and dogged by the Chickamauga defeat.

Impulsively, Grant decided to order four of Thomas's divisions, about twenty-five thousand troops, to attack the rifle pits at the base of the middle of Missionary Ridge. This was simply intended "to help" Sherman.

By diverting the enemy's attention to the center of the line, Sherman might be enabled to attack without facing additional enemy reinforcements, which Grant presumed would be redirected back to the area confronted by Thomas. In all, it was to be merely "a demonstration" to relieve the pressure on Sherman. At a signal of six field guns fired in sequence on Orchard Knob, Thomas's men would advance and take the forward rifle pits, but not approach the main Confederate defensive line on top of Missionary Ridge, some six hundred feet above the lower rifle pits. Indeed, once Thomas began the attack, Sherman was sent a message by Grant: "Now is your time to attack with vigor; do so."

Grant's thinking was severely flawed. He had made a poor tactical decision that was a blueprint for disaster. What he failed to consider was quickly perceived by many of Thomas's frontline commanders. By advancing to capture the rifle pits at the base of Missionary Ridge, Thomas's men would be trapped immediately under the frowning guns of the Confederates atop the ridge and subjected to such a severe fire that "it would be impossible to stay there."

Since this diversionary attack was being made upon an entirely mistaken premise—that Sherman would again attack North Missionary Ridge—it was out of touch with reality and threatened total disaster. With Sherman defeated on the north, Hooker floundering to the south, and Thomas about to take an untenable position directly under the enemy's guns where they might be pounded into oblivion, Grant had seemingly lost the battle.

Yet Grant didn't seem to know that he was beaten. When Thomas's men attacked about 4:00 P.M., Grant was again watching from Orchard Knob. The four divisions easily overran the moderate enemy force at the base of the ridge, capturing the rifle pits without severe opposition. Yet as the scattering Rebels fled up the slopes of Missionary Ridge, Thomas's men fully understood their own predicament. A whirlwind of rifle and shell fire from above raked their position, throwing the milling Union line into chaos. There was no cover from the plunging fire coming from the ridge's crest. To remain where they were "would be destruction," realized a Union officer, and to fall back would involve renewed exposure, defeat, and disgrace.

Slowly but impulsively, the men "on their own hook" lurched forward for the comparative protection of the sharply rising ground ahead and away from the terrible enfilade fire from above. With the fugitive Rebels scattering up Missionary Ridge's steep slopes above them, Thomas's men continued on, eagerly pursuing the enemy, since they were partially sheltered from the enemy's fire by the steep angle of the ridge.

On Orchard Knob, Ulysses Grant stood aghast. Despite the victory at the rifle pits along the base of the ridge, Thomas's men in disobedience of specific orders were seen continuing forward—up the very slopes ringed with more than fifty Rebel cannon and thousands of infantry. The prospect of another bloody repulse such as what Sherman had endured on North Missionary Ridge was stark in Grant's mind. Angrily, he turned to George Thomas and blurted out, "Who ordered those men up that ridge?"

Emotionless, Thomas stood transfixed. Slowly he replied, "I don't know. I did not." Another officer nervously responded, "When those fellows get started all hell can't stop them." Grant wasn't amused. Menacingly, he grumbled that someone would pay dearly for it if the assault failed.

Convinced that the wrath of God was about to descend on the army, a nearby general turned to his chief of staff and told him to find out who ordered the troops up the ridge, saying they should be halted if possible, as it was Grant's order that they not go beyond the first line of rifle pits.

It was an amazing circumstance. Thomas's twenty-five thousand troops, without orders and seemingly out of control, kept surging up the slopes while staff officers raced across the plain seeking to recall them. This awkward, odd race of destiny found its fruition in the comment of one frontline general who was told by a staff officer to recall his men. "Who in Hell is going to stop them?" growled Thomas J. Wood. The matter was thus practically decided. There would be no stopping George H. Thomas's soldiers until the fight was fully won or lost.

In one of the most famous infantry assaults in the history of our nation, Missionary Ridge was carried by Thomas's men, resulting in the complete defeat of Bragg's army. A major frontal attack, almost always unsuccessful in the face of strong natural and military defenses, had improbably succeeded, resulting in the capture of forty cannon, more than four thousand prisoners, and an enormous rout.

Grant, truly amazed at the sudden turn in fortune, rode atop Missionary Ridge when the hazy smoke of battle still lingered over the field. His demeanor was that of relieved gratitude, and he thanked the soldiers, taking off his hat as he passed the lines of cheering men. In his official report he reflected that the tremendous victory could be accounted for only on the theory that the enemy was surprised by the audacity of the unlikely charge, which resulted in their confusion and inaccurate shooting.

Of course, there were technical explanations for the defeat. The Confederate leadership under Bragg had not envisioned a massed frontal assault and was poorly prepared: inadequate breastworks were mistakenly located on the actual crown of the ridge (not the military crest, which would have allowed a full field of fire); and half of each brigade's strength was positioned at the bottom of the slopes, both forcing the routed survivors to flee to the top and interfering with the field of fire.

Yet the technical explanations belie the decision-making process. Grant had made the right decision even if for the wrong reasons. Destiny then had completed the full equation. At the root of the matter was the inner fiber of the man. He had the moral courage to act decisively upon what he knew without worrying about the personal consequences. As at Fort Donelson, at Shiloh, and again at Vicksburg, Grant had overcome adversity with the moral courage that was later attributed to his "bulldog" determination.

After Chattanooga, Grant received the adulation of the Northern people. Already a household name, Grant became the most famous soldier in the nation. Promoted to lieutenant general, a rank specially authorized by Congress and previously held by only George Washington, Grant was called to the east and made general in chief of the combined Union armies.

His subsequent status as a national hero who bested Robert E. Lee in Virginia was in large part made possible by the Chattanooga results. Despite its flaws, the victory on November 25, 1863, was the result of more than good luck. Given a major crisis, Sam Grant could keep his composure and act decisively while under enormous stress. Perhaps William Tecumseh Sherman said it best when he noted that Grant didn't scare worth a damn—he made his own plans and went ahead, caring nothing for what he couldn't see.

He knew how to win.[9]

XVIII

COWARDICE, COURAGE'S COUSIN

The primary sources in this study are letters, journals, and diaries written contemporaneously to the dramatic events depicted. Due to a general lack of censoring (except for letters by prisoners of war), there was a positive freedom of expression that enabled what often became a purging of emotions, following a particularly traumatic or significant event. To tell the family or a close friend of one's experiences and innermost thoughts was, to some, a way to sustain rational equilibrium—the reality confronted, survived, and reported. The experience of combat was not entirely conveyable, but the emotions were. To describe the horror, and admit one's fright, served perhaps as a catharsis of the soul, not only relieving pent-up emotions, but in some cases helping steel the psyche for the next coming fury. As one wise-beyond-his-years Ohio sergeant admitted in 1862 after experiencing battle: "I believe that [any] man does not live, but [he] has fear about him. If he wants to live—and, of course, all sensible men want to live as long as possible—unless he has that noble and patriotic feeling that all Americans should have, he is bound to [run away in combat]."[1]

Patriotism, and a heightened sense of duty, were the best means of coping with the battlefield, according to this soldier. Duty and responsibility overrode the fear of dire consequences. Yet, admitting one's fear was often only the first step. The randomness, and the capriciousness of injury, death, or else survival were apparent to those who faced combat. There seemed to be no rational explanation for why one person survived unscathed, while another met severe injury or death—except perhaps within one's own mind. Here the emotions ranged from a trust in God's divine protection, to the practice of superstitious habits or thoughts. A soldier's fatalism was in essence a concession, an awareness that life was beyond any individual's full control. Obviously, being in the wrong place at the wrong time was not perceptible in advance (although some soldiers had premonitions about their fate in battle that proved accurate).

Nonetheless, there was prudent behavior in the face of danger—a minimal exposure of self within the context of duty and "manliness." How far a soldier might go to shield his body from injury required intense self-evaluation. The mind's computer reaction in confronting battlefield dangers, however, was not always consistent. An awareness of crucial circumstances and practical protocols sometimes conflicted. How the scenario played out varied from situation to situation. Through it all, however, there was usually an overriding self-control based on hope or faith. What the Ohio sergeant saw as patriotism was in essence man's refined sense of purpose, to risk great bodily harm for a worthy object, even for the impersonal—a nation's political goals.

The key to prudent behavior was knowledge. A practical awareness of battlefield circumstances conveyed with it a manageable perspective. Veterans of combat reacted differently from raw recruits when going into battle. Knowing what one was likely to face was important, especially to a veteran, who used his prior experience to help manage the ordeal. An awareness that the soldier had survived past combat was a conscious reminder that there was practical hope of the same in future battles. Hope impelled courage, and specific knowledge sustained it.

The mind required a positive attitude for the dire events faced. A tool for further leverage was having a personal standard of right and wrong. Only when those values crumbled under the pressure of self-perpetuation did a soldier lose self-control. Survival in life-threatening circumstances was a rudimentary, basic instinct, but it was modified by intelligent reason.

To those that failed the test of combat, the primal instinct of survival seemed to justify the means of prioritizing safety. It was sort of a reverse courage; the duty or object at hand was not as important as preserving oneself. Cowardice was a near cousin to courage. It expressed an acute awareness of the deadly prevailing circumstances, and the reaction was both mental and physical. Instead of inspiring bravery and the risking of one's life, however, the essential nature of survival resulted in timidity. Exposure to criticism was secondary at the moment. The short-term benefits outweighed the long-term consequences. Trauma inspired extreme fear or panic in some soldiers, but the breaking point varied according to each individual's circumstances.

A MATTER OF IRONY

Elisha Bourne Bassett seemed to have the world at his beck and call. An experienced and long-established newspaper publisher in Allegan, Michigan, a vestryman of his church, a local county, township, and village official, and the master of his Masonic lodge, Bassett was a community leader, well respected and prominent in this industrious southwestern Michigan community. It wasn't surprising, therefore, when the forty-year-old publisher announced in July 1862 the organization of a volunteer company in Allegan to help defend the Union. From the time Company B of the 19th Michigan Volunteer Infantry was organized to the eve of its departure for the war about the first of September 1862, the townspeople of Allegan were most supportive. Indeed, on the evening of August 25 at a farewell party given by family, friends, and fraternal associates, Captain Bassett was presented with an "elegant" gift—a deluxe

sword, sash, and belt. The fancy nonregulation cavalry officer's model
sword carried a silver band on the scabbard that was inscribed:

The Constitution [Masonic logo] and the Union

Capt. E. B. Bassett

Master of Allegan Lodge No. 111

From the Members of the Craft

August 1862

With the singing of several "soul-stirring" songs, words of encouragement from his friends, and a speech by Bassett "such as to start the
tear from every eye," said the reporter for the *Allegan Journal,* a fond
adieu was bid "to the citizen soldier who goes to save our government
from peril, and country from ruin."[2]

Yet Bassett's behavior as company commander was soon the subject
of anxious talk among his men. He seemed to abandon them when
hardships were encountered, traveling elsewhere with his wife under the
pretext of being sick while his unit was at Lexington, Kentucky, in November. By early February 1863 the 19th Michigan was in an active war
zone near Franklin, Tennessee, and Captain Bassett, noted one of his
soldiers, was "a little shaky."

With the prospect of active campaigning, Elisha Bassett submitted
his resignation, but the paperwork was delayed. A few days later the
19th Michigan was ordered on a reconnaissance toward Columbia, Tennessee. Confronted at Thompson's Station by a large Confederate cavalry force under Nathan Bedford Forrest and W. H. Jackson, the 19th
Michigan found itself fighting for its survival. Once the 19th was heavily engaged, its colonel, Henry C. Gilbert, looked around in the rear.
There, behind a large tree fifteen or twenty yards from the firing line,
stood a cowed Elisha Bassett. Gilbert immediately strode to the spot and
angrily asked the shaking captain "what he was doing there and why he
was not with his company." In Gilbert's words, Bassett croaked out a reply, that "he could not take any part in the fight [and] that I must not
depend upon him for anything; that the lieutenant could command the
company, and [he] begged me to excuse him."

Gilbert's ire was profound. "I repeatedly ordered him to his post, but he refused to obey," wrote the angry colonel. Within minutes, Gilbert saw Bassett run off down the railroad track, where he eventually "crumpled" a horse belonging to one of the cavalry, and rode back to Franklin. "I have never seen a man exhibit so much cowardice and fear as Captain Bassett did," Gilbert bitterly commented.

Yet Bassett survived the heavy fighting in which the 19th lost 20 killed and 92 wounded of 531 present. Moreover, Gilbert and most of the regiment were taken prisoners at Thompson's Station, and were soon sent to Libby Prison in Richmond.

Being one of the few who escaped, and with no one of authority to report his desertion under fire, Captain Bassett wound up being the senior officer and in command of the remnant of the regiment, amounting to about 230 officers and men who had been on detached duty.

Days later, Captain Bassett was in charge of a stockade-fort guarding a railroad bridge near Brentwood, Tennessee. Bassett's lack of composure bordered on the ridiculous, thought the 19th's chaplain, Israel Coggshall. "Captain Bassett is either utterly incompetent to perform the duties of commander, or has deliberately made up his mind that he will do nothing. He has determined that he will leave the service at all hazards, and thus will do nothing in it," complained Coggshall on March 9. "We are in a most deplorable condition. There is no authority; no subordination. Men go where they please and when they please. If the Rebels desire us . . . they only have to come and take us."[3]

On March 25 Nathan Bedford Forrest's cavalry suddenly appeared at Brentwood and captured the entire 521-man town garrison following feeble resistance. Having bypassed Bassett's stockade about daylight, Forrest returned about 9:00 A.M. and surrounded the sturdy fort with his command. The Confederates had a field gun, and a single shot was fired at the stockade, which was observed to be "of great strength against small arms." Some of Forrest's men noted that storming it would likely result in heavy losses. "Take in a flag of truce," Forrest told his aide-de-camp, Lieutenant Charles W. Anderson, "and tell them I have them completely surrounded, and if they don't surrender I'll blow hell out of them in five minutes and won't take one of them alive if I have to sacrifice my men in storming their stockade."

Lacking a white handkerchief, Anderson stripped off his shirt and rode to the fort with his shirt waving in the breeze. Here he confronted Captain Elisha Bassett and demanded a surrender or else no quarter would be given. Bassett didn't hesitate. Promptly the white flag was raised, and the 230-man garrison was surrendered. Soon hastened by forced marches through mud, sleet, and hail to Chattanooga, Bassett and the other officers were sent on to Knoxville, and finally arrived at Richmond on April 11.

Ironically, Bassett wound up in Libby Prison, where his old comrades from the 19th Michigan had been taken. The reception he got there can only be imagined. When the 19th's officers were soon exchanged and sent north, the resentment quickly boiled forth. As soon as Bassett set foot on the wharf at Annapolis, Maryland, on May 7, he was arrested. Colonel Henry C. Gilbert was so furious at the cowardly captain that he refused to see him. Supported by Major General Gordon Granger, who called Bassett one of "our milk and water soldiers," Gilbert had his ex-captain dismissed without trial for cowardice less than thirty days later. Bassett, who feebly protested about not being furnished with the charges, said he "had nothing to say" about his conduct, but he did what "he supposed was his duty." One of his soldiers wryly commented that since Bassett now wasn't with the regiment, he might be found hiding in some "rocky cavern." Had he been with the regiment, wrote the man, he would face dismissal at dress parade in front of the ranks, where a soldier would "cut all the buttons off his coat, cut off his shoulder straps, and break his sword" before he was drummed out of camp.

Seemingly broken in spirit and in health, Elisha Bassett returned to Allegan, but since his old regiment had returned to active duty in the field, he was able to scrub his tarnished reputation by exerting the considerable political clout gained from his newspaper days. Indeed, before the end of the war Elisha Bassett sought election to local office. The stigma of cowardice had seemed permanent to many of his soldiers, but when they returned from the war, ironically, Bassett was the town's mayor![4]

Bassett's experience in combat, analyzed in today's context, reveals much about the behavior of those predisposed to run away. His fundamental emotion of fear in encountering a life-threatening situation seems to have produced a substantial chemical reaction in the brain, resulting in panic. In view of humans' primal flight or fight natural response, his mind was essentially influenced to the point of abandoning his primary task as a soldier. Physically, this panic was so intense that it could produce trembling, nausea, and headaches or dizziness. Genetically, Bassett appears to have been predisposed to this reaction, being "wired" for such as a part of the ancient reaction to fear that aroused our forebears and helped keep them alive. The difference between Bassett's reaction and that of another who stayed to fight was the other person's use of reason in overcoming fear. Many people can maintain proper behavior under severe stress, but according to one estimate as much as half the population might experience dire symptoms or acute disorder in coping with such.[5]

"Cowardice" is a strong word; it involves the raw emotion of self-intimidation. That we all have the potential to be intimidated by various circumstances is apparent. The wonder is that so many exhibit courage when their very survival is at stake.

WHISKEY COURAGE

Captain William C. Morgan, Company F, 3rd Maine Infantry, was respected as a military man of good experience, having served for five years in the British army before immigrating to the United States in 1851. Almost penniless when he arrived here, Morgan had experienced success and prosperity, becoming a printer in Maine prior to joining the army in September 1861. He was relied upon to provide expertise and leadership, and by mid-1863 he and his men had fought arduously at Williamsburg, Seven Pines, Second Manassas, Fredericksburg, and Chancellorsville. His firm, resolute commitment to see the rebellion put down was continually reflected in his many letters to his wife, Amanda. Yet the fatiguing campaigns, intense fighting, and constant responsibility took their toll. After Chancellorsville he informed his wife, "I have had enough of this wholesale butchery and destruction of human life, so that I want to see [it] no more. The sight of a battlefield is sickening. You look at your shattered ranks [lying] on the ground, and see mutilated bodies of brave men, [and] it is enough to set me crazy."

Perhaps it was enough to drive such a distraught officer to strong drink. Although he had once lectured his wife to "live a pure life," Captain Morgan's reputation among his men began to suffer because of his frequent abuse of liquor. Further, his men noted how Morgan seemed incapable of leading them into a fight unless under the influence of alcohol. At Chancellorsville, one of his soldiers saw Captain Morgan remain prone on the ground when his men were ordered to charge. "I saw no attempt on his part to rise and follow, or to accompany the men," wrote Corporal George W. Stewart. The regiment's chaplain even said of Morgan: "[H]e is a man that indulges in spirituous liquor pretty freely."

With the Gettysburg Campaign under way and a battle threatened on July 2, the men of Company F, 3rd Maine, carefully noted their captain's demeanor. Throughout the heavy fighting of that day, Captain Morgan seemed to act the part of an effective officer, rallying his men and staying with them throughout the fighting during Sickles's ordeal at the Peach Orchard. Again on July 3, when required to assist in the repulse of Pickett's Charge, Morgan was present with his men and endured their exposure while supporting a battery near the Angle.

Yet there were dark accusations among the men that Morgan's display of courage was induced by the contents of a whiskey bottle. So incensed was Private Charles N. Maxwell that he wrote a blistering letter to his friend in Maine, complaining that Morgan at Gettysburg was like "a common drunkard, the worst of any of the regiment's officers." At one point, he had lain flat upon the ground, remembered Maxwell, "and when told that his men were shot down, he would not even get up to look at them. He knew nothing of what became of his men except what [we] told him." Maxwell's letter damningly asserted that "for courage, [Captain Morgan] has little unless he is full of liquor."

Suitably outraged, the Maine friend gave the letter to a local newspaper editor, who published it anonymously in the *Skowhegan Clarion*.

When copies of the newspaper arrived in the 3rd Maine's camp, the uproar resulted in Maxwell's being identified, arrested, and subsequently tried by court-martial.

Morgan, who denied it all, boasted to his wife in a letter home after Gettysburg that he had captured a sword from "one of Longstreet's aides" who had "tried hard to put it into my body—but couldn't come it." He was sending the weapon home for her to keep safe, he wrote, "for it has been where thousands of brave men were killed, and where cowards dare not go."[6]

Clearly, Morgan didn't look upon himself as an inebriate or less than a brave soldier. The liquor was a stimulant, taken like medicine to strengthen his resolve and bolster his sinew. It made him feel good—and better about his role as an officer. Yet, was it a crutch to endure the rigors of war and also the ennui of the service? Was it a means to cope, knowing the horror of combat and the prospect of losing everything in a blink of the eye? Would anyone care that his emotions were too raw to tolerate without some relief? Whatever the circumstances, others weren't as tolerant of Captain Morgan's periodic indulgence, as evidenced by the events after Gettysburg.

"The man that said a soldier's life is always gay had not seen the rough side of it," groaned William Morgan to his wife in a letter after Gettysburg. "I wish in my heart it was at an end. We lay down at night, weary and tired from the effects of a march or battle on a pile of rocks, or in a mud puddle, and sleep soundly. But on waking up in the morning we are about as tired as the previous night, and have to begin again on this day's tramp. . . . I don't see how we are going to stand it."[7]

Stand it he did, but increasingly, said some, with the use of whiskey. By the time Private Maxwell was court-martialed in April 1864, Morgan, who had been promoted to major following the loss of the 3rd Maine's major at Gettysburg, was more deeply involved in controversy about his drinking. Indeed, the evidence presented at Maxwell's trial was so related to Morgan's drinking and conduct on the field of battle as to virtually place Morgan himself on trial.

Damaging testimony about Morgan's intoxication came from a variety of the regiment's personnel, including the lieutenant colonel, the chaplain, and a variety of enlisted men. Yet the colonel, Company F's sergeant major, and other noncommissioned officers not only exonerated Morgan, but indicated they had never seen him drunk on duty or incapacitated in command of his company. Even Major General David Birney's brother, a major on the division's staff, testified to Morgan's sobriety.

In all, it was an exercise in contradiction. Quietly, the court acquitted Private Maxwell of all charges except for indiscretion in the language of his private letter to the Maine friend about Morgan, and restored him to duty. To protect him from retaliation, Maxwell was soon transferred to another regiment.

Aware that his clouded reputation was thereafter subject to internal debate, Morgan resolved to exonerate himself. Grant's Overland Campaign was soon in progress, and the 3rd Maine was called upon to fight extensively in the Wilderness. On May 5 Major Morgan was shot with a glancing blow by a rifle ball in the right arm. In an emotional letter, William Morgan told his wife that once he returned home, "I shall never leave you again." Yet he vowed to do his duty, even as the regiment prepared to end its three-year term of service, which would expire on June 4, 1864. Only a few days more, and Morgan and the men could go home to their wives and family. The Army of the Potomac would prevail, he told Amanda, and he would continue to lead his men in combat despite the fact that everywhere he looked the scene was "literally covered with dead and wounded of both sides."

On May 23, 1864, the 3rd Maine was engaged at the North Anna River, and in an evening assault on the enemy's lines at Taylor's Bridge the regiment suffered heavily. Major William Morgan was in the forefront of the charge when a rifle ball passed through his right breast. A wound that testified to his valor on the battlefield, it also heralded a final tragedy. Within hours thirty-three-year-old William C. Morgan died, leaving a grief-stricken wife and two children under the age of four to mourn his passing. With his death the controversies of the past quickly flickered and died. On June 9, 1865, an effort was announced to raise three hundred dollars to obtain a portrait of Major Morgan to be placed in "the National Gallery of American Heroes."[8]

Perhaps a hard drinker, William C. Morgan had paid the ultimate price in laying his body upon the altar of his country. Only a few days had remained in his term of service. Even as he might have suggested, every man has his faults, but it is his virtues that often mean the most.

XIX

WHAT KIND OF COURAGE?

General John Bell Hood is a complex subject. His various descendants and supporters today insist that he is unfairly maligned for his short-comings, whereas his attributes should be emphasized. Certainly, in bat-tle the man was very courageous; his physical courage attracted such attention that it provided great opportunity to achieve at the highest lev-els. Hood became a prominent commander with high responsibility, and he was among the key players of the war. Having courage, fame, and glory, what more could any soldier seek?

Yet where does virtue begin or end? Ultimately, Hood was one of the great failures of the war: a sad, tragic figure who underachieved in his greatest endeavors. Today, his story provides a remarkable insight into the incomplete role of physical courage in his life.

In the beginning, there was little in John Bell Hood's background to suggest that he would become one of the more influential generals of the Civil War. Born in Kentucky to a bluegrass-region doctor, Hood grew up with a streak of wildness and nonconformity about him. He was frequently in trouble, and his appointment to West Point through the influence of his uncle, a U.S. congressman, was looked upon by his father as social conditioning. Known as "Sam" to his associates at West Point, young Hood struggled with the academic curriculum, winding up forty-fourth in his class of fifty-two upon graduation in 1853. Never known for his intellectual qualities, Sam Hood was thought to be rather simplistic in manner and style, yet an aggressive sort who might do the unexpected and sometimes the bizarre.

Once he became a lieutenant in the regular army, however, Hood prospered. As a member of the famed 2nd U.S. Cavalry, he fought Indians with a verve and bravery that earned him praise. During a skirmish against raiding Comanches in July 1857, Lieutenant Hood took an arrow through his left hand that lodged in his horse's bridle. He merely broke off the shaft, freed his hand, and continued to fight. Promoted to first lieutenant in 1858, the tall, muscular Hood seemed endowed with good luck equal to his bravery. When the Civil War began, and upon his resignation from the U.S. Army, he found duty under his old 2nd Cavalry lieutenant colonel, Robert E. Lee.

Beginning as a Confederate cavalry lieutenant, Hood within a few months rose to command of the 4th Texas Infantry and the rank of colonel. Then, when his brigade commander resigned to return to a legislative career, Hood found himself promoted to brigadier general and was given command of the elite Texas Brigade. At the Battle of Gaines' Mill, Hood was personally inspired by Robert E. Lee, who when ordering a crucial frontal assault upon Turkey Hill told him: "May God be with you!"

Hood stormed up the hill with his Texans, forbidding them to fire a shot until the enemy line was reached—or else the men would then halt to reload and thus break alignment. The Texas Brigade took severe losses in its grim attack, but captured the hill after hand-to-hand fighting. Hood miraculously survived the combat without a scratch. As he stood and surveyed the carnage, he saw that nearly an entire Yankee regiment, the 4th New Jersey Infantry, had been captured and fourteen pieces of artillery had been taken by his Texans. Valor and courage had won the big fight. It seemed to be a critical lesson well learned. Praised by Lee and Stonewall Jackson for his remarkable accomplishment, Sam Hood was soon assigned to command of a division.

Hood's reputation as a fighter and his boldness marked him as a rising star who just might be destiny's darling. At Antietam his reputation continued to brighten, and ambition began to burn ever brighter in his mind. He even wrote a letter to his "friend" Robert E. Lee suggesting that smaller army corps might be desirable. Perhaps Lee would favor Hood with such a command? Hood approached the Gettysburg Campaign with further confidence. If his battlefield courage had produced so much already, the thirty-two-year-old Kentuckian keenly sought more opportunity to show his mettle.

But Gettysburg was a disappointment for Hood. Early in the fighting on July 2, 1863, he was struck with multiple shell fragments that tore into his left arm, severely crippling him for life. He was promptly removed from the battlefield and relinquished command of his division. Instead of high praise, there was scant mention of Hood in the official reports. He used his convalescence in Richmond to good advantage, however, being feted as a wounded hero, and falling in love with the beguiling Sally "Buck" Preston, a woman high in Richmond social circles.

When restored to division command in September 1863, Hood journeyed west along with portions of Longstreet's Corps to reinforce Bragg's army. On the grisly field of Chickamauga on September 20, Hood was again quickly taken out of the action by a severe wound. Struck by a rifle ball in the right leg that shattered the bone just below the hip, an amputation was deemed essential. Amazingly, Hood survived although retaining only a four-and-a-half-inch leg stump. His robust physique and strong will to live pulled him through, even though he was horribly disfigured. The pain and trauma of his wounds were but a reminder to Hood that his bravery on the battlefield had earned him recognition as a Southern war hero despite the lack of important results in his new command responsibility. By mid-November, Hood was back in Richmond, marked for promotion to lieutenant general, and very much a celebrity.

At Richmond matters rapidly changed. A burgeoning friendship with President Jefferson Davis resulted in Hood's assignment to the Army of Tennessee, where Hood would be present to inform Richmond of the compliance of General Joe Johnston with the administration's policies. Like a highly placed watchdog, Hood surreptitiously kept up a correspondence with the Davis administration, repeatedly discrediting Joe Johnston in deceitful commentaries about decisions and maneuvers during the Atlanta Campaign. When it became prudent in President Davis's eyes to replace Johnston once he had retreated from Dalton, Georgia, all the way to Atlanta, Hood was selected as his successor with the endorsement of key adviser Braxton Bragg. Having "wire-worked" his way to top command, observed an officer, Hood was now in an unfamiliar spot: the chief rather than the critic.

The essential difference was soon apparent. From his initial aggressiveness on July 20, 1864, in attacking Sherman's troops after they crossed the Chattahoochee River to the desperate battle at Ezra Church eight days later, Hood sacrificed nearly twenty thousand men in a series of failed assaults that had the Union soldiers shaking their heads in disbelief. We kill more Rebs than ever before, noted an Illinois sergeant, for "they come out from their works and charge our men, which is useless, for . . . they only get their men slaughtered."[1]

Hood's recklessly aggressive use of his men clarified the aberration of Gaines' Mill; Southern dash and courage were no substitute for skill and tactical expertise in fighting the enemy. Yet "Sam" Hood, largely by blaming others, managed to avoid removal from command following the loss of Atlanta. During a hurried visit to Georgia, President Davis kept him in command, and approved his plan to raid north with his depleted but still threatening army. While Sherman's columns were marching through Georgia to the sea in late November 1864, Hood's men were struggling northwestward into Tennessee, in the direction of Nashville.

Hood's "invasion" of Tennessee was driven by desperation, a need to do something to forestall the imminent loss of the war. Further, he knew that both his personal career and the fate of the army were at stake. His plight was as obvious as his uncertainty of what to do once he reached the enemy's defenses.

Hood faced greater combined numbers and resources in the Union forces of General George Thomas at Nashville and General John Schofield at Columbia, Tennessee. So Hood decided to outflank the separated Union detachment of about twenty thousand men under Schofield that was retreating toward Nashville across the Duck River at Columbia. Hood's well-conducted maneuver on November 29 to get in the rear of Schofield's force was initially successful, but the greatly fatigued Hood opted to retire to the rear as the critical events unfolded that afternoon. The resulting command confusion and inertia enabled the Union army to escape that night by passing almost directly beneath the Rebels' guns at Spring Hill, Tennessee. When an astounded and angry Hood pursued the fleeing enemy twelve miles to Franklin the following morning, he found the Union force fortified behind extensive earthworks that had been prepared for defense of the town a year earlier.

In one of the most stunning decisions of the war, Hood determined to assault the entrenched enemy directly across two miles of open ground, and without basic artillery support, since all but a few of his cannon were still en route from the rear. Incredibly, despite the great valor of Hood's soldiers from Shiloh in 1862 to Allatoona just a month earlier, an alleged want of courage provided a graphic backdrop to the assault.

Hood was strongly advised against making the frontal attack at Franklin by many of his senior generals. Yet Hood decided it was to be a remedial lesson in courage. His angry reaction to the protesters seemed motivated by smoldering resentment over the fiasco at Spring Hill the previous day. In his memoirs, Hood stated:

> *The discovery that the army, after a forward march of*
> *180 miles was still seemingly unwilling to accept*
> *battle unless under the protection of breastworks,*
> *caused me to experience grave concern. In my inmost*
> *heart, I questioned whether or not I would ever succeed*
> *in eradicating this evil.*[2]

Terming what he saw as the Army of Tennessee's reluctance to fight in the open a "stumbling block," Hood further resolved to place those he blamed for the Spring Hill debacle in the center of the attacking formation, where enemy resistance was certain to be the strongest.

This massive frontal assault made no sense, commented one of the many Confederate commanders who were compelled to make the attack. The enemy had emplaced artillery in its frontline earthworks, cleared a field of fire, and cut trees and thorny Osage orange shrubs to form an all but impenetrable barrier to reaching the breastworks. The enemy's numbers were comparable to the attackers', and it was grimly discussed by various officers and men that their prospects for surviving the attack were few.

The magnitude of the forlorn assault at Franklin on November 30, 1864, was enormous. About the same number of men made the original attack in the center at Franklin as participated in the more famous Pickett's Charge at Gettysburg. Yet Hood's Assault at Franklin resulted in more Confederate casualties (in excess of 7,000 versus about 6,500), and the battle circumstances were more severe than at Gettysburg (minimal artillery support, two miles of open ground to cross, and well-fortified entrenchments to confront).

The results were simply horrendous. In five hours of sustained fighting, the Confederates lost about one-third of the attacking force of twenty-three thousand men. Sixty-five Confederate commanders of divisions, brigades, or regiments were listed as casualties. Thirteen of twenty-eight general officers involved in the fighting were injured, killed, or captured, including the brilliant Patrick Cleburne, who was shot through the heart. The forlorn ditch in front of the Union breastworks was piled so high with corpses that their blood lay in pools. Trapped beneath the enemy's guns and fired into from front and flank, the surviving gray ranks sought shelter behind the bodies of the dead yet continued to fight, so that their valor, questioned by John Bell Hood, was perhaps never so graphically demonstrated.

Although a breakthrough by Cleburne's and John C. Brown's divisions in the center at the Carter house created a momentary crisis, Union reserves under Colonel Emerson Opdycke countercharged and reestablished the lines. This enabled the blue ranks to repulse all further

Confederate attacks. Following darkness, the fighting gradually abated, and after midnight the Union troops withdrew to Nashville, having virtually wrecked the Confederate Army of Tennessee while sustaining a loss of only about 2,300 Union officers and men.

Hood had been directly responsible for one of the saddest events of the war. His decision to sacrifice the lives of so many in an unlikely military gambit was condemned as "murder" by some of his men. Where had been the moral courage to act upon what was right rather than upon unreasoned emotion? Even worse, the enormity of this mistake was never admitted by Hood. Claiming a victory of sorts, Hood informed the government at Richmond, "[W]e attacked the enemy at Franklin and drove them from their center lines of temporary works into their inner lines, which they evacuated during the night. [They] left their dead and wounded in our possession and retired to Nashville, closely pursued by our cavalry. We captured several stand of colors and about 1,000 prisoners." Later, when questioned about the "slaughter pen" at Franklin, he said, "[W]ar means fight, and fight means kill."

The matter of essential character was all but forgotten in the need to obfuscate the terrible reality of what had happened. Hood later resigned to avoid being removed from command and, having lost his sweetheart, Buck Preston, to another man, ultimately wound up in New Orleans after the war, struggling in various endeavors until succumbing to yellow fever in 1879.

The Battle of Franklin, obscured by initial reporting inaccuracies and a lack of publicity in the newspapers, never achieved its rightful status as one of the most terrible and significant battles of the war. Largely unappreciated until recently, its intense fury was termed by one survivor "the thunder drum of war," and even today it is an enduring testimonial to the courage and mettle of the Southern fighting man.

Certainly, the consequences were profound for the South. When given a remedial task, to save Atlanta, Hood had essentially lost an army—the key army that sustained the Confederacy's heartland. The Southern cause could survive without Atlanta, but it couldn't without the heartland army. Lacking a powerful and viable Army of Tennessee, the Confederacy was doomed to a swift demise. Hood's role in the loss of the war was thus prominent; by squandering vital resources, he hastened the certain end. Hood was a man of bold physical courage, but his lack of moral courage and his want of character contributed to both a personal and the South's national defeat.

Courage is a complex matter to evaluate; for the display of physical courage is not necessarily or directly related to the exercise of moral courage. Which of the two is greater? Only God in His infinite wisdom can say. We might reasonably suspect, however, that a person's success in the final judgment is related to choices made of right versus wrong rather than what other humans may consider the ultimate good. Character, the ability to determine and do that which is morally right based upon logic, common sense, and education, may very well be life's ultimate quality. Said John Bell Hood in unintentionally ironic reflection, "To conquer self is the greatest battle of life."[3]

PART THREE

Moral Courage

XX

DECISIONS OF COURAGE

Stress is fundamental to all human life. It is a normal experience, and exists in a variety of forms in both the physical and mental realm. How we cope with stress relates in large measure to the control we exert over the stressful circumstances. The ability to handle intense pressure, to relegate stress to a manageable level, involves an interaction of genetic makeup, education, background, and personality.

Yet, there are practical means of coping. Relief or diversion from the constancy of intense stress is important, as is perspective. The ability to focus on overcoming an obstacle as a challenge versus contemplating the dire consequences is a proactive approach that works for many. Also, the intense meaning of the endeavor, the awareness that a positive value is involved—perhaps a matter of personal accomplishment or achieving a goal of private or public good—serves as a positive incentive to cope well.

Indeed, it is often a matter of fundamental attitude that leads to success or failure.

During the Civil War there were many who either flourished or self-destructed under the enormous stress that involved the fate of thousands of lives and the existence of a future government. Life-and-death consequences meant much to various commanders entrusted with the fate of many soldiers. Others, however, regarded their men, more or less, as expendable tools in the pursuit of an objective.

Courage in managing the lives of others was not necessarily exercised by aggressively ordering an attack, but rather by making the correct decision to fight, defend a position, or withdraw after accurately assessing the benefit versus the cost. Would too many lives be lost in making an attack? What were the true prospects for success? Would they justify the casualties to be sustained? Might the consequences of dire failure outweigh the good results sought?

There are various examples of courage and its counterparts, recklessness and timidity, among combat commanders on both sides during the Civil War. Thousands of lives, and perhaps even the common cause, were at stake; yet making decisions was complex, and the risks and rewards were magnified.

PUTTING IT IN PERSPECTIVE: THE METHODOLOGY OF VICTORY

William J. Srofe was an experienced Union soldier, one who had witnessed the carnage of Shiloh and knew the essence of coping on the battlefield: to act courageously based upon one's patriotic duty and the common objective. A sergeant in Company K, 48th Ohio Volunteer Infantry, Srofe, although not yet twenty-one, understood that prior conceptions of combat and army life were usually not the reality. If boastfulness and ego were commonplace at the inception of soldiering, the ordeal of the battlefield narrowed a man's view of proper decorum. Those who faced the rigors of combat with courage were deeply respected. Fear and despair, however, remained a familiar burden for many soldiers. The all too common youthful spirit of invincibility and eager boastfulness gave way to introspection, trying to explain and interpret what was of sustaining influence in confronting the army's inherent dangers.

If a soldier's fate was unforeseeable, a trust in "Him on high" and intense patriotism were the best ways to find courage under fire, reasoned Srofe. Focusing on the noble task at hand—to put down the rebellion—became the real key. It was, he thought, the difference between fighting courageously in battle, or "skedaddling." He noted in a letter to his family:

> *I have seen so many brave men that "blowed" about as if they would whip Jeff Davis and [his] bodyguard themselves. And at the whistle of the first cannon ball, they would skedaddle if they had a chance. I believe that a man does not live but has fear about him if he desires to live (of course, all sensible men want to live as long as possible). Thus, unless he has that noble and patriotic feeling that all Americans should have, he is bound to skedaddle. . . . You need not be uneasy about me, [however]. I shall trust in providence, believing that all who trust in Him on high are ever ready for any emergency, let the results be as they may. . . . When I think . . . how corrupt the future will be should this wicked rebellion prevail, . . . and the fortune of our nation is dependent upon the success of our arms, . . . it serves to arouse my spirits with renewed determination—and then I feel as if I could fight till the last armed foe expires. . . . When I see a man who gives way to despair, I always feel like doing something for him, and generally find it is very easy to arouse his spirits. I ask them to think what they have to fight for, and this is generally sufficient. Yes, this [will] make any American's blood [swirl] with patriotism.*

In mentally preparing himself for the terrible struggle ahead at Vicksburg, where he foresaw the Confederacy would fight to the bitter end to maintain partial control of the Mississippi River, Srofe anticipated much personal danger. Indeed, mindful of the desperation of the final struggle during the later stages of the siege, Srofe, now a second lieutenant, knew that the ordeal of prolonged combat and danger had taken a heavy toll on him both physically and emotionally. He could sense that the end of Confederate resistance was near, but the lingering uncertainty of what would happen preyed upon his mind. The pending fall of Vicksburg was the subject of the hour; everybody was keyed to the imminent Rebel collapse.

Writing on June 21, only days before the city's surrender, Lieutenant Srofe reflected on the strong emotions running just below the surface of the soldiers' daily existence. While it anticipated the enormous relief and euphoria they would experience less than two weeks later, his letter is a classic depiction of the mental anguish and yet rampant hope of the Vicksburg siege, written at the very height of the pending drama.

Camp Near Vicksburg, Miss./ June 21st 1863

Dr. Mother:

I am still in excellent health. We are slowly but surely nearing the enemy's works. Some of our rifle pits are so near those of the enemy that our boys throw spades of dirt inside of the enemy's forts. On our right (in Gen. Logan's division) they are digging the Rebel fort down. I do not think that this army will be long kept in suspense, for unless they surrender soon, our men will charge them.

They cannot resist another charge—never. All our men will have to do will be to climb their forts. We have no hills, hollows, deep ravines, etc. to charge over, as we had on the 22nd of last month. Our men can get into the rifle pits during the night, and at the break of day advance. One charge will be sufficient to gain the greatest victory on record. It will cost the life of many a brave man; this is why our generals do not advance immediately. They still hope to force a surrender by starvation.

But I fear that our fond hopes which [were] ever so bright and flattering in the beginning will end in sad disappointment. I hope my fears may be unfounded, but this is the thirty-third day of [waiting following] the [unsuccessful Union] charge [and] the *enemy will not surely be idle all this time. They will sooner or later attempt to raise the siege by attacking our rear, though I do not think that they will be successful. Nothing less than fifty or sixty thousand men could render them any aid, and I feel perfectly at ease as to the result if they would even bring fifty thousand more men in our rear, they would not whip us, though they might kill a great many.*

There were thirty deserters [who] came inside our lines yesterday. They reported that there were from three hundred to four hundred citizens and soldiers killed in Vicksburg yesterday by the explosion of our shells. There is still talk of our regiment being consolidated, and in fact, an order to that effect has been received, but will not be enforced until something decisive has transpired in and about Vicksburg. If this order is enforced, I no doubt will be mustered out, at least I hope so, and will be at home in July or August at the furthest. . . .

All the boys are well from New Hope [Ohio], and [are] anxious to get into Vicksburg. I have command of the company now, as the captain [Samuel G. W. Peterson] has been sick for some time, and Lieut. [William H. H.] Rike is detached on Gen. [Jacob G.] Lauman's staff as inspector general. I must close by asking you to write soon. I am your affectionate son, Bud [William J. Srofe][1]

As is evident in Lieutenant Srofe's letter, the raw physical courage of assaulting enemy entrenchments at Vicksburg, which would cost thousands of lives, was not considered prudent. Rather, and in confirmation of such concerns, Union Major General Ulysses S. Grant secured the surrender of the city and garrison on July 4, 1863, by judiciously using moral courage and exercising well-reasoned patience.

Moral Courage, the Essential Element

Courage amid crisis: it often is the popular focus in analyzing crucial events of the past. Yet the most profound and significant courage, or lack of it, often related not to bravery or valor in the physical fighting, but to decision making during the height of an important crisis. There were usually tense moments requiring critical decisions during major Civil War events. Although the key moment wasn't always apparent at the time, there were heavy pressures that weighed on the minds of the senior leaders, who were acutely aware of enormous consequences. The steadfast courage, and the moral turpitude, in making such decisions represent the very best, and worst, of reasoning among mankind.

Risk taking is usually conditioned by the stakes and potential consequences, great or small. A company commander's important decisions generally relate to the lives of his men, perhaps a hundred souls. An army commander's major decisions relate not only to the fate of his army, usually thousands of men, but also to the fabric of the war as a whole, even leading to ultimate success or failure of the cause for which so many are fighting. The weight of the responsibility and the demands of history are burdens that have caused many top commanders to self-destruct. Others have assumed the burden gracefully and competently, providing an insight into the differences in individuals, particularly as to the core attributes that often seem to make the difference.

Intelligence, ability, experience, personality, determination (spirit of competitiveness), and even good luck were all weighty factors in successful crisis decision making. At the very heart of the matter, however, was an often overlooked element that is as valid today as it was in the past. Competence in making important decisions is often a matter of character, of doing the right thing stemming from a knowledge of that which is basically right and wrong. Education may provide an essence of knowledge, but deciding what is proper requires ethical discipline. While that which is collectively good or evil may be difficult to determine on the surface, in one's mind the extent of moral excellence defines motive. And motive equates to a factor that significantly colors key decisions.

To accept blame or praise based upon our actions and decisions is to acknowledge our humanity. There are fundamental lessons of life: Unreasoned fear is self-defeating, and true justice and success are equally elusive to one who cheats in mind or matter. To be a man of great character is not only to be independent in spirit, but to enact the premise that others count as much as oneself in the span of history. To act this part mindful of one's limitations no matter how big the position and responsibilities is to obtain the best chance for an ultimate success, as subjected to the disposition of Providence.

As surely as God knows our every thought, action, and very being, He gives us choices. If a person might be able to fool his fellow man part of the time, he can't fool God any of the time. History is filled with actions that proved either right or wrong based upon decisions stemming from a presence or a want of character. The essence of this understanding is a disciplined perspective of right and wrong.

To be in harmony with God we must do that which we know is right, not that which we want to be right. Man proposes, God disposes, in full. Our understanding is limited, but we can learn from the lessons of our past. There is a plethora of decisions profoundly influencing the Civil War and American history. These decisions, impacting key events, offer crucial insights, including further evidence of God's will.

XXI

SHILOH: THE ROLL OF THE DICE

The Battle of Shiloh was the nineteenth-century version of Pearl Harbor. This famous battle at Pittsburg Landing, Tennessee, witnessed one of the truly outstanding surprise attacks in the history of warfare, yet it degenerated into what one key participant understood as ill-managed chaos. As mentioned earlier, Confederate Brigadier General Patrick Cleburne concluded, "Shiloh was a battle gallantly won, and as stupidly lost." At the heart of the matter were crucial "decision" elements that ordained both disaster and triumph; Shiloh is a graphic case study in moral courage that echoes through the ages as a decisive moment in history.[1]

Albert Sidney Johnston was one of the nation's premier soldiers in 1861. Regarded by Jefferson Davis as the Confederacy's best general, he had traveled east from San Francisco after resigning as a U.S. Army colonel in April 1861, and had finally taken the helm in September as commander of the vast area of the Confederacy west of the Appalachian

Mountains. Ranking as the South's senior field general, Johnston was beset by a variety of inherited problems. The occupation of Columbus, Kentucky, by Major General Leonidas Polk just prior to Johnston's arrival in the west ended Kentucky's neutrality and resulted in the overrunning of the state by both sides.

Committed by the Davis administration to a political and geographic rather than a military-strategic line, Johnston was forced to rely upon several lackluster subordinates for the defense of the river line guarding his western flank. When Generals John B. Floyd and Gideon J. Pillow both failed in the defense of Fort Donelson on the Cumberland River following the loss of Fort Henry on the Tennessee River, a precipitate retreat by Johnston's Central Kentucky Army was imperative. From Bowling Green, Kentucky, to Nashville, then south to northern Alabama, Johnston's retreating forces abandoned thousands of miles of Confederate territory, resulting in widespread criticism and despair.[2]

Johnston had been joined by General P. G. T. Beauregard, who had come west in February 1862 following a political tussle with Joseph E. Johnston in northern Virginia. As the highly publicized hero of Fort Sumter and the victor at Manassas, Beauregard basked in the glow of popular acclaim—in marked contrast to Sidney Johnston, who was severely disparaged following the series of February disasters. Assigned by Johnston to defend the Mississippi Valley, centering on Corinth, Mississippi, Beauregard, although hampered by a lingering respiratory infection, by late February began fashioning an army in the vicinity of Corinth.[3]

Because of the dire situation in the west, Johnston had determined on "a most hazardous experiment," to unite his army with Beauregard's for the defense of the Mississippi Valley. By joining Beauregard at Corinth in mid-March, Johnston successfully integrated both forces into a single army prior to a major strike at the enemy invaders led by Ulysses S. Grant. Grant's troops were preparing to advance on Corinth's major railroad connections from Pittsburg Landing, Tennessee, a Tennessee River site about twenty-three miles distant.[4]

Both Robert E. Lee, the president's adviser, and President Jefferson Davis in Richmond sent letters to Johnston, urging that the enemy be met and defeated before its reinforcing columns, then proceeding from the vicinity of Nashville under Major General Don Carlos Buell, could come up and join Grant's forces. Aware of the critical importance of this campaign, Johnston was fully determined to act aggressively. The faith that Lee and his close friend the president placed in him was more than a personal obligation; it was a matter of the deepest honor and the gravest responsibility. The Confederacy desperately needed a redeeming victory.[5]

Reflecting his great character, Sidney Johnston allowed Beauregard to plan and organize much of the campaign. As a popular hero, Beauregard was given substantial discretion in conducting operations against the enemy. Since Beauregard had been present in the area since mid-February and had greater local knowledge, Johnston conveyed to him the authority for all orders relating to operations.[6]

Aware that he could delegate authority but not responsibility, Johnston wrote at the time: "The test of merit in my profession with the people is success. It is a hard rule but I think it right." Johnston's will remained strong, and he oversaw all offensive plans—which initially anticipated delaying only long enough to bring Major General Earl Van Dorn's trans-Mississippi army to Corinth before attacking the gathering Union forces.[7]

Yet on April 2, 1862, a strong reconnaissance by Confederate troops led that evening to a reaction by Federals under Major General Lew Wallace. Several Union brigades advanced and deployed along the road leading toward Bethel Station. Misinterpreting this Union defensive show of force as an indication that the junction of Buell's and Grant's armies was near at hand, Beauregard, when informed after 10:00 P.M. by telegraph of the incident, endorsed the telegram, "Now is the moment to advance and strike the enemy at Pittsburg Landing." Coincidentally, word had been received that day from Confederate cavalry scouts in mid-Tennessee that Buell's troops, thirty thousand strong, had crossed the Duck River and were en route to Savannah, Tennessee, nine miles downriver from Pittsburg Landing. It was a crisis that precipitated a major decision.[8]

When handed Beauregard's endorsed telegram by his adjutant general, Thomas Jordan, Johnston was compelled to make a key decision:

the timing of the planned attack on the enemy at Pittsburg Landing. Jordan, arguing on Beauregard's behalf (Beauregard was not present, having gone to bed), stated the urgency of an immediate advance. Johnston, acting on the data at hand, complied with the request, and a general advance from Corinth was ordered for six o'clock the following morning.[9]

The irony and agony of this decision were soon apparent. Beauregard had been in the region for forty-six days. He knew as early as March 12 that one of the likely sites for the Union to launch a river-based invasion was Pittsburg Landing, where the high bluffs enabled access to a good staging area despite the heavy spring rains. On that date he had telegraphed to Sidney Johnston, then at Decatur, Alabama, "[T]hey [Union forces] will stop at Pittsburg [Landing] or Eastport." Yet the Confederates suffered from a glaring lack of information about what was one of the most important sites to watch and know about. The lack of intelligence about the enemy's Pittsburg Landing campsite led to severe complications.[10]

First, the April 2 reconnaissance that led Beauregard to think that the Union forces were acting aggressively because of the imminent arrival of Buell's reinforcements had originated to rectify an absence of specific data about the location and extent of the enemy's camps. Even an accurate, detailed map of the region was lacking, thus the Confederates didn't have vital information about routes and terrain.

The Confederate patrols' mission to discover vital target information had resulted in a large reconnaissance. This in turn had led to Wallace's entire Union division advancing and forming for battle to confront the supposed heavy Rebel advance. Instead of learning of the enemy's dispositions and strength, Beauregard only precipitated the direct enemy action that swiftly led to an overall confrontation. Ironically, access to vital information about the terrain and location of the enemy's campsites had been available to the Confederates for much of the crisis period.

As early as March 1 a Confederate regiment had occupied Pittsburg Landing, and it had remained in the vicinity for two weeks. Yet no map or detailed survey of the region had been made. So on the eve of the

Confederate army's march to strike the enemy's Pittsburg Landing camps, there was only an inaccurate map to use in planning the attack. Prior to March 11, at the direction of the local region commander, Brigadier General Dan Ruggles, Captain James Trezevant of Louisiana had made a rough sketch of the country along the river between Eastport and Pittsburg Landing without compass, square, or rule. His purpose was only to locate possible defensive positions. So ignorant of the Pittsburg Landing region were Beauregard and his staff that on March 26 Sidney Johnston himself sought to organize a group of twenty former residents who knew the area. They were to be consulted and used as guides.[11]

Clearly, the Confederate rush to advance was predicated on hasty and careless staff and administrative work. Beauregard's plans were formulated with notes he had jotted on the backs of telegrams and envelopes before 5:00 A.M. on April 3. Beauregard's thinking involved a raid in force, to strike a sudden blow at the enemy, drive them back upon their gunboats in the river, and then gather up munitions and spoils of war before the Confederate army quickly withdrew back to Corinth.[12]

This raid concept did not encompass what Johnston wanted: a decisive victory. Further, Beauregard's operational plans called for an advance of the various Confederate corps—which were scattered over the countryside—by separate roads that converged on the Pittsburg Landing region. Since no preliminary orders had been prepared, despite that an attack was being considered for more than a week, the initial instructions were given verbally so that the march could begin by noon that day. Of course, in the absence of maps and written orders, confusion and congestion resulted, especially in Corinth. All of this served to seriously delay the march.[13]

When finally present (a day late) in the vicinity of the enemy's camps at Pittsburg Landing, the Confederates remained hampered by a lack of information as to the location of the specific enemy camps—where resistance was certain to originate. On April 5 Confederate cavalry companies scouted the outlying areas, attempting to locate the outer Union perimeter. Their presence resulted in several sightings and some shooting.

The Confederate plan called for an attack along the Tennessee River flank so as to drive the Yankees back from their outer perimeter, which was about three miles removed from the landing site. Sidney Johnston knew from his rough map that the Union army was essentially trapped in a triangle of ground bordered by three major watercourses: the Tennessee River on the right, Owl Creek (a tributary of Snake Creek) on the left, and Lick Creek along the three-and-one-half-mile-wide base of the triangle. His premise of attack was that the enemy could form no greater front in this limited-area triangle than he could. By rolling up the enemy's flank along the Tennessee River side of the triangle, he would drive the Yankees back against Owl Creek, where they might be cut off from the landing site. It was an admirable and logical plan on paper.[14]

Yet Johnston had no direct knowledge of the topographical features of the terrain upon which the enemy was to be driven back. Unknown to him, Dill Branch ravine, deep and nearly impassable because of spring flooding, virtually blocked this path in the close vicinity of Pittsburg Landing. It made the tactical plan highly impractical if not impossible. Beauregard's failure to provide key intelligence about the presence of this crucial ravine as fundamental topographical data soon led to serious consequences.

Moreover, what was even more damaging was that Beauregard or his chief of staff, Jordan, authored a model of attack based upon Napoleon's order for the Battle of Waterloo. Whereas Sidney Johnston had informed the president in a dispatch on April 3 that the Confederate army would attack with corps abreast, Beauregard's man Jordan drew up orders calling for an attack by succeeding lines of infantry with each corps aligned one behind the other across the entire front. The thinking, later said a staff officer, was that no force the enemy could bring to bear could resist three double lines of Confederates. This unwieldy battle formation was a severe flaw. In the rough, wooded terrain, the troops of each corps would become badly intermixed with others. Then, since there was no clear line of authority for a given sector, the various commanders would have to improvise who was to command and where.[15]

After the Confederate attack began at first light on Sunday, April 6, a serious crisis was soon in focus. Unbeknown to the Confederates, a single Federal camp, David Stuart's, had been placed beyond the normal Union campground perimeter. Stuart's brigade was camped on the far Union left flank, being sent there early in the occupation of the region merely to guard a bridge over nearby Lick Creek. In the haste of planning a sudden attack, no one had bothered to determine the location of each enemy campsite along the outer perimeter. Only on the morning of April 6 was General Braxton Bragg's chief engineer, Captain S. H. Lockett, sent to scout the critical region along the Tennessee River.

When the main Confederate attack began that morning, Johnston didn't know of Stuart's presence beyond his right flank. Later, when Captain Lockett found Stuart's soldiers—they were what he thought was an entire division—lurking beyond the critical Confederate right flank zone of attack, he sent an urgent dispatch to warn Johnston. When this message arrived, Johnston's troops had just routed Brigadier General Benjamin M. Prentiss's division from its camps along the center of the Union army's outer perimeter. The way was now open in front to push directly toward Pittsburg Landing.

Yet Lockett's discovery compelled Johnston to halt pursuit of the fleeing enemy and divert two frontline brigades to check these recently located Yankee troops. Since Johnston then didn't have sufficient strength to continue the main drive north, he had to wait for the arrival of Brigadier General John C. Breckinridge's Reserve Corps, coming up from the rear as one of the succeeding-waves lines of battle.[16]

This resulted in about a four-hour delay. The lengthy time lapse was critical, for it allowed the beaten enemy under Prentiss to re-form and help occupy the soon to be famous Hornets' Nest defensive line held primarily by Generals W. H. L. Wallace's and Stephen Hurlbut's divisions. Because of the great loss of time and lives in attacking and overwhelming the Hornets' Nest, the battlefield victory was incomplete for the Confederates as night fell on April 6.

At the root of the problem was not only faulty intelligence by Captain Lockett in estimating that a full division of the enemy was present beyond the right, but more seriously, the omission of earlier scouting patrols by Beauregard, who had control of operational details. Stuart's chance presence on Lick Creek to guard a bridge became one of the critical elements of the battle. Although his brigade made only a brief resistance and was ultimately driven back, Stuart's undetected original location cost the Confederates much time and thus helped change the course of history.

It seems that Sidney Johnston was already fed up with the critical lack of information, which forced him to make key decisions based upon guesswork rather than facts. Indeed, so disgusted was he with Beauregard's indiscretions and want of expertise in conducting operations that he had already altered his basic reliance on the Creole general.

To Sidney Johnston, on the evening of April 5 and again on the morning of April 6, it appeared that Beauregard had lost his nerve if not his reason. In several roadside councils of war Beauregard had suggested that any prospect of surprising the enemy was gone due to a wanton disregard of secrecy on the part of the approaching Confederates, and that the Yankees would be found "entrenched to the eyes." Accordingly, said Beauregard, the army should retreat to Corinth without giving battle.[17]

To an army commander on the eve of a decisive conflict, it was a critical command crisis. His principal subordinate, who had pressed for an immediate attack and was allowed to plan and direct much of the operation, suddenly seemed to abdicate his role once combat was imminent. Johnston was appalled. This was not understandable conduct to the determined Johnston. Where was the moral courage so necessary in a successful commander? After conferring with his physician, Dr. D. W. Yandell, who suggested that Beauregard was a sick man and that perhaps his mind had been affected, Johnston instructed Beauregard to remain behind in the army's rear on April 6. His meager role was confined to forwarding munitions and troops to the front.[18]

Johnston was not prone to blame others; the battle was his own responsibility, and as a manager he could delegate only authority, not responsibility. That Beauregard had failed him was quite evident, and the unorthodox last-minute replacement of a senior commander in the conduct of the battle reveals Johnston's dismay.

Ultimately, there was heavy irony in this command circumstance. Despite the menial task initially assigned to Beauregard, he became the battle's primary manager and the Confederate commander when Sidney Johnston was killed by a stray bullet about 2:30 P.M. Following Johnston's death, the disastrous loss of life in many piecemeal assaults that after-noon, the withdrawal of the Confederate troops from their confrontation with the final Union line near Pittsburg Landing, and the subsequent sur-prise attack on April 7 by Union reinforcements led by Generals Buell and Lew Wallace were but further evidence of the dire Confederate fate under Beauregard's leadership.

Although P. G. T. Beauregard displayed considerable personal brav-ery in grasping a flag and leading forward wavering troops amid intense fire at the end of the action on April 7, his physical valor did not atone for his want of expertise and moral courage. His earlier omissions, mis-calculations, and want of determination were a primary basis of the Southern defeat.[19]

Albert Sidney Johnston had been right; battle was like rolling dice—one never knew what might result. He had been at the fulcrum of the teeter-totter of fate on that momentous Sunday, April 6, 1862. He was later regarded by some historians as a lackluster leader who had been in-decisive and overtrusting in his command responsibilities, and his repu-tation ultimately suffered from the absence of success. Yet close scrutiny shows that at Shiloh, Johnston performed with remarkable physical and moral courage. Unlike Ulysses S. Grant and William Tecumseh Sher-man, who made severe mistakes at and before Shiloh, the dead Albert Sidney Johnston did not have the opportunity to learn from events and rectify the errors. Destiny tipped the scales on that momentous day, but there is no doubting the quality of Johnston's effort. His luck was bad, but his courage was outstanding.

SHILOH: ULYSSES S. GRANT AND A TEST OF WILL

"Sam" Grant was a man redeemed in mid-March 1862. As the lauded victor of Fort Donelson, he had been heralded throughout the United States as a man of action and victory. Once an obscure Illinios ne'er-do-well, he was now known as "Unconditional Surrender" Grant, a favorite newspaper nickname, reflecting the toughness of character that had en-abled victory at a crucial moment of decision. Yet, stunningly, he had been removed from command only a few weeks after Fort Donelson for allegedly neglecting his duty in filing reports and for reported whiskey-drinking binges.

Grant, stunned, was at a loss to explain the sudden ire of his superior, Major General Henry Halleck. Perhaps sensing an emerging rival in the arena of popular esteem, Halleck had conspired to remove Grant from field command on March 4. Grant, who was handicapped in his efforts to communicate rapidly with Halleck in St. Louis by having to forward his dispatches by boat to Cairo, Illinois, and from there by telegraph to Halleck, became despondent and bitterly asked to be relieved from further duty.[20]

President Lincoln was soon involved, however. Grant was the only Union general who had won a major victory in the war's first eleven months, and Lincoln made it known that specific allegations and a court of inquiry would be necessary. Halleck then backed down and reinstated Grant to command of the Tennessee River expedition on March 15.[21]

Newly arrived at Savannah, Tennessee, on March 17, 1862, Grant assumed operational control from Major General Charles F. Smith, who was sick with a blood infection. Grant forwarded all the troops at Savannah to the Pittsburg Landing campsites on the Tennessee River's southern bank, pending the arrival of Major General Don Carlos Buell's Army of the Ohio, then marching overland from Nashville to Savannah.

Because Pittsburg Landing would be a staging area for both armies, which would then advance on Corinth, Mississippi, Grant regarded the campaign and campsite as strictly offensive. As late as the afternoon of April 5 he told an inquiring officer, "There will be no fight at Pittsburg Landing; we will have to go to Corinth, where the Rebels are fortified." Grant was waiting only for the arrival of Buell's troops and the roads to dry before advancing on Corinth.[22]

His lack of urgency in bringing some of Buell's advanced troops forward following their arrival at Savannah on April 3 reflected his lack of anticipation of an enemy attack. He knew that Sherman and the other outer-division commanders had not entrenched, and were merely camped in the open woods, but was confident that the enemy would act only defensively. Indeed, his instructions to Sherman, following a clash of outposts on April 4, had been to do nothing that would tend to "bring on a general engagement until Buell arrives." Grant's final telegram to a restless Halleck in St. Louis on the night of the fifth reassured his department commander: "I have scarcely the faintest of an attack [general one] being made upon us, but will be prepared should such a thing take place."[23]

The morning of Sunday, April 6, 1862, found Ulysses S. Grant anything but prepared for the events in store for him that day. Having been up until nearly midnight the night before (following a routine journey to Pittsburg Landing aboard his steamboat, the *Tigress*), Grant was late in ordering breakfast at his Cherry mansion headquarters. He was eating after 7:00 A.M. when an orderly came in and reported the sound of artillery fire coming from upriver. Grant left his breakfast unfinished and went out on the back porch, where he heard the rumble of "heavy firing." By this means he learned of the attack upon "our most advanced positions."

Not knowing if the enemy was advancing in the vicinity of Pittsburg Landing, or toward Crump's Landing, where an isolated division under Lew Wallace was positioned, Grant hastened upriver once the *Tigress* got up steam. After stopping briefly at Crump's Landing, he arrived at Pittsburg Landing about 9:00 A.M., four hours after the fighting began near Shiloh church.[24]

Immediately, Grant found himself in the midst of a disaster. Even worse, he was now virtually a spectator, with his army already on the brink of collapse. The unprepared victim of an enormous surprise attack, Grant must have known that the battle under way would likely impact his army career. Grant visited and encouraged his division commanders in their defensive perimeters, but control of the battle was beyond his means. About 12:30 P.M. he returned to his temporary headquarters, a small trader's log cabin atop the hill at Pittsburg Landing.

On his way there he was nearly killed while slowly passing through the northern border of Duncan field. Here he and his staff were fired upon with canister by Captain Melancthon Smith's Mississippi battery. Grant was taken by surprise. "The shells and balls whistled about our ears very fast for about a minute," he later remembered. After he and his staff dashed to cover, one of his aides' horses was found to have been struck, the missile passing through the animal just behind the saddle. In a few moments the horse fell dead. Grant then discovered how close he had come to being seriously wounded. Looking at his sword, he found that a projectile had struck the metal scabbard just below the belt and broken it nearly off.[25]

That evening, following the collapse of the Hornets' Nest defensive perimeter and the appearance of the Confederates in front of the last defensive line guarding the landing area, Grant watched the enemy's approach. A line of siege cannon had been rolled up to provide a final zone of defense across deep Dill Branch ravine, but below the landing lay the wreck of his army. Union troops huddled in panic-stricken masses. Some were so desperate that they were attempting to swim across the broad Tennessee River to the opposite shore. Amid the chaos and mayhem bullets were zipping about, and shells screeched through the air. If ever there was a supreme crisis, a moment of trial where the road forked toward the unknown, for Grant this was it.

Grant remained unruffled. About 6:30 P.M., with darkness gathering, he was seen sitting motionless on his horse, like a statue. Soon the fighting began sputtering to a halt as the limited number of Confederates present found the Federal siege cannon too formidable and Dill Branch ravine too difficult to attack across, and they withdrew to ransack the captured Yankee camps. A staff officer heard Grant mutter something. He leaned over and saw that Grant was talking to himself. "Not beaten by a damn sight," the general repeated.[26]

Bolstered that evening by the arrival of advance elements of Buell's army, which were even then being ferried over the river in transports, plus the near approach of Lew Wallace's missing division from Crump's Landing, Grant pondered the prospects for a battle the following day. When asked by one of Buell's staff officers if he planned to retreat, Grant fiercely replied, "No, I propose to attack at daylight and whip them!"[27]

When on April 7 the battle was decisively won by the combined Union forces, and the exhausted enemy retreated to Corinth, Grant became the victor rather than the ultimate victim. "Sam" Grant had made one of the greatest military mistakes of his life at Shiloh, suffering an enormous surprise attack for which he was fully responsible. Yet the man didn't scare worth a damn. He kept control of his wits and gave his troops a chance to win when the odds were heavily against them. His state of mind was similar to that when confronted by a major crisis several months earlier at Fort Donelson. He remembered the Fort Donelson lesson well, and feeling that "a great moral advantage would be gained by becoming the attacking party," at Shiloh he decided on a broad offensive thrust rather than opting for a retreat.

At Shiloh he stared destiny squarely in the eye. The risks and rewards were self-evident: perhaps a crushing defeat that might lead to the destruction of his army and an end to his military career, or else a critical reversal of fortunes and a redeeming victory. With so much at stake, Grant simply refused to panic or wilt under the pressure. He intended to manage events to the extent possible rather than be managed by them. It was characteristic of the composure and dogged perseverance that later made Grant so successful and famous. His moral courage in making a calculated decision to risk everything by planning to win rather than to minimize his losses reflected his capacity to make proper, if hard, decisions while under severe stress.

In marked contrast, his opponent P. G. T. Beauregard, when compelled to decide on the afternoon of April 6 either to press forward or retire to the captured camps, reacted conservatively. Because of the bursting Union gunboat shells in the rear echelon near Shiloh church, where he had remained analyzing various reports from the front, Beauregard became concerned about his troops' vulnerability and knew of their confusion and fatigue. Without bothering to investigate personally along the front lines, and believing he had Grant's army trapped where he might destroy it the following day if it didn't retreat across the Tennessee River, Beauregard ordered a halt to the fighting about 5:30 P.M. Unaware of the nearby presence of heavy Union reinforcements, Beauregard was in turn surprised on the morning of April 7. While the Confederate army fought arduously, the large numbers of fresh enemy troops helped turn the former tide of victory into defeat.[28]

After the emotional furor and enormous publicity about the fighting had abated, implicit in the final results of the Battle of Shiloh were the psyche and extent of moral courage of the senior commanders on both sides.

XXII

ROBERT E. LEE, A MAN FOR ALL AGES

The good qualities of any man may or may not shape his most significant deeds in life, but in retrospect we often tend to think of the best rather than the worst of most individuals, as a matter of both decency and emotional allowance. In the case of a Southern icon such as Robert E. Lee, "Marse Robert," his virtues have been emphasized to the virtual exclusion of his faults. His noble character, keen mind, and dedication to his men have endeared Lee to millions of Americans, both North and South.

Because we often learn the most from our failings, however, it is important that the life lessons evident in personal defeat be put in perspective. Lee's greatest military failure was at Gettysburg. He lost there the key battle of the war. It was his responsibility, self-determined, to win a peace militarily for the South before the overwhelming numbers and resources of the North sealed the issue. He failed, and he accepted blame for such—it was "his fault," he said of the key frontal assault on July 3 that became such a spectacular failure.[1]

The Battle of Gettysburg remains the focus of technical arguments about Lee's management that endure to this day. Was Lee's aggressive decision making proper despite the failed results?

In an analysis of victory won or denied, frequently all but lost is the perspective of reason versus deed. Winning a battle is beyond the capability of any one participant, no matter how perceptive and talented. Lee's plans, for example, were carried out by his subordinates. Their deeds were more important than a concept of action, no matter how wise or foolish. However, what is personally relevant upon close examination is the decision-making process, the thinking and rationale that provided the impetus for appropriate action. Revealed in this sense is Lee's great character and valor in the moral sense, which had as its goal more than just winning a battle.

To better understand the extent of Lee's courage within the Gettysburg defeat it is important to analyze the circumstances as a matter of strategy. Certainly the high crisis Lee found himself confronted with in mid-1863 greatly influenced his thinking and his actions.

Following the stunning Confederate victory at Chancellorsville in May 1863, Lee had anticipated swift, aggressive follow-up action. Yet, a month later, his army was still bogged down awaiting key Davis administration directives.

Lee's view of the Confederacy's military situation in mid-1863 was far different than the popular conception that the war was going well for the South. Lee was aware that the South's military resources were diminishing rapidly even while the enemy's were increasing. "Conceding to our enemies the superiority claimed by them in numbers, resources, and all the means and appliances for carrying on the war, we have no right to look for exemptions from the military consequences," he warned Jefferson Davis on June 16, 1863. "We should not therefore conceal from ourselves that our resources are constantly diminishing, and the disproportion in this respect between us and our enemies . . . is steadily augmenting. . . . [The strength of our army] falling off in its aggregate shows that its ranks are growing weaker, and that its losses are not supplied by recruits." Accordingly, wrote Lee, the enemy should be made "to feel some of the difficulties experienced by ourselves. It seems to me that the most effectual mode of accomplishing this object . . . is to give all the encouragement we can . . . to the rising peace party of the North."[2]

In other words, Lee was thinking ahead. His diminishing assets in the Army of Northern Virginia made it imperative in his mind that something decisive be done to achieve a peace before it was too late. Militarily conquering the North was beyond the realm of possibility. The best way to win a peace was by playing upon the will of the Northern populace to continue the war. Mindful that 1864 would witness the presidential election in the United States, Lee foresaw that a convincing military victory on Northern soil might materially influence the outcome.

In essence, the true means to ultimate victory in "winning the peace" was his superb army, in which Lee had supreme confidence. "There never were such men in an army before," he told one of his division commanders. "They will go anywhere and do anything if properly led. But there is the difficulty," he continued. "Proper commanders. Where can they be obtained?"[3]

In the wake of the loss of Stonewall Jackson at Chancellorsville, the crisis in high-level commanders was great. The fighting ability of the army was never in question, but it had lost irreplaceable experienced officers and men. "Our army would be invincible if it could be properly organized and officered," Lee told President Davis in May 1863.[4]

At a time when nearly all were reflecting about recent successes and the bright prospect for more, Lee was expressing great concern about what lay ahead. Thus when the invasion of Pennsylvania began in June, Lee knew that the pending crisis demanded a decisive result before the onset of truly devastating circumstances.

Initially, Lee appeared to steal the march and hence create an enormous opportunity to defeat the scattered elements of the Union army, which lagged behind in the march from Virginia northward. According to one subordinate, Lee now intended to "throw an overwhelming force against the enemy's advance" and crush the separate columns so as to effectually destroy the Yankee army.[5]

Because of the absence of General J. E. B. Stuart's cavalrymen, who were away on a raid far to the east, Lee was unable to anticipate the rapid approach of the Union columns to the vicinity of some of his troops near Gettysburg, Pennsylvania. What subsequently occurred was a "meeting engagement," where the two great armies blindly collided during a chance encounter of advance elements at Gettysburg on July 1.

"Coming unexpectedly upon the whole Federal army," wrote Lee in his official report, to withdraw or merely await attack would have been "difficult and dangerous." Aware of the difficulty of gathering food in an enemy's country while its army was present, Lee reasoned that a battle "in a measure was unavoidable." And, considering the successes already achieved on July 1 in driving back the Union forces beyond the town to a long ridgeline, Lee was prompted to renew the chance-meeting fight as it "gave great hope of a favorable issue."[6]

Despite the obvious alteration of his original concept of the campaign, and his tendency to carefully plan a battle before engaging the enemy, Lee was now required to improvise. As a comfort to the grimly determined Lee, his army was in high spirits, and had the precedent of recent victories. The men were deemed as nearly invincible as any soldiers could be. Nonetheless, already there had been serious trouble involving the failure of key subordinates.

On July 1, prior to Lee's presence, Lieutenant General A. P. Hill had overaggressively initiated the contest by committing a heavy number of troops. Then, that afternoon, with three Federal corps beaten and in disarray, General Richard S. Ewell, Stonewall Jackson's replacement, failed to press an attack on the high ground of Cemetery Hill, where the Yankees were desperately attempting to re-form. Ewell's excessive caution carried over into the second day, when Lieutenant General James Longstreet's turning movement was less than inspired.

Lee wanted Longstreet to attack along an oblique line north of Little Round Top, since a reconnaissance at sunrise by Captain S. R. Johnston had found no Yankees on the high ground. Yet Lee was deceived; Little Round Top was under enemy occupation by the time Longstreet approached late that afternoon. Moreover, a Union corps commander, General Dan Sickles, had unilaterally moved his entire command forward from Cemetery Ridge to the Emmitsburg Road so as to occupy high ground there. What Lee had intended to be an oblique attack against the lower portion of Cemetery Ridge became instead a protracted firefight on ground well in advance of the ridge. Before the fighting sputtered out after dark, Longstreet and other supporting troops had been unable to penetrate to the crest of Cemetery Ridge, with one notable exception. Brigadier General A. R. Wright's lone brigade had attacked and nearly breached the main Yankee line on Cemetery Ridge about 6:30 P.M. before being driven off by enemy reinforcements under Brigadier General Alexander S. Webb.

Lee was duly impressed. Wright maintained that had he been supported he could have penetrated the enemy line, and assessed that it was quite vulnerable. That seemed to raise a red flag in Lee's mind. Throughout the day on July 2 it was evident that Confederate success was incomplete because attacks were not coordinated. Lee anticipated that masses of troops would strike together and thus apply extreme pressure in breaching the enemy's lines. Yet Longstreet's and a portion of A. P. Hill's corps had largely fought that day in a series of piecemeal attacks.[7]

In developing plans for the critical third day of fighting at Gettysburg, Lee wanted a continuation of the major assault against the Union left, concurrent with an attack by Ewell's troops against the enemy's right flank on Culp's Hill. His reasoning was explained in his prior statements of purpose, and by his official reports.

On the first day, July 1, the capture of an estimated five thousand prisoners and many field guns was evidence that the enemy was not only partially beaten, but severely crippled. By July 2 Lee's primary intention was to drive the enemy from Cemetery Ridge. This he intended to facilitate by capturing adjacent high ground, which would provide commanding positions for his superb artillery to pound the specific segments of the Union line to be attacked. The "steep ridge" (Cemetery Ridge) was the true objective point. Thus Longstreet's protracted fight and the slaughter of many men on July 2 without reaching the ridge was of secondary importance. Longstreet had "succeeded in getting possession of and holding the desired ground," wrote Lee. This terrain was the elevation adjacent to

the Peach Orchard and the Emmitsburg Road that was to be the key location for Longstreet's artillery. Here the artillery "could be used to advantage in assailing the more elevated ground beyond [Cemetery Ridge]
and thus enable us to reach the crest of the ridge," Lee concluded. His superb infantry, if given strong artillery support, would probably win the
fight.[8]

Lee's fixation on Cemetery Ridge was predicated on his extremely aggressive approach to the battle. Lee wanted a devastating, army-destroying
victory rather than a barren success where the enemy merely withdrew in
frustration or discomfiture. Lee wanted to win a peace by demonstrating
the superiority of the Confederate army so as to sap the North's fighting
spirit.

An enormous Confederate victory on Northern soil would perhaps
be decisive in initiating and negotiating peace. To do this Lee was willing to make certain concessions and take serious risks. His focus was not
so much on the cost to his own army, but on the losses suffered by the
Union army. This he emphasized in his first official report by stressing
"the enemy suffered severely" before discussing his own heavy losses.
Defeating the opposing commander, General George G. Meade, not
avoiding his own defeat (which he believed the fighting spirit of his own
army would prevent), was paramount. Getting his men into a position
from which they could devastate and rout Meade's army required attacking. To win decisively rather than to merely win was foremost in
Lee's mind. It is the reason why there was a critical confrontation with
Longstreet on the morning of July 3, when his senior subordinate strongly
objected to Lee's plan.[9]

James Longstreet was perhaps Lee's most trusted commander, but
he disagreed about the concept of the July 3 battle. Lee's "Old War-
horse" wanted to swing south in a circuitous march beyond the Round
Tops to reach the Taneytown Road beyond Meade's lines. This would
allow the Confederates to attack the Union lines in the rear (which also
would have directly struck the huge and unengaged Union VI Corps,
then positioned to block this move and thus likely thwart any such attack). Longstreet was so confident of his own plan that he had already
given orders to his troops for its execution when it was vetoed by Lee.

Crestfallen, Longstreet, after strenuously objecting to Lee's plan for a direct assault, became depressed and objected to using his entire corps in the assault. Pointing to Little Round Top, Longstreet warned that the enemy could attack his men in the rear as they advanced, and was so insistent about this danger that Lee altered his plan accordingly. Instead of Longstreet's entire corps, only Pickett's Division would go, with his two other divisions remaining in place to guard against a sortie from Little Round Top. Two replacement divisions, Pettigrew's and Trimble's, both from A. P. Hill's Corps, would advance in their place.[10]

Unfortunately for Lee, there was already a command failure to cope with that morning. Based upon the lack of timely and mutually supporting attacks on July 2, Lee had ordered Ewell to attack Culp's Hill simultaneously with Longstreet's pending attack, set for the morning of July 3. Yet Longstreet hadn't been ready that morning, and Ewell's isolated attack was beaten back.

Lee's plans had already gone awry, and he must have been gravely upset, but he maintained a calm demeanor. When Longstreet asserted that "there never was a body of 15,000 men who could make that attack [against Cemetery Ridge] successfully," Lee replied, "The enemy is there, and I'm going to strike him!" Lee was placing full confidence in his men, the troops that would go anywhere and do anything if properly led. Lee also counted on the massive artillery bombardment that would accompany the assault.[11]

Indeed, beginning two hours before the famous assault, more than a hundred Confederate cannon bombarded the Union lines with a fury unprecedented in the war. Then, about 3:00 P.M., Lee watched as the weathered gray ranks of his troops deployed and advanced toward the main target, an umbrella-shaped clump of trees one mile distant on Cemetery Ridge.

Immediately, another severe problem occurred. All but a few Confederate cannon became silent. Whereas it was Lee's intention that the artillery actively support the actual attack, most batteries had run out of ammunition before the assault began. Further, an ample reserve supply of ammunition had been removed to a considerable distance during the previous cannonade to avoid the danger from incoming Union shells.

Lee was especially candid in his subsequent official report: "[During the attack] our own [guns] having nearly exhausted their ammunition . . . [they] were unable to reply, or render the necessary support to the attacking party. Owing to this fact, which was unknown to me when the assault took place, the enemy was enabled to throw a strong force of infantry against our left."

Lee implied that had he known of this stunning development before the Pickett-Pettigrew-Trimble Charge, the assault might not have been made. Lee had planned for the artillery fire to be a key element in enabling his superb infantry to penetrate the enemy lines.[12]

What happened soon became a spectacle of glory, frustration, and defeat. The clash of Armistead's Virginians with Alexander Webb's Philadelphia Brigade at the Angle on Cemetery Ridge was spectacular, but mostly anticlimatic. The majority of the other attackers never made it to the crest, much less fought hand to hand like Armistead's men. Fired into from the front by withering musketry, double charges of canister, and enfilading shell fire by unengaged distant Union guns, the essence of the massive frontal attack was defeated before reaching the main Union lines.

"It's all my fault!" Lee reportedly stated as the broken ranks of men stumbled past him along Seminary Ridge following the attack. Many of the officers and men seemed panic-stricken amid the enemy's continuing artillery fire. It was a sad spectacle for Lee to witness—the very men he had regarded as nearly invincible fleeing from the enemy's fire. Later in assuming responsibility for the tactical failure, Lee wrote: "More may have been required of them [the troops] than they were able to perform, but my admiration of their noble qualities and confidence in their ability to cope successfully with the enemy has suffered no abatement."[13]

Because of the repulse of Lee's grand assault, the battle was admittedly lost, and the saddened Confederate commander soon withdrew his army to Virginia, acknowledging "the unsuccessful issue." Lee's great character forbade him to blame others, even when heavy censure was due, and his official reports and demeanor served to obfuscate the role of others in the Gettysburg defeat. Characteristically, he reacted to the disaster in Pennsylvania by accepting full responsibility, and when he became the subject of implied or direct criticism in some newspapers, Lee offered to resign.

Lee's attitude was reflected in his comments after he learned about the capture of his second-eldest son, William H. "Rooney" Lee, during a Federal raid shortly before Gettysburg. He then told his wife: "We must bear . . . this affliction with fortitude and resignation and not re-pine at the will of God. It will eventuate in some good that we know not of now."[14]

Lee's ability to cope with disaster, both public and personal, was a trait reflecting his supreme courage and also his faith in God. "The re-sult [of battle] is in the hands of the Sovereign Ruler of the Universe, and known to Him only," he advised his wife shortly after Gettysburg. Thus he would go forward with his duty, in the hope that all would eventually go right. "That it should be so, we must implore the forgive-ness of God for our sins, and the continuance of His blessings. There is nothing but His almighty power that can sustain us."[15]

His requiem for the Gettysburg Campaign was written in self-appraisal: "The army did all it could. I fear I required of it impossibili-ties." As for his future role: "Success is so necessary to us [the cause] that nothing [less than everything] should be risked to secure it."[16]

Robert E. Lee was truly a man whose moral courage is indelible for all ages.

XXIII

WHAT IS JUSTIFIED CAUTION?

The matter was infuriating. As a veteran commander, the hero of Chicka-mauga, the general who had won countless battles with his stalwart fight-ing, and the man who had turned down command of an army because he believed an injustice was being done to the old commander, George Henry Thomas was extremely upset.*

His judgment and, even worse, his competence were being called into question by the highest authority in the army, the implacable Lieu-tenant General Ulysses S. Grant.

Grant, the commander of all Union armies and now conducting the war against Robert E. Lee in Virginia, in early December 1864 wanted

---

* Thomas was offered command of the Army of the Cumberland before the Battle of Per-ryville in 1862 but refused, believing the commander, Don Carlos Buell, to be improperly treated by government officials. Hence after Perryville, William S. Rosecrans was appointed.

Thomas to take the offensive immediately at Nashville, Tennessee. Here the "besieging" Confederate army was threatening to seize the initiative, and there was no basis for delay, according to Grant. Either attack the enemy now or be removed from command.

Despite Thomas's past brilliance as the "Rock of Chickamauga"—a reference to his tenacious defense of the final ridgeline on September 20, 1863, which saved the Union army from a rout—Grant was adamant. The stakes were bigger than ever at Nashville, and in the wake of the November presidential election nothing must disrupt the political impetus to successfully prosecute the war.[1]

Thomas, while mindful that Grant disliked his cautious methods and seeming lack of celerity, was the on-site commander and knew what was or wasn't possible based upon the exact circumstances he faced. Grant was hundreds of miles away in Virginia, attempting to micro-manage a major confrontation to be carried out hastily with an impro-vised force. The war of wills and fortitude thus continued.[2]

The problem was in part a matter of personalities—including that of the enemy commander's. Grant knew that Confederate General John Bell Hood was impetuous and aggressive to the point of recklessness. Indeed, Hood was prone to do the unlikely and unconventional so long as a fight was involved. Thus Hood appeared to worry Grant more than he did Thomas. Grant feared that Hood with his veteran Confederate Army of Tennessee, after "invading" Tennessee in mid-November 1864, would detour around and beyond Thomas at Nashville, cross the Cumberland River, and raid wildly into Kentucky all the way to the Ohio River. In this event, reasoned Grant, the political and practical embarrassment would be profound.[3]

William Tecumseh Sherman, marching with his troops through Georgia to the seacoast in the wake of the successful Atlanta Campaign, had dropped out of sight. Grant was bogged down in a protracted stale-mate around Petersburg, Virginia. Now Thomas was penned up by a weaker Rebel army in Nashville. The war was going nowhere.

Grant, angry and impatient, wired Thomas on December 6, 1864, "Attack Hood at once and wait no longer for a remount of your cavalry. There is great danger of delay resulting in a campaign back to the Ohio

River." Grant was so on edge over this matter that on December 7 he wired the administration in Washington, D.C., that if Thomas didn't attack promptly he should be superseded by his second in command, Major General John M. Schofield.[4]

George Thomas was duly pressured by the Union army's chief of staff on Dec. 9: "General Grant expresses much dissatisfaction at your delay in attacking," wired Henry Halleck from Washington, D.C. Even President Lincoln was worried. "[Thomas's laying in his fortifications until ready] looks like the McClellan and Rosecrans strategy of do nothing and let the Rebels raid the country," he told Secretary of War Edwin Stanton.[5]

But Thomas was equally firm. Concerned about the presence of the feared Confederate "Wizard of the Saddle," Nathan Bedford Forrest, who commanded about six thousand Rebel cavalry, Thomas wanted his own cavalry under Major General James H. Wilson reorganized and reequipped before attacking Hood. This would enable Thomas to protect his flanks while assaulting Hood's fixed positions.

As for Hood crossing the Cumberland River and raiding north, this he deemed highly improbable. The Union navy's gunboats, in full control of the river, would prevent a major crossing. With various Union garrisons throughout the Tennessee countryside from Murfreesboro to Chattanooga, Thomas believed he could wait until his newly formed army was in proper condition to fight. Especially since Hood had been severely bloodied, losing more than seven thousand men at the Battle of Franklin on November 30, Thomas knew the enemy's supposed "siege" of Nashville was more a desperate gambit than a meaningful campaign.[6]

Matters continued to deteriorate with each passing day. Cavalry commander Wilson was having trouble impressing horses from the countryside as far north as Kentucky, and the weather turned bitterly cold, with freezing rain, sleet, and even snow. Travel about the city of Nashville virtually came to a standstill from December 9 to December 13. Thomas warned the authorities at Washington that it was impossible to launch an attack with any probability of success until the weather moderated.

Another urgent dispatch from Ulysses S. Grant to Thomas on the evening of December 11 clarified the seriousness of the situation: "If you delay attack[ing] longer the mortifying spectacle will be witnessed of a Rebel army moving for the Ohio River, and you will be forced to act, accepting such weather as you find. Let there be no further delay. . . . Delay no longer for weather or reinforcements." To remind Thomas of the severe consequences, Grant informed him that his removal as commander at Nashville was actively under consideration.[7]

Thomas sat at his desk and pondered the future on "Cold Sunday," December 11, 1864, a day the temperatures plummeted to about ten degrees below zero in Nashville. The grim skies and whistling wind must have mirrored his despair. He could but look at the frozen countryside from the window at his St. Cloud Hotel headquarters and wait. The lonely burden of command was never more evident. Thomas was later found sitting at the window "for an hour or more," not speaking a word and forlornly gazing off into the distance.[8]

Although the strong north wind moderated on the twelfth, the weather remained exceedingly cold. The hard-frozen ground and ice-covered streets were still as slippery as a skating rink. Cavalry moving across the river from Edgefield into Nashville floundered and fell. The many accidents and mishaps only reaffirmed Thomas's intransigence. When a council of war was called among the senior Union generals at 3:00 P.M. on December 12, Thomas was resolute and adamant. The Washington authorities might relieve him from command, but in no case would he go against his own judgment and fight before the local conditions were favorable. Indeed, noted Thomas with emotion, Grant's favorite, William Tecumseh Sherman, was virtually unopposed on his "holiday excursion" through Georgia, but had taken the cream of the western Union army with him, leaving Thomas with mostly reserves, recruits, and combat-depleted units that he had to fashion into an effective army. Grant, who was unmercifully pressuring him, had the temerity to try to rush him into hasty action after Hood had been present at Nashville only ten days, even when Grant himself had been deadlocked in Virginia for seven months. It was enough to depress any commander. Thomas remarked to a friend: "The Washington authorities treat me as if I were a boy. They seem to think me incapable of planning a campaign or of fighting a battle. But if they will just let me alone until [a thaw] . . . I will show them what we can do."⁹

The problem was that Grant and the others wouldn't wait. On December 13 Grant was sitting at his City Point, Virginia, headquarters visiting with Major General John A. Logan, one of Sherman's corps commanders, who had just returned from a leave of absence and was seeking a new assignment. Grant was obviously distraught, having just received a copy of Thomas's telegram from Nashville on December 12 reporting that he hadn't advanced due to the inclement weather and that "an attack at this time would only result in a useless sacrifice of life." Grant surprised Logan when he wrote out a conditional order for Logan to take command of Thomas's army. The understanding was that Logan would proceed immediately to Nashville, and if on his arrival Thomas hadn't moved, Logan would replace him.¹⁰

A day later, Grant had misgivings. Having sent Logan to relieve Thomas, he realized, was a spur-of-the-moment decision. On second thought, he believed it would likely cause divisiveness among the senior subordinate generals with Thomas. Accordingly, on the afternoon of December 14 Grant decided to go himself to Nashville, and proceeded by steamboat to Washington, D.C., where he arrived on the fifteenth. That afternoon he met with President Lincoln, Chief of Staff Halleck, and Secretary of War Stanton.¹¹

Grant insisted that Thomas should be removed. When the chief telegraph operator, Major Thomas T. Eckert, was called in and confirmed that no new information had been received from Nashville, Lincoln and Stanton gave their approval. Grant then wrote out the order for Thomas's removal and gave it to Eckert for transmittal. Since the telegraph lines were then down, Eckert had to wait for the wires to be restored. Grant, meanwhile, returned to Willard's Hotel and prepared to journey to Nashville.¹²

Thursday, December 15, 1864, had dawned warm and foggy in Nashville. Despite the muddy and soft terrain, it was the day George H. Thomas had committed to attack the Rebel army under Hood. With moderating weather on the fourteenth, Thomas had ordered a major flanking movement to envelop the enemy's western flank for the morning of the fifteenth. Despite the fog and inevitable delays and confusion, on December 15 Thomas's cavalry found few of Forrest's cavalrymen present to hinder their wide-swinging attack. Days ago Hood had sent most of Forrest's men to harass the garrison at Murfreesboro, and now there were few gray cavalry available to resist as a mixed command of Union cavalry and infantry overran several of Hood's defensive redoubts. By that evening the collapse of the Confederate left flank caused Hood's entire force to stream south in disorder before finally halting along a line of high hills several miles distant. As the fruits of victory, Thomas had sixteen pieces of captured Rebel artillery and about a thousand prisoners. Moreover, the entire Confederate defensive perimeter was shattered. As he headed back to Nashville that evening, Thomas could hardly wait to get to the telegraph office.[13]

In Washington, Major Thomas Eckert learned that evening that the telegraph lines were again open to Nashville. It was his duty to transmit Grant's order relieving Thomas. Yet Eckert decided to await the daily transmittal of news from Nashville, perhaps suspecting that action had occurred. Indeed, at 11:00 P.M. the wires began to hum. Eckert was overjoyed to learn of Thomas's great victory and hastened to see Stanton, with the unsent telegram from Grant still in his pocket. Both Stanton and Eckert then hurried to the White House to rouse the president. Minutes later Lincoln, in his nightshirt, read the good news and was elated. Grant, when notified at Willard's Hotel that night, immediately sent a telegram to Thomas: "I was just on my way to Nashville, but receiving [the] dispatch . . . detailing your splendid success . . . I shall go no farther. Push the enemy now and give him no rest until he is entirely destroyed."[14]

In a fateful few minutes Thomas's career had been saved, and to complete the turn of events, in Washington a hundred-gun salute was ordered in Thomas's honor.

The next day, December 16, 1864, witnessed the most complete major victory of the war, the decisive combat at Nashville that wrecked Hood's army and sent the remnants fleeing south in wild confusion. It was George H. Thomas's shining hour, the true epitome of his military career.

When the final count was made, Thomas's men over the span of little more than a month had taken seventy-two Rebel cannon and more than thirteen thousand prisoners, including eight generals, and won three major victories that resulted in the destruction of about two-thirds of Hood's Confederate army. Never in American military history had there been such an overwhelming major combat victory.[15]

George H. Thomas was rewarded with promotion to major general in the regular army, but later declined to consider command of the postwar U.S. Army when proposed for that post by President Andrew Johnson.

Although an outcast Southerner and soon largely shunted aside following the war's end, George H. Thomas today looms as one of the nation's greatest military men. Having triumphed over mind and matter at Nashville, he was distinguished not only by his deeds, but equally by what was in his heart.

XXIV

A TALE OF TWO PRESIDENTS

Understanding the difference between courage and stubbornness is often subtle: knowing the objective right from the subjective opinion about such. To act with courage versus stubbornness is to weigh effectively the contrasting evidence and focus not upon the personal effect but rather on the practical result. How we perform is more readily analyzed by scrutinizing the total context of reality versus the emotion of the moment. Thus we often understand belatedly what we failed to see at the time of a crucial decision or action.

The purpose of an action is often best served by goal-oriented thinking. That may seem obvious, yet how often in our history have decisions of importance and major impact been predicated upon emotionalism, favoritism, or personal prejudice? To accomplish the lofty and difficult goals of national importance, history's chief decision makers have long exhibited considerable courage in perspective and action.

Yet there are other examples of outright failure to perceive and understand, and thus to enable the very sought-for means of accomplishing great undertakings.

In the Civil War the presidents of the respective combatant entities were the crucial decision makers whose performance keyed the difference in results. If the greatness of Abraham Lincoln were to be defined in one all-inclusive quality, it might very well involve his practical wisdom as reflected in various courageous decisions. In contrast, the smart and accomplished statesman Jefferson Davis, whose ability was perhaps equal to Lincoln's, was best known for the stubborn pride that often exceeded his concentration of purpose. The dramatic effect in terms of performance was perhaps never more evident than in the crucial fall of 1863.

SHOULD I CHANGE HORSES?

It was a most critical moment in the nation's history. At the Battle of Chickamauga, September 19 and 20, 1863, the Confederate forces swept General William S. Rosecrans's once mighty Army of the Cumberland from the cedar-laden forests about Chickamauga Creek, Georgia, and penned the surviving troops up in mountain-ringed Chattanooga, Tennessee. Not only a major defeat, but gradual starvation was the consequence, since supplies dwindled to a trickle.

Ringed by Missionary Ridge on the east, Lookout Mountain to the south, and rugged Walden's Ridge on the west, Chattanooga was a town easily besieged. With travel on the broad Tennessee River restricted by shoal obstructions and low water in the winter, the town was so difficult to supply that within weeks of the Chickamauga battlefield disaster Rosecrans put the army on severely reduced rations.[1]

William S. Rosecrans was a most curious personality. Regarded as a very competent and successful general, as recently as the past summer "Old Rosy" had been looked upon by many as the premier Union general in the western theater. In July 1863, however, U. S. Grant's victory at Vicksburg had assured him of such great public stature and fame that he dominated the war scene as the army's leading general. Ironically, while Grant was winning at Vicksburg, Rosecrans had outmaneuvered Braxton Bragg in a relatively bloodless campaign that reclaimed virtually all of Tennessee and sent Bragg reeling back into the mountains of northern Georgia.

But the brilliant Tullahoma Campaign had been only the precursor to the ensuing mess at Chattanooga, and Rosecrans's subsequent lack of inspired action only made matters worse. Assistant Secretary of War Charles A. Dana had been sent by Edwin Stanton essentially to spy on Rosecrans prior to the debacle at Chickamauga (he had been on a similar mission with Grant at Vicksburg). Dana was appalled by Rosecrans's seeming negligence, and Dana's repeated confidential denunciations of the Ohio general, together with Dana's statements that he should be replaced, constantly reminded the Lincoln administration of the unfolding crisis.[2]

Abraham Lincoln, as the nation's chief decision maker, knew the matter would eventually be placed in his hands. Lincoln had much to consider in the potential replacement of Rosecrans. Old Rosy had achieved much success in the past, and the president remembered his significant victory at Stones River. Not wanting to do Rosecrans an injustice, and mindful of the forthcoming Ohio gubernatorial election, in which Rosecrans as a prominent Ohioan might influence the voting, Lincoln delayed making a command change. Yet the pressures kept growing.

Dana's ongoing crisis communiqués were accentuated by the receipt of a controversial letter from Rosecrans's chief of staff, James A. Garfield. In this private letter Garfield warned that Rosecrans was "singularly disinclined to grasp the situation [at Chattanooga] with a strong hand." The result, Garfield asserted, was "a fatal delay," and accordingly, "if this inaction continues long I shall ask to be relieved and sent somewhere where I can be a part of a working army."[3]

Lincoln waited until after the Ohio election on October 9, when the prowar Republican governor, John Brough, decisively defeated the Democratic antiwar candidate, Clement L. Vallandigham. The president was grateful for Rosecrans's ardent support of Brough and that 97 percent of the Army of the Cumberland's votes had gone to the governor. Yet matters suddenly came to a head on October 16, 1863. That day another telegram arrived from Assistant Secretary Dana, stating that "nothing [except the opening of the Tennessee River] can prevent the retreat of the army from this place within a fortnight." Furthermore, wrote Dana, the "dazed and mazy" Rosecrans did not perceive the approaching disaster.

Lincoln's reaction was to place U. S. Grant in charge as the department commander in the West, with authority to fully manage events. Still mindful of Rosecrans's contribution as a general and a patriot, Lincoln did not specifically order the removal of the Ohioan, but instead allowed Grant to determine who would command the Army of the Cumberland as his subordinate.

Lincoln's profuse magnanimity and great character thus allowed for the possibility that Grant might choose to retain Rosecrans, but above all else Lincoln was goal oriented. He would simply not allow persons or perspectives to get in the way of achieving results. Grant had repeatedly demonstrated his capacity to win victories and remain cool in a crisis. Even Lincoln assessed that Rosecrans was acting "confused and stunned like a duck hit on the head" following the debacle at Chickamauga. Although Old Rosy was "a true and very able man," Lincoln couldn't accept less than full success in this great crisis. The loss of Chattanooga would set a precedent for perhaps an even greater loss the following year, with the presidency itself at stake.[4]

Grant, who had a poor relationship with Rosecrans dating from their personal squabble at Iuka, Mississippi, in September 1862, opted to remove Old Rosy and replace him with the hero of Chickamauga, George H. Thomas. Under Thomas's able leadership the Union troops won the major victory at Missionary Ridge to end the siege of Chattanooga in November 1863, propelling Grant to a national level of command, even as Rosecrans was relegated to a minor role as commander of the Department of Missouri.[5]

Lincoln undoubtedly was mindful of the personal trauma inherent in making this major command change, but his was a fully pragmatic view. His duty, the first order of priority, was to do that which he knew was right in an ultimate sense. It was his responsibility; it was his pain. It was also his courage.

"Continuance in the Patient Endurance"

Braxton Bragg's troops had won the crucial Battle of Chickamauga. The Southern people were enthralled by the greatest victory ever of the Army of Tennessee, and one of the Confederacy's proudest moments. More than anything it was the profound renewal of Southern hope that fired the imagination of all. In the aftermath of the disasters at Vicksburg and Gettysburg only a few months earlier, Chickamauga inspired enthusiasm. There was the real prospect of regaining Chattanooga and much of Tennessee. The initiative in the West had shifted to the Confederacy's victorious forces. Greater success seemed imminent, rekindling the spirits of the very fighting men who had so long suffered in the shadow of despair. "Having before been accustomed to defeat and retreat, no one can conceive what a change a victory so brilliant would make," wrote a jubilant Southern lieutenant.[6]

Once considered by some as the greatest general in the Confederacy, Braxton Bragg had seemingly redeemed the faith President Jefferson Davis had placed in him in mid-1862. Davis had then named him commander of the Confederacy's principal western army, the Army of Tennessee, following the death at Shiloh of Albert Sidney Johnston and the incapacity due to sickness of P. G. T. Beauregard. Bragg, who had won laurels in the Mexican War and earned high praise for outmaneuvering the Yankees after the loss of Corinth, Mississippi, seemed at last to be shedding his controversial image. Bragg saw the victory at Chickamauga as vindication of his methods and perspectives. Once termed a "master genius" by the governor of Alabama, Bragg was quick to bask in the glory of it all even though he said his "mind and body [were] taxed to the utmost. Thank God the latter has not failed me," he told his wife a few days after Chickamauga.[7]

What Bragg was alluding to was his new order of business. The Battle of Chickamauga hadn't so much defeated the Yankees as it had brought new prospects for personal vindication in the matter of his command of the army. Rather than attempting rapidly to follow up and extend the only major Confederate victory of the war in the West, Bragg's personal priority was a vendetta against the various senior subordinate generals whom he regarded with contempt. He intended to purge from the army those commanders who had long differed with his views and had offered petty insults and snide remarks about his lack of leadership. Bragg was now in a position to repay their resentment with steep interest.[8]

Braxton Bragg was perhaps the most despised commander on either side in 1863. Regarded as "either stark mad, or utterly incompetent" by one observer, Bragg was a much maligned general, many of whose troops regarded him with disgust and disdain. Denounced in mid-1862 for ordering multiple executions for desertion, Bragg had frequently bungled battles such as Perryville and Stones River, wasted tactical opportunities, and made poor battlefield command decisions. Both officers and men had long damned Bragg as a wretched general. "No one man that ever lived . . . had as much hatred expressed against him as Bragg," said one of his soldiers following Stones River. So many officers had complained and sought his removal from command that even Bragg had polled his principal subordinates for their opinion, offering to resign if they believed him wanting. Despite their lack of support, Bragg abruptly ignored their candid negative opinions. Following the debacle of the Tullahoma Campaign and the wasted aftermath of Chickamauga, the severe criticism reached a crescendo.

Bragg's mental and physical disability was the talk of the army, and some of his officers were so outraged that they circulated a petition among the army's ranking officers, demanding Bragg's removal. Bragg struck back, however, seeking the ouster of Lieutenant General Leonidas Polk from corps command, and chastising Generals Daniel H. Hill, Simon B. Buckner, Thomas C. Hindman, and James Longstreet, all of whom he sought to get rid of. What resulted was in effect a revolt among many of the senior officers. Twelve key commanders signed the formal petition for Bragg's removal, and Jefferson Davis's aide-de-camp, Colonel James C. Chesnut, sent to investigate, found such a storm of

open hostility that he urged the president to come to Georgia and resolve the matter.[9]

By October 8, 1863, Jefferson Davis was at Atlanta, conferring with
his old friend from West Point days, Leonidas Polk, who had been ban-
ished from the army by Bragg. Polk adamantly refused to serve again
under Bragg, and raged against the acerbic North Carolina general for
his "incapacity." Davis, first hoping to dissipate the whirlwind of discontent, saw that he would have to give up as impractical any attempts
at reconciliation. Traveling to Bragg's headquarters, on October 10
Davis sat down for a meeting with the army's ranking generals. The petition for Bragg's removal was still circulating among the army, and
Davis listened impassively to the storm of criticism that issued from the
subordinate generals in Bragg's presence. The army's best fighter, Major
General Patrick Cleburne, said a change in leadership was absolutely essential. Others added that Bragg's ineffectiveness had removed all confidence within the army and destroyed his usefulness as commander.
Humiliated, Bragg listened with intense resentment as his subordinates
depicted his woeful performance.[10]

The whole matter was a charade. In a meeting with Davis on October 9, Bragg had offered to resign, but Davis had said no. Davis's mind
had been made up even before he left Richmond. He then implied to
Secretary of War James Seddon that he had no intention of removing
Bragg. Jefferson Davis abhorred the only ranking generals who might be
persuaded to replace Bragg. Both P. G. T. Beauregard and Joe Johnston
were severe critics of Davis, and he regarded them much as personal enemies. Davis had no personal fondness for James Longstreet, whom
Robert E. Lee thought might become Bragg's successor. Longstreet's
burning ambition to succeed Bragg was evident in his ardent criticism
of that general. Davis, it seems, was clearly miffed about Longstreet's
flagrant ambition. As for Robert E. Lee, that favorite general had refused to go west, insisting on staying in his Virginia command.

Davis firmly announced to all the dissident generals that Bragg
would be retained. He admonished them that "shafts of malice" would
be harmless against him. Instead of criticizing their commander, they
should support him for the common good.[11]

Davis then returned to Virginia, and Bragg moved quickly to exploit his personal victory. He summarily dismissed or had transferred the key "conspirators" against him, including the irate Nathan Bedford Forrest, who called Bragg to his face a coward and a damned scoundrel, and threatened to kill him if he ever crossed his path again.

Bragg continued to bristle with vindictiveness. He reorganized the army and shuffled units into new brigades to weaken the political influence of former detractors, all to the ire of many officers and men. These moves didn't quell the budding mutiny among the army; instead, by the middle of November so many of his men were deserting that one amazed Yankee soldier thought that if the current rate kept up Bragg would lose his entire army in a matter of days.[12]

Instead of focusing on the military task at hand, forcing the Union army to retreat from Chattanooga, Bragg and Davis had been intent on strictures to "discipline" the army. When Davis departed from the army, he left behind a message to the soldiers, telling them that "patient endurance of toil and danger" would result in the common good, and also warning them that "he who sows the seeds of discontent and distrust prepares for the harvest of slaughter and defeat."[13]

It was now clear that Jefferson Davis had visited the army solely to dispel the anger and discontent. That he thought he could end the rampant discord by merely hearing complaints and speaking out on Bragg's behalf was characteristic of Davis's exaggerated self-image. Jefferson Davis had just sustained his reputation as the true sphinx of the Confederacy. Although a mystery to many because of his famed stubbornness and stoicism, Davis had long prided himself on his perceptive military judgments, based on long experience in army matters. An 1828 graduate of West Point, a much publicized Mexican War hero, and the Pierce administration's secretary of war, Davis harbored strong opinions about most of the principal generals North and South. His personal assessments often resulted in favoring personal friends and seeing to their appointments in high commands. Davis's assessments were sometimes valid, as in the case of Robert E. Lee and Albert Sidney Johnston. Yet in many cases his opinions were so poor as to be ultimately ruinous.

As the war progressed increasingly unsatisfactorily for the South, Davis's decisions about his generals and a stubborn pride in sustaining them perhaps contributed the most to the ultimate defeat of the Confederacy. His unbending attitude seemed to accept the risk of widespread destruction rather than personal defeat. "He retains his favorites long after they have blundered themselves out of the confidence of all their troops," wrote one angry observer, "and would rather lose a battle or give up a state than admit Jeff Davis could have made an injudicious promotion."[14]

Davis's flawed personality thus reflected not only an intense stubbornness but an inability to admit or correct serious mistakes. Having risen to power on the basis of mostly intuitive judgment, Davis was self-righteous and largely uncompromising in his conduct of affairs. He simply would not allow himself to be proven wrong in his personal judgments. The consequences were apparent for the Confederacy when Braxton Bragg lost the critical battle at Chattanooga in a stunning defeat on Misssionary Ridge and was compelled to resign from command of the army shortly thereafter.

Ironically, on the very October 1863 day that Jefferson Davis had departed from the Army of Tennessee on his return to Richmond, another president, in a similar crisis, had opted for a basic change in commanders at Chattanooga.

The striking contrast in moral courage was never more apparent.

$\mathcal{XXV}$

THE UNTHINKABLE

The war was being lost! The South's best blood had been spilled. In early 1864, after nearly three years of fighting, nothing had been gained "but long lists of dead and mangled." Confederate-controlled territory had been reduced by about two-thirds. The Union army was poised with superior forces to subjugate the remaining portion. A "fatal apathy" had stricken Southern soldiers, who were "growing weary of defeats, hardships, and slaughters, which promise no results." Desertion was rife, supplies were faltering, and much of the South was in ruins. Unless something was done quickly, the Confederacy would be conquered.

This stark indictment was like a message from hell. Nobody in the Davis administration wanted to acknowledge its accuracy. However, these dire assessments were not those of an enemy, but words from one of the best combat generals in the Confederacy, division commander and congressional honoree Major General Patrick R. Cleburne.[1]

In the emergency, Cleburne and other prominent signers of a special petition urged the responsible authorities to act with "common sense," to alter the old, failed ways and make "extraordinary change" to prevent losing the war and keep the South from being placed under oppressive enemy control. The way to do this, said Cleburne and his supporters, was to change slavery from an inherent weakness to a strength—by enlisting blacks in the army as combatant soldiers. They should be given an incentive to fight by emancipating them and their families.

Cleburne's extraordinary document was explicit. There were three basic reasons for the impending Southern defeat: (1) the Confederacy's armies were far outnumbered by those of the enemy; (2) there wasn't enough remaining unused white manpower to replenish the army's great losses; and (3) slaves were a source of troops, information, and cooperation to the enemy, thus being a military liability rather than a strength to the South.[2]

The North was raising an army of one hundred thousand blacks, noted the petitioners, and they were being recruited from escaped slaves, especially in Southern regions overrun by Union troops. Added to the conscription of the general Northern population, and European immigrants being recruited literally "off the boats"—induced by antislavery rhetoric and bounty cash—it was a program that had turned Southern slavery into a significant weakness.

That facing an overwhelming number of enemy soldiers was tantamount to defeat few would deny. So why not make the South's black population a source of victory? The South should bring forth sufficient numbers of blacks to replace white combat losses, create a large reserve of troops, and repair the severe military imbalance between North and South. By utilizing its black resources to the fullest, the South might even take the offensive and occupy enemy territory, gaining access to vital local foodstuffs and supplies.[3]

It was an astounding proposal, one of the most important if controversial of the war. The overt issue was the military success of the Confederacy, a paramount objective. The deeper issue was a test of the soul: the sacrifice of a traditional Southern institution.

The logic on both sides was intense. Cleburne's proposal would replenish the tremendous loss in manpower the Confederate armies had sustained over nearly three years of warfare. It would further deny to the enemy much of that very same source of manpower, which it was already exploiting. It would restore to the rank and file a crucial boost in morale by renewing hope for the South's ultimate success. Most substantially, being a "concession to common sense," it would be a practical means of preventing the South's imminent military defeat.[4]

It was also to many the unthinkable, an outrage against Southern culture and principles that provoked an emotional firestorm. The proposal to enroll slaves as combatant soldiers in the Confederate army burned in the minds of many like a white-hot poker. Hadn't the South resorted to war to save the "peculiar institution"—its cheap, self-perpetuating labor force in a heavily dependent agricultural economy? Emancipation of the slave who fought for the South (the major incentive for serving) would surely cause social upheaval, economic chaos, and emotional despair. A way of life more than two centuries old was threatened. The idea that blacks would be armed and placed on an equal combat status with white soldiers was treasonable to some. That the matter even came to the forefront at the decision-making level reflected an extraordinary circumstance.

As was evident to various close observers, the crucial crossroads had been reached. The military results of the devastating war would determine if the Confederacy survived. Was it best to make concessions requiring bitter sacrifices for an ultimate benefit—independence—or to continue down the increasingly desperate path of no compromise and risk everything?

The handwriting was seemingly on the wall. Robert E. Lee's defeat at Gettysburg, and the loss of Vicksburg and control of the entire Mississippi River, foretold the beginning of the end and the coming total defeat.

This terrible truth was evident to many in the Army of Tennessee, where despair had manifested itself after a succession of bloody and demoralizing defeats, from Fort Donelson in early 1862 to, most recently, Missionary Ridge. Losses in the South's primary ranks of experienced troops were not now replaceable. Outnumbered by the North in white population more than six to one, the Confederate states by 1864 were largely depleted of white manpower resources. Only the aged, young, and indifferent or reluctant conscripts were yet untapped—a poor prospect for replacing the vital core of the essential army. Even Robert E. Lee acknowledged as much in his 1863 correspondence, fretting about diminishing resources and the irreplaceable loss of experienced officers and men.[5]

The essence of this critical issue was perhaps best expressed by a Confederate private, James Hamner of the 21st Tennessee Cavalry: "There is no use in fighting unless we can accomplish something by it. I think we have one of the best armies in the world, but still if they outnumber us too far, we must not fight them, for when the army we have now is gone, I cannot see where the next one is to come from."[6]

In fact, the want of fighting men was perhaps the most crucial aspect of the war for the South at the beginning of 1864. The South's aggressive, offensive-minded tactical methods of attacking in many battles had resulted in an unsustainable casualty rate. The disparity in available numbers of troops was pronounced, especially since the North could generally replace its losses from a population of about twenty-two million. "Every soldier in our army already knows and feels our numerical inferiority," reasoned a veteran Confederate general. Faced with a wasting war of defense, involving the loss of more territory, greater civilian hardships, and diminishing resources, it was obvious that the war was being slowly, inexorably lost.[7]

The best answer seemed to be black Southerners. The black population of the South numbered about four million in 1860 (more than a third of its total population), and perhaps one million might be regarded as males of military age, representing a potential addition of perhaps 500,000 soldiers to the Confederacy's armies (which had dwindled to about 480,000 men under arms in early 1864).* In fact, the entire Federal army numbered only 861,000 at that time.[8]

Would blacks fight for the South? They knew little but their Southern heritage, reasoned some. If the North was enlisting blacks as United States Colored Troops and using them in a combat role, why not the

---

* Confederate Secretary of State Judah P. Benjamin estimated there were in the South 680,000 black men of fighting age (*Richmond Daily Examiner,* February 10, 1865, p. 2; see also Purdue and Purdue, *Pat Cleburne, Confederate General,* p. 283, n. 43).

reverse? "If they can be made to face and fight bravely [as Union soldiers] against their former masters, how much more probable is it that with the allurement of a higher reward, and led by those masters, they would submit to discipline and face [our] dangers?" asked a keen observer. Giving a slave "not only his own freedom, but that of his wife and child" and "securing it to him in his old home [the South]" would be a more effective incentive than the North could offer, he continued. Indeed, hadn't many slaves gone off to war with their masters in 1861, and served faithfully as servants and auxiliaries? Their loyalty seemed evident.[9]

There were other reasons for enrolling blacks as combatants in the Southern war effort. Under present circumstances, slaves often served as guides or aided the enemy with vital information, enlisted in the Union ranks, and caused some owners in occupied areas to take the United States oath of allegiance so as to save their property. Further, slaves in quest of freedom were prone to abandon their plantations upon the enemy's approach. Moreover, England and France would not recognize the Confederacy so long as it practiced slavery.

As Southerners had increasingly acknowledged following Lincoln's Emancipation Proclamation, it made practical sense to utilize blacks in the fighting army. Few men in the Confederate ranks were slaveholders, and most seemed to espouse independence at any cost. The African American soldier could be counted on to sustain the South's war effort indefinitely—but there was a catch.

The matter was an issue for the South's hierarchy. Only if the leadership embraced the idea would the masses become involved.

The impetus devolved on a select few, and history tottered on a tenuous fulcrum. Indeed, this momentous question effectively rested in the lap of one man: the supreme decision maker of the Confederate States of America, its president. It took an extraordinary act of moral courage even to bring the matter up for his consideration.*

---

* Many historians have regarded the idea of arming slaves as soldiers as unacceptable to the white population of the Civil War South, and therefore not a realistic option. That slaves were generally considered "inferior" to whites and thus not to be placed on an equivalent status seems to be much of the basis for this rationale. Having examined dozens of soldiers' letters

While the idea had been bandied about at various times by newspaper editors and several local functionaries, there had been no prominent champion to propel it forward. A man of stature, respect, and integrity was needed to provide impetus.

Major General Patrick Ronayne Cleburne was just such a man. He saw it as simply a question involving the priority of Southern independence. What was more important: to forgo slavery to win the war, or at least achieve a stalemate leading to a negotiated settlement; or retain slavery to the bitter end, and face ruin? Moreover, the issue was time sensitive; any changes in policy would have to be implemented soon, before it was militarily too late.

In January 1864 Cleburne understood the gravity of the war, and the best hope of altering its foreseeable devastating outcome.* Black soldiers would help turn the tide; their influence as a major force to be confronted by the enemy might be decisive. How would the North maintain the will to continue a war already too costly in lives and treasure in the face of such unpromising odds?

---

touching on this issue, many both pro and con, it is my conclusion that the Southern public's unwillingness to accept blacks and fight alongside them is overstated. The individual views of soldiers, while often emotional, did not necessarily predict their actions. There is every reason to believe that if the Confederate government had embraced the idea and implemented the policy effectively, supported by the endorsement of well-respected leaders such as Robert E. Lee, the program would have succeeded.

There were comparable highly emotional and divided sentiments in Northern ranks upon the introduction of black soldiers within their fighting army and also after the Emancipation Proclamation that gave rise to few defections. The prevailing sentiment seems to have been: we may complain about it and not like it, but collectively we will support our cause as the government officially directs. That a similar situation would have occurred in the Confederate armies upon the introduction of black combat soldiers seems likely.

* The actual impetus for Cleburne's proposal likely came from a memorial letter of December 17, 1863, prepared under General William J. Hardee's lead and signed by twenty-nine senior Confederate commanders in the Army of Tennessee (including Cleburne), requesting of the Confederate Congress emergency measures to increase troop strength so as to prevent the South's "destruction." Inherent in this memorial was the proposal to enroll in the army "able bodied negroes and mulattoes, [both] bond and free" as noncombatants (i.e., cooks, laborers, teamsters, and hospital attendants). It is easy to see how Cleburne, a few weeks later, would be inspired to go one step further and advocate incorporating blacks into the fighting ranks. Yet Hardee's tenure in command of the army was short, and within a few weeks a new, far less receptive commander, Joe Johnston, was present. An original printed copy of the Army of Tennessee's December 17, 1863, memorial is in the Wiley Sword Collection.

After preparing the groundwork and consulting many of his subordinates and friends, Cleburne carefully drafted his proposal and offered it for endorsement to a few key officers. Some readily signed it, although there were mixed emotions and advice. Pat Cleburne then asked for a special meeting of generals who were division commanders and higher at the headquarters of the new Army of Tennessee commander General Joseph E. Johnston. Cleburne believed that if they approved the idea, it would reach government officials in Richmond and receive due consideration.[10]

Cleburne's special 7:00 P.M. meeting on January 2, 1864, at the Dr. James Black home in Dalton, Georgia, began with a simple announcement by the former temporary army commander and now corps commander, William J. Hardee. The distinguished Patrick Cleburne had a matter of importance to present to those present, he said. With a noticeable Irish brogue, Cleburne read the multipage document, already endorsed by fourteen of his comrades.

The subject was soon revealed, and an astonished audience contemplated its implications in stark silence. Indeed, the assembled throng, stunned by the unforeseen and heretofore almost unmentionable subject, undoubtedly pondered the author of this remarkable petition.

The man was a brilliant general, a battlefield genius of the first order. No one was a better fighter, more dedicated or hardworking. His grasp of tactical combat was not exceeded by that of anyone in the Confederacy. He was an exceptionally smart and brave general whose ability seemed limitless. Pat Cleburne, in fact, had become almost a cult within the army and was virtually idolized by his men. If the Army of Northern Virginia had Robert E. Lee and Stonewall Jackson, the Army of Tennessee had Pat Cleburne.

Yet Cleburne was not larger than life, as Lee and Jackson later came to be regarded. If truly a soldier's icon, he had already become a political liability—so dangerous that others (such as Braxton Bragg) sought to suppress his ideas. Among rival generals and various aristocratic commanders, Cleburne had political enemies and detractors. Cleburne was an outsider, not native to the land, and seemed to be regarded by some as having insufficient cultural perspective to address fundamental Southern values and concepts. What did "a bloody Irishman," a former common British soldier, know of the real South? Here was no West Point–trained commander or member of the aristocracy—or "first rank"—who had been tutored in formal military and social protocols, but rather a naive upstart, seemingly ignorant of fundamental Southern perspectives. Beyond this, for anyone to advocate using slaves as combat soldiers was "monstrous" and tantamount to treason, reasoned some. In fact, the more a few thought about it, the more outraged they became.

That night there was immediate strong reaction among the generals both pro and con, but the reaction of the senior commander, Joe Johnston, was not favorable. Considering the proposal more political than military, Johnston tabled the matter and directed that no further discussion of it was to occur. Although formally noncommittal about his position, Johnston, mindful of his difficulties with the Davis administration, anticipated that it would not be well received in Richmond. He apparently pondered forwarding the memorial to Davis's officials, but later decided against it.

Despite Johnston's reluctance, the subject was too important and too emotional to go unresolved. Major General W. H. T. Walker, a division commander from Georgia, was so upset that he defied Johnston and forced the issue upon the Davis administration. Walker, regarded by one of his contemporaries as "a crack-brained fire-eater, always captious or caviling about something," saw fit to go beyond everyone and everything to get the proposal quashed at the highest level. Believing that Cleburne's proposal would incite such a controversy that it "would ruin the efficacy of our army, and involve our cause in ruin and disgrace," Walker became an activist in getting the paper into Jefferson Davis's hands. Even when directly ordered by Johnston not to forward the proposal to Richmond, Walker surreptitiously sent a copy of it to Davis via a Georgia congressman, who hand carried it to Richmond. "The gravity of the subject" warranted this action, Walker later huffed.

Joined in his dissent by generals Patton Anderson and William B. Bate, Walker continued to be indignant, and even queried every officer who had been at the January 2 meeting to determine their stance on the matter: "[Do] you favor the proposition or sentiments of the document in any form?" Angered by the obvious attempt to isolate and single out anyone who would be so bold as to support the idea, one general— Thomas C. Hindman (who favored the proposal)—wrote: "I do not choose to admit any inquisitorial rights in you."[11]

Clearly the proposal to arm the slaves would be at the storm center of intense controversy. It was forward thinking, a means of military survival. Placed in the hands of Jefferson Davis about January 12, 1864, it took less than twenty-four hours to elicit a reply.

Jefferson Davis was stunned, like most of the others. He immediately wrote to Walker thanking him for the information and sent his personal condemnation of the slave proposal: "Deeming it to be injurious to the public service that such subject should be mooted or even known to be entertained by persons possessed of confidence and respect of the people, I have concluded that the best policy under the circumstances will be to avoid all publicity, and the Secretary of War has therefore written to General Johnston requesting him to convey to those concerned my desire that it should be kept private. If it be kept out of the public journals its ill effect will be much lessened."[12]

That was it. There would be no last resort, at least so long as the noose was not in sight. It was an idea that the administration forbade even talking about. Davis's spokesman, Secretary of War James A. Seddon, advised Joe Johnston that the matter could produce only "discouragement, distraction, and dissension." The proposal was to be suppressed, and likewise "all discussion" of it. Although Seddon remarked that "no doubt or mistrust" was made of Cleburne's patriotism, clearly the Irish-born general had made a serious political blunder.[13]

Braxton Bragg, posted by Davis as his special military adviser charged "with the conduct of military operations of the armies of the Confederacy," wrote soon thereafter that a great sensation had been stirred up by the emancipation project of "Hardee, Cheatham, Cleburne & Co.," but "it will kill them," he smirked. Even several of Cleburne's own staff had warned their general that the slave proposal might ruin his chances for promotion. The Irishman grimly responded that it was his duty to present the proposal regardless of its effect on his career. If worse came to worst, he would be court-martialed and cashiered, but then he would enlist as a private in his old regiment, the 15th Arkansas, and still do his duty. "An honest heart and a strong arm should never succumb," he had once written to his family. Cleburne, who never owned a slave but saw their great potential as soldiers, was soon effectively blacklisted as a military leader, largely because of his slaves-as-soldiers concept.[14]

Thereafter, although clearly the Army of Tennessee's ablest combat general, Cleburne was repeatedly denied promotion through four corps commander vacancies in eight months. The fulcrum of opportunity wasn't to be ability, but the often crucial alignment with protocol and politics. Nonetheless, Cleburne never wavered, either in his loyalty to the system or in his mental fortitude. When informed of Davis's decision, Cleburne wrote to a close friend, "After such an opinion . . . from the highest officer of our government I feel it my duty to suppress the memorial and to cease to advocate the measures mentioned." He caused all copies of the proposal but one (the original) to be destroyed in full compliance with the president's wishes. When he was later killed at the Battle of Franklin in November 1864, Cleburne's courage and leadership in raising this momentous issue were unknown to the general public.[15]

The great question of the war—to what extent would the Confederacy's leaders go to establish its independence—had been answered. At the critical moment, pride and tradition, not practicality, had seemed foremost in their minds.*

For those who knew Jefferson Davis well, this result seemed foreordained. In fact, how this great issue was resolved told much about aristocratic Southern thinking involving sweeping change. Of courage, Jefferson Davis spoke in his second inaugural address, saying he was "securely relying on the patriotism and courage of the people of which the present war has furnished so many examples."[16]

---

* Cleburne's logic reflected keen innovative and practical reasoning, even while his proposal ignored the deeper ordeal of social tragedy engulfing the South. Change of a basic way of life was involved. Nonetheless, had Cleburne's proposal been implemented in early 1864 as he advocated, the complexion of the war would have changed drastically. Possibly, the South might have even won its independence. Ulysses S. Grant estimated in his *Memoirs* that: "Anything that could have prolonged the war a year beyond the time that it did finally close, would probably have exhausted the North to such an extent that they might have abandoned the contest, and agreed to a separation." See Purdue and Purdue, *Pat Cleburne, Confederate General*, p. 277.

His conception of courage did not match its essence, however. From a modern perspective, the war had been irreversibly lost following Jefferson Davis's emotionally charged decision. Unfortunately for the South, so was one of its best generals, who never had the chance to permanently command a corps.

Ultimately, there was a heavy irony. When faced by the gathering whirlwind of final defeat in the early spring of 1865, reconsideration of using slaves as combat soldiers was inevitable. It was by then a desperate grasping at straws, the impetus for which had been building throughout the bitter defeats of the final months of 1864. Atlanta had been lost, Richmond and Petersburg were under heavy siege and about to fall, and the vital seacoast ports were all but gone. Robert E. Lee, in a private letter on January 11, 1865, to Confederate senator R. M. T. Hunter (Virginia), urged that slaves be brought immediately into the fighting army as soldiers. It was a simple matter: "[W]e must decide whether slavery shall be extinguished by our enemies and the slaves be used against us, or use them ourselves."[17]

His arguments were much the same as Cleburne's: Enemy access to a large population of the South's blacks within conquered territory would ensure thousands of additional black soldier recruits for the enemy's ranks. These, in turn, would occupy more Southern territory, being used to hold the white population "in subjection, leaving the remaining force of the enemy free to extend his conquest." Freedom for the black Confederate soldier and his family was necessary to ensure that they fought with personal incentive, reasoned Lee. But whatever was done, it must be quickly implemented, for "every day's delay increases the difficulty [of implementing the same before] . . . it is too late."[18]

Even Jefferson Davis by this point was willing to compromise principle for practicality. A year after harshly condemning Cleburne's proposal, he endorsed the idea of black soldiers serving in combat within Southern ranks. Although this had once been anathema to his intent to maintain the Southern institution of slavery at any price, survival with the enemy at the gates brought into perspective what Cleburne had said twelve months earlier. The South had no alternative but to give up slavery, either by conquest or by choice. As Lee and others urged, incentive and politics were now aligned, and the result was foreordained.

Approval by Congress on March 13 finally generated active recruitment of blacks as Confederate combat soldiers. Several companies of blacks with white officers were raised in Richmond in early April 1865. Thus a great irony was evident in the final days of the Confederacy; its leaders adopted the very measure that had been unthinkable only months earlier.[19]

Of course, it was far too late. Cleburne was dead, and so too was his moral courage. Perhaps it was poetic justice that Jefferson Davis at the very end proclaimed that he was endeavoring "without much progress to advance the raising of negro troops." Passage of the laws allowing such "had taken too long," and if only Congress had acted earlier, he complained, Lee and the other major commanders might have had thousands more men to fight off the Yankees.

"If the Confederacy falls," Davis mused, "there should be written on its tombstone, 'Died of a theory.' "[20]

XXVI

COPING AMID THE SHADOWS

It was an occasion that had long been pondered. The war was coming to an end, and to those who had fought the many hard battles it was a godsend. Even the earth seemed to rejoice in the spring of 1865; the blossoming flowers foretold a new uplifting mood and an end to the winter of darkness and despair. To Private Daniel C. Dodge of the 26th Michigan Infantry, one of the last soldiers to become a casualty in the Civil War, the news that Lee had surrendered meant "the war will stop soon." He wondered what lay ahead as he walked about the hospital at City Point, Virginia, on April 14, 1865.

Wounded in the flurry of fighting at Farmville, Virginia, on April 7, Dodge had been fortunate. A week later he was "feeling first rate," even though his hospital ward seemed depressing and he "hate[d] to see so many of our boys with their hands and legs cut off." Dodge had plenty of time, and he began writing to a friend that day about his feelings: "It is pleasant here today. I went out this morning before sunrise and looked around. I could see the cherry trees in blossom. But when I looked in another direction I could see the graves of 14,000 of our boys laid low by the cursed Rebs." With peace imminent, Private Dodge thought of the costly effort and the courage it had taken: "God bless the wounded soldiers and the [nation's] reunion," he continued.

In the afterglow of victory, he especially thought now of "Old Abe," President Lincoln, who had paid a visit to the soldiers just before the last fight in which Private Dodge had been wounded. Dodge had listened to his eloquent words: "I saw him going into the field after we had taken Petersburg. He made a speech to the boys. [He said] he could not bring to life the noble boys that fell on the field, but he called on God to bless the living."

Lincoln had been right, Dodge thought; the living deserved to be honored and to enjoy peace. To Private Dodge it seemed fitting that the war was thus "played out" and he would likely be home before July 4.[1]

There was a deep irony in Dodge's words, for it was Friday, April 14, and like Private Dodge, Abraham Lincoln was at that same moment preparing for some relaxation from the rigors of a long war that was finally ending. That very night he would view the popular play *Our American Cousin* at Ford's Theatre.

The war was all but over, but there was yet another shot to be fired in anger.

The end of the Civil War didn't obviate the need for courage in deed and thought. In fact, perhaps a greater courage was required to face what seemed to be the bitter, never-ending aftereffects of the tragic war. Especially in the South, where all appeared to have been lost but one's own life—the cause, family members, property, financial well-being, and perhaps even home—the devastating ordeal of facing life from day to day without much progress was an excruciating hardship requiring steadfast courage of the soul. Instead of a collective endeavor in the army where sustenance, clothing, and essentials were typically provided, the war's aftermath involved an individual's own dilemma in acquiring the very means to live. Comfort was a standard that seemed unobtain-able to many. The quest to survive and provide adequate means for one's family was a grueling task in a war-torn land.

Popularly known as the era of Reconstruction, the immediate post-war years in the South involved travail and a meager existence that few could have imagined a few years earlier, when patriotic ideals seemed at stake. The enormous trauma of coping amid the war-ravaged land is in-herent in a September 1, 1865, letter from an aged Newnan, Georgia, farmer, Andrew J. Berry, to his son, who had left home and gone to New York to escape the prospect of imprisonment.

> *[We] are sorry to hear of your destitution, but the war has placed us all in the same condition, and the people—almost every man in the country—is ruined. Those that were wealthy are now the poorest of all men. This country is almost entirely without money. There has been nothing made [in produce] to bring money [in] for the last four years. Consequently, there is no money . . . and nothing to sell to bring money in the country. . . . We have had a drought of six weeks in July and August, which has ruined the crops. Scarcely will there be bread made to supply the country. The last wheat crop was a total failure. Not a bale of cotton has been made in all my knowledge for the past four years. . . .*
>
> *We have a Yankee garrison here [at Newnan] and [it] has been [here] ever since the war, which is the case in nearly all the towns in Georgia, particularly on railroads. The negroes in Georgia are all free, and are trying to live on freedom without work. You can scarcely hire them to work for money or anything else. There are about 600 of them loitering about Newnan stealing hogs, cattle, and everything else. All our negroes left us long since, except old Peter and Amy. Most of them left us during the war; the balance after Gen'l Lee's surrender. . . . When the Yankees had possession of Atlanta, just before Lee's surrender, I sold in Columbus [Georgia] a few of our negroes for Confederate money and lost every dollar when the money "went up." I have it now on hand, $25,000. As the war progressed our negroes became demoralized*

*and we could not make them work. Consequently we did not
make . . . anything for market except a little, and that we sold for
Confederate money, and [thus] lost it all, [even though] it is still
on hand.*

> *Our army was as destructive to us as the Yankee army, only
[they] did not burn [our] property as the Yankees did. . . . The
Yankee raid [before the war's end] took every mule on the
place. . . . The next loss was the failure of the wheat crop, and
lastly the almost failure of the corn crop this year. We are like
everybody else in this section, poor and without anything but land;
and that is worth nothing, scarcely. In fact, our farm is useless, and
I know not how we are to live in the future. All is gloom and
uncertainty. . . . Money is like angel's visits here. Everything I sold
for you or from your place, amounting to nearly $10,000, was in
Confederate currency, and is all lost—not worth one cent—and is
on hand. You can only count on your land, [but] that would bring
little at this time. In fact, it could not be sold at all. Therefore, I
know not what we are to do for a living. Everybody is lying on
their oars and doing nothing. Almost everybody in the country
considers and acknowledges themselves broke.*[2]

To another Southerner living in the New Orleans area, who had
avoided participating in the war but was experiencing great difficulty in
the aftermath, living amid a defeated culture was a devastating experience. Yet his spirit remained resolute. He informed a friend:

> *The war has completely ruined me. I still own a fine tract of land,
but unfortunately I owe more than it is worth. You will probably
be astonished that I haven't made any money . . . , [but] the water
came three feet deep on my highest land so that I lost the crop; and
'66 finds me without money. I was in New Orleans yesterday and
made arrangement with a man to work my place this year. He
furnishes the money; I furnish the land and mules, and we divide
the crop. I have a great fear of another overflow this year, but . . .
if we are not overflowed I will make something. I do not repine*

over what I have lost. I can see no good in grieving. "Let the dead
past bury its dead." I look into the future and feel confident that I
can support my family. I feel that I have a great deal to be
thankful for, and so long as God spares me, my wife, and children,
I can be happy in the affliction.[3]

To wallow in self-pity was alien to the mind-set of most Southerners, and a staunch heritage of rising above adversity ordained an intense
effort to overcome the ordeal. Call it courage or determination, Maria
Louisa Fleet was not going to allow the war to ruin her family's future.
Once a prosperous, even wealthy family that owned "Green Mount," a
three-thousand-acre Virginia plantation in King and Queen County,
the Fleets found that the war had brought severe change. The head
of the family, Dr. Benjamin Fleet, a country doctor, had unexpectedly
died just before the war's end of a streptococcal infection at age forty-
six. Maria Louisa was devastated by her husband's death, but she had a
large family of seven children, six of whom were still alive to care for.
Time and the distress of the immediate postwar days wouldn't allow a
respite. To Maria Louisa, at age forty-two, the pressures of life were un-
forgiving.

Their plantation had largely been ruined by soldiers on both sides
during the war years. In June 1864 Union General Phil Sheridan and his
cavalry troopers had camped on the Green Mount property for three
days prior to their Trevilian Raid, and Sheridan had made the Fleet home
his headquarters. Soldiers had ransacked the property of livestock and all
manner of valuables, even destroying the fences and driving off about
fifty slaves. Maria Louisa's pluck was well demonstrated when Sheridan,
while being serenaded on the veranda by a military band, asked her what
she'd like to hear. "Dixie" was her reply, and Sheridan had the band play
the tune, much to her amusement. Even after the Yankee columns left,
stragglers continued to harass the family, and Maria Louisa, who had
once professed concern for soldiers of either side, by now had an intense
hatred of the enemy. "My heart is hardened; if I were a man I would
never take a prisoner, but would consider it my duty to rid the world of
such monsters," she wrote following Sheridan's "visit."[4]

Thereafter, matters had only continued to worsen. Her teenaged son, Benny, on the eve of joining Mosby's command, had been killed during the Kilpatrick-Dahlgren Raid on Richmond when ambushed by a Yankee cavalry patrol. When her eldest son, Fred, a captain on Brigadier General Henry A. Wise's staff, returned home after Appomattox, he brought with him the only working animal on the farm, his faithful mare Alice. The barns and stables were empty, there were no workers to plant the weed-choked fields, and the large quantity of Confederate money and bonds the family had was worthless. Maria Louisa had attempted to borrow money on their plantation, but she sadly wrote: "I never thought I'd see the day when I'm unable to borrow $200 on 3,000 acres of land."

With no money to hire hands, she had to rely on Fred to farm the land just to provide food. As Fred later remarked, the situation was both quasi-ludicrous and devastating. He told the story of a friend who was a Southern cavalry officer during the war. "He came home to devastation and desolation, but got hold of a mule which he hitched to a plow as best he could. 'Proceed!' he shouted. Nothing happened. 'Advance!!!' Again nothing happened. Sinking to his knees, he said, 'Oh Lord, why wasn't I killed at Second Manassas?' "[5]

It was a godsend that a former slave, Joshua Gaines, and his wife, Millie, found their way back to the Fleet plantation bringing along a mule. Joshua and Fred planted corn and a garden, and the two families survived the winter. Said Joshua, "We all get along the best we kin."

Through it all, "Ma," Maria Louisa, kept the family's spirits up, refusing to accept despair. When Fred became depressed, she counseled, "I know the way is dim, but God will guide you through the tunnel to the light, with which you children can make your own way. I am determined that you shall be educated at any cost." Indeed, she managed to sell one of the local ferry sites the family had operated on the Rappahannock River, and paid for Fred's entry to the University of Virginia in the fall of 1865. When Fred, who at first sought to study medicine and become a doctor in his father's footsteps, determined instead to become a teacher, there were many anxious thoughts.

Yet Maria Louisa Fleet would have none of it. She told Fred, "What is the good of an education but to take you along this life wherever the path may lead. I expect you to be more courageous than to shrink from the battle of life after going through the war as honorably as you did." As for her own philosophy, she told her son, "You need never expect that I will not have trouble—it is the lot of man[kind]. Rather, pray for me that I will have strength equal to my day and task."[6]

To combat the prospect of endless poverty at home, Maria Louisa arranged in early 1866 to sharecrop her land with thirteen men in planting corn. As Fred reminded her in a letter, "You can do anything with the energy you show," and now that the war was over, "you don't have to fear that at any moment it [property] might be taken from you." "The people about here are getting poorer and poorer," she had told Fred a few years after the war, "and I hope you will never think of coming back here to live—or starve."[7]

Fortunately, there was always hope. "These times can't last always" became words of encouragement from her sons, and Maria Louisa bore up under the many burdens of home and family. "Into each life 'some rain must fall,'" she proclaimed to another son. "But what would we have without rain!" Maria Louisa humorously continued. Her attitude was as game as her practicality. The sharecropping effort proved favorable by 1871, and Maria Louisa began to feel "we are exceedingly fortunate" considering the less-successful fate of so many of her neighbors.[8]

Fred and the other children began to prosper. Marriages and grandchildren eased the mental burden, and the pride of her life, Fred, after his college graduation in 1867 became a teacher at a local academy, then moved to Missouri in 1868 as a professor. From his work with the University of Missouri, to his organization of a military academy at Mexico, Missouri, Fred Fleet reflected the confidence his mother had in him. When he died in 1911, it followed a distinguished and successful career as an educator, and a forty-year marriage that produced eight children.

At home, Maria Louisa Fleet ran the Green Mount Home School for Young Ladies from 1878 to 1890. When she died from pneumonia in January 1900, her last sentiments, spoken with the conviction and dogged courage that had always graced her life of hardship, proclaimed an ultimate understanding: "Love one another and help each other all you can." It was truly a message for everyone, for all ages.[9]

Maria Louisa Fleet well knew that love reflects perhaps an ultimate courage.

XXVII

MATTERS OF ENLIGHTENMENT

Why is the American Civil War so important? Aside from deciding the momentous issues of secession, at what level governmental power rested, and the abolition of slavery, in large measure it resulted in altered perspectives about our lives. Our long-standing naïveté in terms of life's potential had given way by 1865 to a new, more sophisticated and informed thinking. The value of life was more pronounced. Thousands upon thousands of dead American youths had altered the mind-set of the nation. The world had greatly changed amid the grief of it all, and it was the precursor of a better way. The ongoing industrial and educational revolutions ensured an enlightened path for the masses, while the war's dire consequences had refocused awareness of life's realities.

The 1861–65 warfare's school of hard knocks had conveyed far more than just experience under fire. It produced a perspective that set the tone for modern America in ordeals confronted and understood. At the root of the matter was a form of revised thinking, of better equating the conception with the reality. What was once utopian or ideal was now largely considered in more practical terms. In the past, physical courage had been regarded as a fundamental means of success in war as in life. A less-sophisticated rationale had held sway, producing an attitude of "Where there is a will, there is a way." Yet, instead of blood, sweat, and toil achieving a given result, the efficacy of raw physical endeavor now tottered precariously on wisdom in the use of information and technology. It was more than ever a thinking man's world. The use of myriad resources and complex means had led to a paradigm shift in reasoning. How to do it was now as significant as the task itself.

In combat, the ability to win on a battlefield was far more complex than physically confronting the enemy with superior bravery and manpower. One had to understand the new essential technical components and assess the merits and liabilities of a tactical situation in terms of employing the proper methods. This meant relying more on technology than on physical prowess to achieve success.

This was an alien concept in 1861. Combat had always been personal, close and up front. Disciplined valor had provided the means and method of victory. Now there were new technologies that refined killing to such an extent that reason, rather than physical effort, was often the key. The battlefield was a far more dangerous place. The means had altered the methods, and fighting smart meant coping amid all factors. Physical courage just wasn't enough. The perspectives of a combat commander were never more crucial. Success revolved around the use of common sense and intelligent reason more than textbook doctrine.

Certainly, the validation of this concept was a painful ordeal. There were many who never learned, or saw only a distorted picture. At the point of confrontation of diametrically opposed methods and rationales was moral courage. One might know what was right based upon one's experience and reasoning, but disobeying orders or evading long-established protocols involved great personal risk. Strong moral courage was often contrary to the old methods of conducting combat.

Such mental courage was comparatively rare in the early war years. As experience and specific knowledge became more prevalent, so too did an awareness of the dire consequences of not doing the right thing. Tactical expertise was essential in combat, and the courage to implement such in the face of outmoded traditional methods was critical. One's survival increasingly depended upon it. Matters often came down to how much moral courage would be used in conducting the war at the grassroots level. Courage on the Civil War battlefield and elsewhere thus reflects a fascinating story in the evolution of man's thinking.

Its revelations are as old as time itself, yet as new as the next second.

XXVIII

THE ROLE OF COURAGE TODAY

Mankind's ability to reason based upon education, logic, common sense, and experience is foremost in the management of the future so far as the quality of our existence is concerned.

Thus the role of courage. Change is involved in the progress of any society, and it often takes courage to enact fundamental change, which is typically sought for the purpose of our mutual betterment. Yet courage is ambiguous; it can enable evil. That change or courage does not always involve progress or a better way is apparent in the current terrorist threat to civil society. A suicide bomber may act in an ostensibly courageous manner by sacrificing his life for a cause; but the effect is usually chaos. That chaos and embitterment over the loss of innocent bystanders will promote a reasoned solution is contrary to both logic and practical experience. History teaches us that there is a fine line between stupidity and courage. What is proper or wise in any circumstance is a matter of knowledge and reason.

A basic premise of human existence—to live and let live (love and respect one another)—is self-evident in our ideal actions. This principle tells us to act with courage and even independence in our convictions, yet to be aware of the full spectrum of the rights of others.

The terrorist threat of our current era attempts to alter the behavior and moral character of individuals or a nation by random acts of violence. Inherently these acts are byproducts of desperation, which breeds extremity in actions and conduct. Some individuals perceive a need to resort to desperate conduct because existing circumstances seemingly cannot be addressed effectively by conventional means. The vicious circle of cause and effect is thus tied to perspective.

Therefore, a society constantly needs the courage to resist lawless violence. The ascendancy of the United States in world history is predicated on the fullest utilization to date of human talent for the purpose of both self-interest and national interest. Resolute courage is perhaps the defining quality of the American people. However, as surely as we have succeeded in the past, there is no guarantee for the future, as is evident by the fates of other once dominant civilizations.

In the common interest, can mankind perceive and do that which will be best both now and for future generations? The answer is obscured at present. But at the fulcrum of present and future issues is the utilization of courage in thought and deed. Do we have the right stuff, or are we to slide down the slippery slope of dissension, driven by fear and despair? God alone knows, but the echo of our forefathers' voices sounds a profound call to act with courage in both thought and deed.

THE MEANING OF PERSONAL COURAGE

That gritty, time-worn adage—"Have courage, my son"—is an all too familiar admonition that millions have offered their offspring as a means of coping with adversity from time immemorial. Bravery, be it on the field of battle or in a more mundane setting—perhaps that first speech in front of your classmates, or facing that intimidating Little League pitcher with the wicked fastball—plays out as a matter of self-control. Fear of physical distress or personal embarrassment must be coped with. Indeed, how we react to the prospect of injury, either physical or emotional, is a stimulus for self-appraisal and hence how we feel about ourselves.

If often the key to coping well is a deeper understanding of oneself, it is the awareness that others struggle with similar choices and temptations that helps provide insight and thus valuable perspective. The personal risks or rewards may be self-evident within any given crisis, but why do some seem manageable, while other circumstances might produce extreme anxiety and loss of self-control?

If the answers vary from person to person, there appears to be a common perspective and rationale to consider in attempting to resolve these issues in a practical manner. It is through experience (knowledge) that we cope the best. Awareness of what to expect tends to promote solutions of how to cope. That we know what to expect is sometimes a matter of using well the means at hand to investigate and understand. Mastering one's own life often translates into a willingness to study, observe, and learn from others' experiences.

Indeed, history, the reservoir of human experience, is crucial in the promulgation of knowledge. Circumstances do, in fact, change; but not the human decision-making equation. A crisis in 1861, or 1492, or 2007, involved similar elements of human choices: to act on a variety of factors that included emotion, responsibility, advice, and logic or reason. The facts of life involve consequences good or bad, and the history of mankind is rife with lessons to ponder and analyze. Yet, we too often overlook the central theme.

Simply stated, history tells us to do that which we truly believe is right within the context of nonwarped moral values. It is a valid lesson from the past. What is right is a function of properly understanding all the circumstances. Yet no man has all knowledge possible, even in any given discipline. Thus we make mistakes. Our mistakes, however, are generally not immutable, except perhaps in a life-and-death situation. That is why we have so much to gain from better understanding our history. Remembering those crucial decisions involving courage that our forefathers faced in an era of extreme personal danger and risk is both an object lesson and an inspiration.

The American Civil War is distant in time, yet as immediate as the next confrontation with adversity or an ordeal. How our ancestors reacted is how many of us would have reacted. Those life-and-death decisions are of consequence in our existence if we utilize them to better understand the full realm of life. Those in the future will study our lives and look for meaning. As we peer into the past, they will likewise ponder our efforts and accomplishments. To say they or we lived with courage in thought and deed will be perhaps the greatest compliment any generation might achieve.

So it is with our nation's legacy as epitomized by the last words of our very anthem: "and the home of the brave!"

Yet the essential question remains, for today and tomorrow: How long will that legacy continue?

Notes

PART ONE

I. To Obey Orders or Not

1. Sergeant Eugene A. "Casey" McWayne, Company E, 127th Illinois Infantry, letters August 8, 11, 1864; Sergeant Andrew McCornack, Company I, 127th Illinois Infantry, letter August 19, 1864, Wiley Sword Collection, Suwannee, Ga.;
   U.S. War Department, *War of the Rebellion: A Compiliation of the Official Records
   of the Union and Confederate Armies*, 128 vols., 1891–1902, ser. 1, vol. 38, part
   3, 204 (hereafter cited as *O.R.*).

II. The Reason Why

1. Lieutenant Edgar N. Wilcox, 18th U.S. Infantry, diary 1863, entry August 16,
   1863, Wiley Sword Collection.
2. Private Samuel W. Wolcott, Company F, 7th Connecticut Infantry, letter, November 19, 1863; Adjutant General's Office, *Record of Service of Connecticut
   Men in the Army and Navy of the United States During the War of Rebellion* (Hartford, Ct., 1889), 291.
3. Private Samuel W. Wolcott, 7th Connecticut Infantry, letter June 12, 1864, Wiley Sword Collection.

4. Private Horace B. Ensworth, Company B, 81st New York Infantry, letter April 20, 1862, Wiley Sword Collection.

5. Private Horace B. Ensworth, Company B, 81st New York Infantry, letter December 1, 1864, Wiley Sword Collection.

6. Private Winfield S. Waterhouse, Company I, 17th Maine Infantry, letter November 14, 1862, eBay no. 2160941705, February 27, 2003.

7. Private Isaac B. Jones, 3rd Battalion, 18th U.S. Infantry, letter July 10, 1862, Wiley Sword Collection.

III. *"To Win Glory Enough"*

1. Captain David W. Norton, Company E, 42nd Illinois Infantry, letter September 30, 1861, Wiley Sword Collection.

2. Captain David W. Norton, Company E, 42nd Illinois Infantry, letters November 1, 1861, December 2, 1861, Wiley Sword Collection.

3. Captain David W. Norton, Company E, 42nd Illinois Infantry, letter December 2, 1861, Wiley Sword Collection.

4. Captain David W. Norton, Company E, 42nd Illinois Infantry, letter September 24, 1862, Wiley Sword Collection.

5. Captain David W. Norton, Company E, 42nd Illinois Infantry, letter November 12, 1862, Wiley Sword Collection.

6. Captain David W. Norton, assistant inspector general (a.i.g), letter November 19, 1862, journal transcript (1894), Wiley Sword Collection.

7. Captain David W. Norton, a.i.g., letter January 13, 1863, journal transcript (1894), Wiley Sword Collection.

8. Captain David W. Norton, Company E, 42nd Illinois Infantry, letter November 19, 1862, journal transcript (1894), Wiley Sword Collection.

9. Captain David W. Norton, a.i.g., letter June 24, 1863, Wiley Sword Collection.

10. Captain David W. Norton, a.i.g., letter May 10, 1863, journal transcript (1894), Wiley Sword Collection.

11. Major David W. Norton, a.i.g., letters November 21, 23, 1863, January 24, 1864, journal transcript (1894), Wiley Sword Collection.

12. Major David W. Norton, a.i.g., letters November 21, 23, 1863, January 24, 1864, March 10, 1864, journal transcript (1894), Wiley Sword Collection.

13. Major David W. Norton, a.i.g., letter May 20, 1864, journal transcript (1894), Wiley Sword Collection.

14. *O.R.* 1-38-1-806, 819.

15. Ibid.; Major David W. Norton, a.i.g., letter March 10, 1864, journal transcript (1894), Wiley Sword Collection.
16. Archive of Major David W. Norton, including personal army papers, Wiley Sword Collection.
17. Captain James A. Sexton, "The Observations and Experiences of a Captain of Infantry at the Battle of Franklin, November 30, 1864," *Military Essays (MOLLUS*, Illinois Commandery) (Chicago, 1907), 4:483; Private James Perry Campbell, Company D, 79th Illinois Infantry, letter October 17, 1863, Wiley Sword Collection.
18. Private James Perry Campbell, Company D, 79th Illinois Infantry, letter October 17, 1863, Wiley Sword Collection.

IV. The Face of Courage

1. [*Memorial of*] *Adjutant Stearns* [First Lieutenant Frazar A. Stearns, 21st Mass. Infantry], [by his father, W. A. Stearns] (H.O. Houghton, 1862), 64, 118.
2. Ibid., 154–55.
3. Ibid., 92.
4. Ibid., 94–95.
5. Ibid., 101, 153–54.
6. Ibid., 107–8.
7. Ibid., 154–55.
8. Amanda Ripley, "How to Get Out Alive," *Time,* May 2, 2005, 59–62.
9. Lord Moran, *The Anatomy of Courage* (1945; repr. Garden City Park, N. Y.: Avery Publishing, 1987), 3ff.
10. Ibid.
11. Ibid., 170–72.
12. Private George W. Davis, Company E, 15th Massachusetts Infantry, letter September 28, 1862, Wiley Sword Collection; Earl J. Hess, *The Union Soldier in Battle: Enduring the Ordeal of Combat* (Lawrence: University Press of Kansas, 1997), 113–17.
13. Captain Fred E. Ranger, Company F, 22nd New York Infantry, letter December 17, 1862, Wiley Sword Collection.
14. Private Emmet M. Irwin, Company C, 82nd New York Infantry, letters December 15 and 30, 1862, Wiley Sword Collection.
15. Private Robert Nevill, Company E, 103rd Ohio Infantry, letter June 1, 1864, Wiley Sword Collection.

V. *Two Wars in Concept*

1. Hess, *The Union Soldier in Battle,* 74–82.
2. Byron R. Abernethy, ed., *Private Elisha Stockwell, Jr., Sees the Civil War* (Norman: University of Oklahoma Press, 1958), 8ff.
3. Private James P. Campbell, Company D, 79th Illinois Infantry, letter October 17, 1863, Wiley Sword Collection.
4. See Gerald Linderman, *Embattled Courage: The Experience of Combat in the American Civil War* (New York: Free Press, 1987), 135–39.
5. Wiley Sword, *Southern Invincibility: A History of the Confederate Heart* (New York: St. Martin's Press, 1999), 201–11.
6. Quoted in Richard A. Baumgartner and Larry E. Strayer, eds., *Echoes of Battle: The Atlanta Campaign* (Huntington, W. Va.: Blue Acorn Press, 1991), 153.
7. Ibid.
8. Ibid.
9. *O.R.* 1-38-5-792.

VI. *Ordeal at Atlanta*

1. Military service records, Frank S. Curtiss, F. & S., 127th Illinois Infantry, National Archives, Washington, D.C.; Sergeant Eugene A. McWayne, letter August 11, 1864.
2. Sergeant Andrew McCornack, letter August 10, 1864.
3. Frank S. Curtiss, military service records.
4. Ibid.
5. Albert Castel, *Tom Taylor's Civil War* (Lawrence: University Press of Kansas, 2000), 161–63.
6. *O.R.* 1-38-3-198, 236.
7. Frank S. Curtiss, military service records; Sergeant Eugene A. McWayne, letter March 29, 1865.

VII. *Pat Cleburne, a Man Who Understood*

1. For a general reference on Cleburne's background see Howell Purdue and Elizabeth Purdue, *Pat Cleburne, Confederate General* (Hillsboro, Tex.: Hill Junior College Press, 1973).

2. Ibid., 23ff.

3. Ibid., 86–87, 96.

4. Ibid., 106ff., 119; Wiley Sword, *Shiloh: Bloody April* (1974; repr. Dayton: Morningside Press, 2001), 192ff.; also for general reference, Sword, *Southern Invincibility,* 261–63; Wiley Sword, *Embrace an Angry Wind: The Confederacy's Last Hurrah; Spring Hill, Franklin, and Nashville* (New York: HarperCollins, 1992).

5. Purdue and Purdue, 120.

6. Ibid., 186–87.

7. Sword, *Embrace an Angry Wind,* 42–44.

8. Purdue and Purdue, 147ff.

9. Ibid., 148; Captain Henry Haymond, 18th U.S. Infantry, letter January 7, 1863, Charles S. Peace Collection, Navarro College, Corsicana, Texas.

10. Purdue and Purdue, 182–83.

11. Ibid., 203ff.; see also Sword, *Mountains Touched with Fire.*

12. Sword, *Embrace an Angry Wind,* 40.

13. Purdue and Purdue, 270.

14. Ibid., 67.

15. Ibid., 348.

16. Sword, *Embrace an Angry Wind,* 179–180.

17. Ibid., 180ff., 187, 218–19, 223–24, 263–64, 266.

VIII. What Do You Say When You Know You're About to Die?

1. Newspaper clipping: "Col. Broadhead's Last Letter," n.d., n.p., ca. 1862; *O.R.* 1-12-2-737, 747; see also Broadhead's biography, *Appleton's Encyclopedia,* 2001, Internet edition.

2. Brown University, *Alumni Quarterly,* November 1990, 38–42; *O.R.* 1-2-396, 400; U.S. House of Representatives, 37th Congress, 2nd Session, 1861–62, "Barbarities of the Rebels at Manassas."

3. Dallas T. Herndon, "Letters of David O. Dodd, with Biographical Sketch" (pamphlet), n.d., n.p., [ca. 1930]; anon., *The True Story of David Owen Dodd,* Memorial Chapter no. 48 (Little Rock, Ark.: United Daughters of the Confederacy, 1929).

4. William S. Moore, Confederate soldier, letter July 23, 1863 (copy dated June 19, 1939), Wiley Sword Collection.

5. William Brown Jr., 7th Illinois Infantry, letter October 8, 1862 (dictated to George M. Harrison), collection of Paul Larkin, North Falmouth, Mass.

PART TWO

IX. *Extraordinary Bravery, a Special Virtue*

1. Colonel Charles G. Harker, U.S. Volunteers, letter October 1, 1863, Wiley Sword Collection.

2. Richard A. Baumgartner, *Yankee Tigers II: Civil War Field Correspondence from the Tiger Regiment of Ohio* (Huntington, W. Va.: Blue Acorn Press, 2004), 110–11, 150, 152; Baumgartner and Strayer, *Echoes of Battle,* 47.

3. *O.R.* 1-38-5-91.

4. *Webb and His Brigade at the Angle Gettysburg, in Memoriam, Alexander Stewart Webb, 1835–1911* (Albany, N.Y.: n.p., 1916), 12, 14, 94, 95 (hereafter cited as *Webb at the Angle*).

5. Alexander S. Webb to wife, June 24, 1863, Yale University Library, New Haven, Ct.; Alexander S. Webb to father, June 21, 1863 (hereafter cited as Webb Papers).

6. Webb to wife, June 17, 1863, Webb Papers; *O.R.* 1-27-1-429; Joseph R. C. Ward, *History of the 106th Regiment Pennsylvania Volunteers* (Philadelphia: F. McManus, Jr., 1906), 178–188; *Webb at the Angle,* 81.

7. Ward, *106th Pennsylvania,* 180–88.

8. George R. Stewart, *Pickett's Charge: A Microhistory of the Final Attack at Gettysburg, July 3, 1863* (Boston: Houghton Mifflin, 1959), 192.

9. *O.R.* 1-17-1-427; *Webb at the Angle,* 82, 89.

10. Stewart, *Pickett's Charge,* 114, 115, 127; John Gibbon, *Personal Recollections of the Civil War* (New York: G. I. Putnam's Sons, 1928), 146–47; Webb to father, July 17, 1863, Webb Papers; David L. Ladd and Audrey J. Ladd, *The Batchelder Papers: Gettysburg in Their Own Words,* 3 vols. (Dayton: Morningside Press, 1994–95), 1:18; *Webb at the Angle,* 89.

11. Webb to wife, July 27, 1863, Webb Papers.

12. Stewart, *Pickett's Charge,* 172–82; Webb to wife, July 5, 1863, August 3, 1863, Webb Papers.

13. Ward, *106th Pennsylvania,* 199; *O.R.* 1-27-1-427–429; Stewart, *Pickett's Charge,* 167.

14. Anonymous, "The Pinch of the Fight at Gettysburg," soldier's letter dated July 23, 1863, *Cincinnati Daily Commercial,* August 11, 1863; Stewart, *Pickett's Charge,* 200–202.

15. Stewart, *Pickett's Charge,* 214; Charles S. Wainwright, *A Diary of Battle: The Personal Journals of Col. Charles S. Wainwright, 1861–1865* (New York: Harcourt, Brace & World, 1962), 214; Webb to father, July 17, 1863, Webb Papers.

16. Stewart, *Pickett's Charge*, 216; "Pinch of the Fight"; Webb to father, July 17, 1863, Webb Papers.

17. Webb to wife, July 5, 1863, Webb Papers; Ladd and Ladd, *Batchelder Papers*, 1:18.

18. Webb to wife, July 27, 1863, Webb to father, July 17, 1863, Webb Papers; Stewart, *Pickett's Charge*, 218.

19. Webb to father, July 17, 1863, Webb to wife, July 5, 1863, Webb Papers.

20. Webb to father, July 17, 1863, Webb Papers; Stewart, *Pickett's Charge*, 219–22.

21. "Pinch of the Fight"; *O.R.* 1-27-428, 439; Webb to father, July 17, 1863, Webb Papers; Frank Aretas Haskell, *The Battle of Gettysburg* (Madison: Wisconsin History Commission, 1908), 129–30.

22. "Pinch of the Fight"; Stewart, *Pickett's Charge*, 244; *O.R.* 1-27-1-353, 428; Webb to wife, July 5, 17, 1863, Webb Papers.

23. Webb to wife, July 5, 17, 1863, Webb Papers.

24. Webb to father, July 17, 1863, Webb to wife, July 5, 21, August 8, 1863, Webb Papers.

25. Webb to father, July 17, 21, 1863, Webb Papers.

26. Webb to father, June 14, 1864, Webb to wife, June 24, 1863, Webb Papers; *Webb at the Angle*, 104–5; Walter F. Bever and Oscar F. Keydel, *Deeds of Valor: How America's Heroes Won the Medal of Honor*, 2 vols. (Detroit: Perrien Keydel Co., 1901), 1:224–25.

27. Norton Galloway, "Hand to Hand Fighting at Spotsylvania," in Robert Underwood and Clarence C. Buel, eds., *Battles and Leaders of the Civil War*, 4 vols. (New York: Century Company, 1887–88), 4:170–75; Surgeon George T. Stevens, 77th New York Infantry, letter August 4, 1863, Wiley Sword Collection.

X. *"The Sun Shines Brightly; I See It for the Last Time"*

1. Scott Rye, *Men and Ships of the Civil War* (Stamford, Ct.: Longmeadow Press, 1995), 197–205; *Richmond Examiner*, March 1, 1865, article on the execution of Beall; Isaac Markens, *President Lincoln and the Case of John Yates Beall* (New York, 1911); John Ely Briggs, ed., *Palimpsest*, vol. 4, no. 2 (February 1923); Confederate States Navy Research Center, Mobile, Ala., Internet copy of the *Southern Historical Society Papers*, vol. 32 (1904), 99ff.

2. Ralph J. Roske and Charles Van Doren, *Lincoln's Commando: The Biography of Commander William B. Cushing* (1957; repr. Bluejacket Books, 1995).

XI. "Rally 'Roun de Flag, Boys"

1. *O.R.* 1-30-4-482, 483; *O.R.* 1-45-1-698; see also Tennessee Gen. Web Project, Tennesseans in the Civil War, 13th U.S. Colored Infantry Regiment, www.TNGenWeb.org.
2. *O.R.* 1-39-2-460; *O.R.* 1-45-1-542ff.
3. *O.R.* 1-39-2-460; O.R. 1-45-1-542ff.
4. *O.R.* 1-45-1-542ff., 548ff.
5. *O.R.* 1-45-1-288ff., 542ff., 548ff.
6. *O.R.* 1-45-1-705.
7. *O.R.* 1-45-1-543–44, 548–49, 705ff.
8. G. W. Lewis, *The Campaigns of the 124th Ohio Volunteer Infantry* (Akron: The Werner Co., 1894), 209–10; Assistant Surgeon Joseph B. Griswold, letter December 29, 1864, Bentley Historical Library, University of Michigan, Ann Arbor.
9. Sword, *Southern Invincibility,* 15–18, 30–31, 144, 356–57.

XII. A Woman's Ordeal: Coping on the Home Front

1. Personal military service and pension records, William H. Morse, Company C, 3rd Michigan Volunteer Infantry, National Archives, Washington, D.C.; Private William H. Morse, Company C, 3rd Michigan Infantry, letters July 28, November 18, 1861, to wife; Lucy Morse, letters to husband, August 7, 1861, June 12, 13, 1862, Wiley Sword Collection.
2. Personal military service and pension records, Captain Job H. Aldrich, Company G, 17th U.S. Colored Troops, National Archives, Washington, D.C.; Colonel William R. Shafter, 17th U.S. Colored Troops, letter December 19, 1864; letter fragment, Ann Shafter Aldrich, n.d., Wiley Sword Collection; *O.R.* 1-45-1-538–539; Mrs. William R. "Hattie" Shafter, letter December 20, 1864, collection no. 838, Library of Congress, Washington, D.C.

XIII. Of Agony Extended and Endured

1. Sergeant Thomas Hart Benton, Company B, 19th Indiana Infantry, letters January 25, July 18, 1862, Wiley Sword Collection.
2. Ibid., letters March 1, July 2, 1862.

3. Ibid., letter August 14, 1862.

4. William T. Venner, *Hoosier's Honor: The Iron Brigade's 19th Indiana Regiment* (Shippensburg, Pa.: Burd Street Press, 1998), 63–79, 339–50.

5. Sergeant Thomas Hart Benton, Company B, 19th Indiana Infantry, letters January 25, July 2, 1862, Wiley Sword Collection.

6. R. O. Dormer to Thomas Benton Sr., letter September 2, 1862, Benton Archive, Wiley Sword Collection; Thomas Benton Sr. to wife, September 5, 1862, Wiley Sword Collection.

7. R. O. Dormer to Thomas Benton Sr., letter September 2, 1862, Benton Archive, Wiley Sword Collection.

8. Sergeant Thomas Hart Benton, letter to parents, September 11, 1862, Wiley Sword Collection.

9. Mrs. Roche, army nurse, to Thomas Benton Sr., October 20, 1862, Wiley Sword Collection.

XIV. Of Valor Less Than Glory

1. Captain James Vance Jr., Company K, 37th Virginia Infantry, letter to Kate Fulkerson, August 22, 1861, Wiley Sword Collection.

2. Corporal John S. B. Matson, Company I, 120th Ohio Infantry, letter to Friend Lyman, January 20, 1863, Wiley Sword Collection.

3. Sergeant Lewis Hanback, Company K, 27th Illinois Infantry, letter October 22, 1861, Wiley Sword Collection.

4. Lieutenant Joseph G. Younger, Company F, 53rd Virginia Infantry, letter August 18, 1864, Wiley Sword Collection.

5. Thomas L. Livermore, *Numbers and Losses in the Civil War in America, 1861–1865* (1900; repr. Bloomington, Ind., 1957), 63–64.

XV. The Workings of the Mind

1. John McCain and Marshall Salter, *Why Courage Matters: The Way to a Braver Life* (New York: Random House, 2004), 14.

2. Private William H. H. Winston, Company G, 11th Virginia Infantry, CSA, letter June 13, 1863, Wiley Sword Collection.

3. First Sergeant John S. Harris, Company E, 11th Massachusetts Infantry, letter January 17, 1862, Wiley Sword Collection.

4. Sergeant Chester C. Ellis, Company H, 80th Illinois Infantry, letter January 4, 1864, Wiley Sword Collection.

5. Private John S. Daniels, Company D, 2nd New Hampshire Infantry, letter August 13, 1863, Wiley Sword Collection.

6. Sergeant Russell T. Knight, Company C, 6th Iowa Infantry, letter September 5, 1862, Wiley Sword Collection.

7. Sergeant Martin V. Miller, Company E, 7th Illinois Infantry, letter April 19, 1862, Wiley Sword Collection.

8. First Sergeant Hiram Talbert Holt, Company I, 38th Alabama Infantry, letter June 16, 1862, Wiley Sword Collection.

9. Private Asbury Fouts, Company I, 9th Iowa Infantry, letter January 16, 1865, Wiley Sword Collection.

10. Sergeant George W. Tallman, Company E, 20th Iowa Infantry, letters September 30, December 29, 1862, Wiley Sword Collection.

11. Captain Alfred J. Sofield, Company A, 149th Pennsylvania Infantry, letters May 29, June 3, 1863, Wiley Sword Collection.

12. Lieutenant Lewis Bodine, Company A, 149th Pennsylvania Infantry, letter April 23, 1864; George Jones, n.p., November [1863], Wiley Sword Collection.

13. Captain Alfred J. Sofield, Company A, 149th Pennsylvania Infantry, personal military service and pension records, National Archives, Washington, D.C.

14. Private J. P. Graves, Swett's Battery Light Artillery, Army of Tennessee, CSA, letters April 25, June 1, September 7, November 5, n.d. [ca. March], 1864, Wiley Sword Collection.

15. Ex-major Frank S. Bond, former aide-de-camp, Rosecrans's staff, letter January 2, 1885, Wiley Sword Collection.

16. Sergeant Jesse Waltner, Company K, 49th Ohio Infantry, letter November 28, 1863, Wiley Sword Collection.

XVI. Our Consciousness Prevails

1. Private Isaac Miller, Company E, 93rd Ohio Infantry, letter December 2, 1864, Wiley Sword Collection.

2. Corporal John S. B. Matson, Company I, 120th Ohio Infantry, letter January 20, 1863, Wiley Sword Collection.

3. Corporal Amos Kibbee, 1st Battalion, 4th Illinois Cavalry, letter May 11, 1862, Wiley Sword Collection.

4. Assistant Surgeon Jesse W. Brock, 66th Ohio Infantry, letter August 4, 1862, Wiley Sword Collection.

5. Private Erastus Gregory, Company C, 114th New York Infantry, letter May 31 to June 13, 1863, Wiley Sword Collection.

6. Private Bernard Fuller, Company C, 36th Massachusetts Infantry, letter January 27, 1865, Wiley Sword Collection.

7. Colonel William R. Shafter, 17th USCT, letter December 19, 1864, Wiley Sword Collection.

8. Private Cecil Fogg, Company B, 36th Ohio Infantry, letter August 14, 1863, Wiley Sword Collection.

9. Private Barnard Fuller, Company C, 36th Massachusetts Infantry, letter January 27, 1865; Corporal Amos Kibbee, 1st Battalion, 4th Illinois Cavalry, letter May 11, 1862; Private Erastus Gregory, Company C, 114th New York Infantry, letter May 31 to June 13, 1863, Wiley Sword Collection.

10. Private Henry Webb, 50th Virginia Infantry, CSA, letters May 20, June 10, 1864, to Mrs. Jacob Smiley, Historical Collectible Auctions, Graham, N.C., Catalog, November 6, 2003, item 141; eBay auction item no. 2173137005, May 9, 2003.

XVII. Doing What Is Right

1. See Nancy Sherman, *Stoic Warriors: The Ancient Philosophy Behind the Military Mind* (New York: Oxford University Press, U.S.A., 2005).

2. Private John D. Compton, Company G, 105th Ohio Infantry, letter February 19, 1863, Wiley Sword Collection.

3. Private John Downes, Company E, 35th Iowa Infantry, letter April 23, 1863, Wiley Sword Collection.

4. Mark W. Johnson, *That Body of Brave Men: The U.S. Regular Infantry and the Civil War in the West* (Cambridge, Mass.: Da Capo Press, 2003), 133ff.; Lieutenant Benjamin H. Arthur, 1st U.S. Infantry, letter January 29, 1840, Wiley Sword Collection.

5. Wiley Sword, *Sharpshooter: Hiram Berdan, His Famous Sharpshooters, and Their Sharps Rifles* (Lincoln, R.I.: Andrew Mowbray, 1988), 71–76.

6. Lieutenant Anthony B. Burton, 5th Ohio Independent Battery, diary 1863, transcript in the Vicksburg National Military Park Library, Vicksburg, Miss., 46–47 (July 3, 1863).

7. Lieutenant Calvin Shedd, Company A, 7th New Hampshire Infantry, letter November 15, 1862, Wiley Sword Collection.

8. Colonel Emerson Opdycke, 125th Ohio Infantry, letter to wife, October 25, 1863, Ohio Historical Society, Columbus, Ohio.

9. For a comprehensive history of the Chattanooga campaign, including Grant's actions in the crisis, see Wiley Sword, *Mountains Touched with Fire: Chattanooga Besieged, 1863* (New York: St. Martin's Press, 1985).

XVIII. Cowardice, Courage's Cousin

1. Sergeant William R. Srofe, Company K, 48th Ohio Infantry, letter September 22, 1862, Wiley Sword Collection.
2. Wiley Sword, "Carried Under Two Flags," *North South Trader,* vol. 8, no. 2 (January–February 1981): 16ff.
3. William M. Anderson, *They Died to Make Men Free: A History of the 19th Michigan Infantry in the Civil War* (Barrien Springs, Mich.: Hardscrabble Books, 1980), 116.
4. Ibid., 133.
5. Amanda Ripley, "How to Get Out Alive," *Time,* May 2, 2005, 59–62.
6. Captain William C. Morgan, Company F, 3rd Maine Infantry, letter July 22, 1863, Wiley Sword Collection.
7. Ibid.
8. General reference: see Wiley Sword, "Capt. William C. Morgan, 3rd Maine Infantry, Hero or Scoundrel at the Peach Orchard," *Gettysburg Magazine,* no. 25 (2001): 75ff.

XIX. What Kind of Courage?

1. Sergeant Eugene McWayne, Company E, 127th Illinois Infantry, letter August 1, 1864, Wiley Sword Collection.
2. John Bell Hood, *Advance and Retreat: Personal Experience in the United States and Confederate Armies* (1889; repr. Bloomington: Indiana University Press, 1959), 290.
3. John Bell Hood, letter to Stephen D. Lee, January 9, 1866, S. D. Lee Papers, Southern Historical Collection, University of North Carolina, Chapel Hill, N.C.; Richard M. McMurry, *John Bell Hood and the War for Southern Independence* (Lexington: University Press of Kentucky, 1982), 196, 211; for general reference see Wiley Sword, *Embrace an Angry Wind: The Confederacy's Last Hurrah; Spring Hill, Franklin, and Nashville* (New York: HarperCollins, 1994).

PART THREE

XX. Decisions of Courage

1. Sergeant William J. Srofe, Company K, 48th Ohio Infantry, letters September 22, 1862, June 21, 1863, Wiley Sword Collection.

XXI. Shiloh: The Roll of the Dice

1. Purdue and Purdue, *Pat Cleburne, Confederate General,* 119.
2. Sword, *Shiloh: Bloody April,* 49ff.
3. Ibid., 63ff.
4. Ibid., 68ff., 82.
5. Ibid., 91.
6. Ibid., 85.
7. Ibid., 72, 83.
8. Ibid., 94ff.
9. Ibid., 96ff.
10. Telegrams (headquarters copies), General P. G. T. Beauregard to General A. S. Johnston, March 12, 1862, Wiley Sword Collection.
11. Sword, *Shiloh: Bloody April,* 92ff.
12. Ibid., 98ff.
13. Ibid., 99ff.
14. Ibid., 108ff.
15. Ibid., 113–14.
16. Ibid., 224ff.
17. Ibid., 107–8.
18. Ibid., 108.
19. Ibid., 413.
20. Ibid., 16ff.
21. Ibid., 17.
22. Ibid., 132.
23. Ibid., 134.
24. Ibid., 134ff, 214ff.
25. Ibid., 352ff.
26. Ibid., 369ff.

27. Ibid., 382.
28. Ibid., 347, 366ff.

XXII. *Robert E. Lee, a Man for All Ages*

1. Edwin B. Coddington, *The Gettysburg Campaign: A Study in Command* (New York: Charles Scribner's Sons, 1968), 526.
2. Clifford Dowdey and Lewis H. Manarin, eds., *The Wartime Papers of Robert E. Lee* (Boston: Little, Brown and Co., 1961), 504–9.
3. Ibid., 488.
4. Ibid.
5. Coddington, *The Gettysburg Campaign,* 170, 622; *O.R.* 1-27-2-316.
6. *O.R.* 1-27-2-308, 318.
7. Sword, *Southern Invincibility,* 175ff; *O.R.* 1-27-2-319.
8. *O.R.* 1-27-2-318.
9. Sword, *Southern Invincibility,* 175ff.
10. Ibid.; *O.R.* 1-27-2-308, 320, 359.
11. George R. Stewart, *Pickett's Charge,* 19–22.
12. *O.R.* 1-27-2-308, 321, 322.
13. Coddington, *The Gettysburg Campaign,* 526; *O.R.* 1-27-2-309.
14. Dowdey, *Wartime Papers of Robert E. Lee,* 540–44.
15. Ibid., 543, 551.
16. Ibid., 540, 544, 561, 589.

XXIII. *What Is Justified Caution?*

1. *O.R.* 1-45-2-15–18; see Sword, *Embrace an Angry Wind,* 277ff.
2. Sword, *Embrace an Angry Wind,* 76ff.
3. Ibid., 290ff.; *O.R.* 1-45-2-55, 70, 84, 96–98, 106, 114–16, 195.
4. *O.R.* 1-45-2-70, 84, 96, 104.
5. *O.R.* 1-45-2-114, 115.
6. Sword, *Embrace an Angry Wind,* 239ff.
7. *O.R.* 1-45-1-114, 115–18; *O.R.* 1-45-2-122.
8. *O.R.* 1-45-1-115; *O.R.* 1-45-2-115–17, 130, 143; Johnson and Buel, *Battles and Leaders,* 4:455.
9. James Harrison Wilson, *Under the Old Flag,* 2 vols. (Westport, Conn.: Greenwood Press, 1971): 2: 100–106.

10. Ibid., 2:93; *O.R.* 1-45-2-46, 141.

11. Wilson, *Under the Old Flag,* 2:94ff.; Horace Porter, *Campaigning with Grant* (New York: The Century Co., 1897), 348; David Homer Bates, *Lincoln in the Telegraph Office* (New York: The Century Co., 1907), 314–15.

12. Bates, *Lincoln in the Telegraph Office,* 314–15.

13. Sword, *Embrace an Angry Wind,* 344.

14. Bates, *Lincoln in the Telegraph Office,* 314–19; *O.R.* 1-45-2-180, 194–96, 210.

15. *O.R.* 1-45-2-227–30, 248, 370, 405.

XXIV. A Tale of Two Presidents

1. See Sword, *Mountains Touched with Fire,* general reference.

2. Ibid., 4ff.; William Lamers, *The Edge of Glory: A Biography of General William S. Rosecrans, U.S.A.* (New York: Harcourt, Brace & World, 1961), 301–6.

3. *O.R.* 1-30-1-198–219, 1051; Carl Sandburg, *Abraham Lincoln, the War Years,* 2 vols. (New York: Harcourt, Brace & Co., 1939), 2:433; Theodore Clarke Smith, *The Life and Letters of James Abram Garfield,* 2 vols. (New Haven: Yale University Press, 1925), 2:868ff.; Sword, *Mountains Touched with Fire,* 49ff.

4. *O.R.* 1-30-1-198–219; *O.R.* 1-30-4-404; Sword, *Mountains Touched with Fire,* 51ff.; Lamers, *The Edge of Glory,* 407.

5. Ulysses S. Grant, *Personal Memoirs of U.S. Grant,* 2 vols. (1885; repr., New York: DaCapo Press, Inc., 1982), 281–308; *O.R.* 1-30-4-404, 429; John Y. Simon, ed., *The Papers Of Ulysses S. Grant,* 9:281.

6. Larry Daniel, *Soldiering in the Army of Tennessee: A Portrait of Life in a Confederate Army* (Chapel Hill: University of North Carolina Press, 1991), 136; Sword, *Mountains Touched with Fire,* 29ff.

7. Sword, *Mountains Touched with Fire,* 20ff.; Peter Cozzens, *This Terrible Sound: The Battle of Chickamauga* (Urbana: University of Illinois Press, 1992), 368ff.; *O.R.* 1-30-1-635.

8. Sword, *Mountains Touched with Fire,* 29ff.

9. Ibid., 20ff.; Thomas Lawrence Connelly, *Autumn of Glory: The Army of Tennessee, 1862–1865* (Baton Rouge: Louisiana State University Press, 1971), 236.

10. Connelly, *Autumn of Glory,* 241–42; *O.R.* 1-30-4-735; William C. Davis, *Jefferson Davis: The Man and His Hour* (New York: HarperCollins, 1991), 516, 522.

11. Connelly, *Autumn of Glory,* 241–42; *O.R.* 1-30-4-735; William C. Davis, *Jefferson Davis,* 516, 522; Judith Lee Hallock, *Braxton Bragg and Confederate Defeat* (Tuscaloosa: University of Alabama Press, 1999), 2: 97.

12. John Allan Wyeth, *Life of Nathan Bedford Forrest* (1901; repr., Dayton: Morningside Press, 1988), 264–66.

13. *O.R.* 1-30-4-744; William C. Davis, *Jefferson Davis,* 522.

14. Sword, *Mountains Touched with Fire,* 34–35; William C. Davis, *Jefferson Davis,* 523, 526.

XXV. The Unthinkable

1. Gen. Patrick Cleburne's proposal is printed in its entirety in Purdue and Purdue, *Pat Cleburne, Confederate General,* 454–61. (See also *O.R.* 1-52-2-586ff.).

2. Ibid.

3. Ibid.

4. Ibid.

5. See Sword, *Southern Invincibility,* 242ff.

6. Private James Hammer, 21st Tennessee Cavalry, letter April 11, 1863, West Tennessee Historical Society, Memphis.

7. Purdue and Purdue, *Pat Cleburne, Confederate General,* 277, 278, 455.

8. Thomas L. Livermore, *Numbers and Losses in the Civil War in America* (1900; repr., Bloomington: Indiana University Press, 1957), 45, 47, 48.

9. Purdue and Purdue, *Pat Cleburne, Confederate General,* 454–61.

10. Sword, *Southern Invincibility,* 242ff.; Purdue and Purdue, *Pat Cleburne, Confederate General,* 267–78.

11. Mark M. Hull, "Concerning the Emancipation of the Slaves," in Mauriel Phillips Joslyn, ed., *A Meteor Shining Brightly: Essays on Maj. Gen. Patrick R. Cleburne* (Milledgeville, Ga.: Terrell House, 1997), 143–177.

12. Purdue and Purdue, *Pat Cleburne, Confederate General,* 272–73.

13. Ibid.

14. Ibid., 67; General Braxton Bragg to Marcus J. Wright, letter February 5, 1864, Marcus J. Wright Papers, Southern Historical Collection, University of North Carolina, Chapel Hill.

15. Purdue and Purdue, *Pat Cleburne, Confederate General,* 273.

16. Dunbar Rowland, ed., *Jefferson Davis, Constitutionalist: His Letters, Papers, and Speeches,* 6 volumes (Jackson, Miss.: Jackson Department of Archives, 1923); see letter of February 22, 1864, 5:198–201.

17. Purdue and Purdue, *Pat Cleburne, Confederate General,* 276; *O.R.* 4-3-1013.

18. Ibid.

19. Purdue and Purdue, *Pat Cleburne, Confederate General,* 276–77.

20. Jefferson Davis, *Rise and Fall of the Confederate Government* (1881; repr., New York: Thomas Yoseloff, 2 volumes, 1958), 1:518.

XXVI. Coping amid the Shadows

1. Private Daniel C. Dodge, 26th Michigan Infantry, letter April 14, 1865, Wiley Sword Collection.
2. Andrew J. Berry to Joel W. Berry, letter September 1, 1865, text published on eBay Internet auction, item no. 6550907629, August 9, 2005.
3. Unknown, letter fragment, n.d., n.p. [ca. 1866, New Orleans, La.], Wiley Sword Collection.
4. Betsy Fleet, ed., *Green Mount After the War: The Correspondence of Maria Louisa Wacker Fleet and Her Family, 1865–1900* (Charlottesville: University Press of Virginia, 1978), 10.
5. Ibid., 22.
6. Ibid., 19, 26.
7. Ibid., 19, 54.
8. Ibid., 22, 72.
9. Ibid., 63, 266; see also Betsy Fleet and John D. P. Fuller, eds., *Green Mount: A Virginia Plantation Family During the Civil War, Being the Journal of Benjamin Robert Fleet and Letters of His Family* (Charlottesville: University Press of Virginia, 1962).

Bibliography

MANUSCRIPT MATERIALS

Aldrich, Captain Job H., Company G, 17th U.S. Colored Troops. Military service and pension records. National Archives, Washington, D.C.

Aldrich, Mrs. Ann Shafter. Letter n.d. Wiley Sword Collection, Suwanee, Ga.

Arthur, Lieutenant Benjamin H., 1st U.S. Infantry. Letter January 29, 1840. Wiley Sword Collection, Suwanee, Ga.

Beauregard, P. G. T. Telegrams (headquarters copies) to General A. S. Johnston, March 12, 1862. Wiley Sword Collection, Suwanee, Ga.

Benton, Sergeant Thomas Hart, Company B, 19th Indiana Infantry. Letters 1861–1862. Wiley Sword Collection, Suwanee, Ga.

Berry, Andrew J., to Joel W. Berry. September 1, 1865. Text published eBay Internet auction, item 6550907629, August 9, 2005.

Bodine, Lieutenant Lewis, Company A, 149th Pennsylvania Infantry. Letter April 23, 1864. Wiley Sword Collection, Suwanee, Ga.

Bond, Frank S., former aide-de-camp Rosecrans's staff. Letter January 2, 1885. Wiley Sword Collection, Suwanee, Ga.

Bragg, Braxton. Letter to Marcus J. Wright, February 5, 1864. Marcus J. Wright Papers, Southern Historical Collection, University of North Carolina, Chapel Hill.

Brock, Assistant Surgeon Jesse W., 66th Ohio Infantry. Letter August 4, 1862. Wiley Sword Collection, Suwanee, Ga.

Brown, William, Jr., 7th Illinois Infantry. Letter October 8, 1862 (dictated to George M. Harrison). Collection of Paul Larkin, North Falmouth, Mass.

Burton, Lieutenant Anthony B., 5th Ohio Independent Battery. Diary 1863. Transcript in the Vicksburg National Military Park Library, Vicksburg, Miss.

Campbell, Private James Perry, Company D, 79th Illinois Infantry. Letter October 17, 1863. Wiley Sword Collection, Suwanee, Ga.

Compton, Private John D., Company G, 105th Ohio Infantry. Letter February 19, 1863. Wiley Sword Collection, Suwanee, Ga.

Curtiss, Frank S. Military service records, F. & S., 127th Illinois Infantry. National Archives, Washington, D.C.

Daniels, Private John S., Company D, 2nd New Hampshire Infantry. Letter August 13, 1863. Wiley Sword Collection, Suwanee, Ga.

Davis, Private George W., Company E, 15th Massachusetts Infantry. Letter September 28, 1862. Wiley Sword Collection, Suwanee, Ga.

Dodge, Private Daniel C., 26th Michigan Infantry. Letter April 14, 1865. Wiley Sword Collection, Suwanee, Ga.

Downes, Private John, Company E, 35th Iowa Infantry. Letter April 23, 1863. Wiley Sword Collection, Suwanee, Ga.

Ellis, Sergeant Chester C., Company H, 80th Illinois Infantry. Letter January 4, 1864. Wiley Sword Collection, Suwanee, Ga.

Ensworth, Private Horace B., Company B, 81st New York Infantry. Letters April 20, 1862, December 1, 1864. Wiley Sword Collection, Suwanee, Ga.

Fogg, Private Cecil, Company B, 36th Ohio Infantry. Letter August 14, 1863. Wiley Sword Collection, Suwanee, Ga.

Fouts, Private Asbury, Company I, 9th Iowa Infantry. Letter January 16, 1865. Wiley Sword Collection, Suwanee, Ga.

Fuller, Private Bernard, Company C, 36th Massachusetts Infantry. Letter January 27, 1865. Wiley Sword Collection, Suwanee, Ga.

Graves, Private J. P., Swett's Battery Light Artillery, Army of Tennessee, CSA. Letters April 25, June 1, September 7, November 5, n.d. [ca. March], 1864. Wiley Sword Collection, Suwanee, Ga.

Gregory, Private Erastus, Company C, 114th New York Infantry. Letter May 31 to June 13, 1863. Wiley Sword Collection, Suwanee, Ga.

Griswold, Assistant Surgeon Joseph B. Letter December 29, 1864. Bentley Historical Library, University of Michigan, Ann Arbor.

Hammer, Private James, 21st Tennessee Cavalry. Letter April 11, 1863. West Tennessee Historical Society, Memphis.

Hanback, Sergeant Lewis, Company K, 27th Illinois Infantry. Letter October 22, 1861. Wiley Sword Collection, Suwanee, Ga.

Harker, Colonel Charles G., U.S. Volunteers. Letter October 1, 1863. Wiley Sword Collection, Suwanee, Ga.

Harris, First Sergeant John S., Company E, 11th Massachusetts Infantry. Letter January 17, 1862. Wiley Sword Collection, Suwanee, Ga.

Haymond, Captain Henry, 18th U.S. Infantry. Letter January 7, 1863. Charles S. Peace Collection, Navarro College, Corsicana, Tex.

Holt, First Sergeant Hiram Talbert, Company I, 38th Alabama Infantry. Letter June 16, 1862. Wiley Sword Collection, Suwanee, Ga.

Hood, John Bell. Letter to Stephen D. Lee, January 9, 1866. S. D. Lee Papers, Southern Historical Collection, University of North Carolina, Chapel Hill.

Irwin, Private Emmet M. Irwin, Company C, 82nd New York Infantry. Letters December 15 and 30, 1862. Wiley Sword Collection, Suwanee, Ga.

Jones, George. n.p. Letter November [1863]. Wiley Sword Collection, Suwanee, Ga.

Jones, Private Isaac B. Jones, 3rd Battalion, 18th U.S. Infantry. Letter July 10, 1862. Wiley Sword Collection, Suwanee, Ga.

Kibbee, Corporal Amos, 1st Battalion, 4th Illinois Cavalry. Letter May 11, 1862. Wiley Sword Collection, Suwanee, Ga.

Knight, Russell T., Company C, 6th Iowa Infantry. Letter September 5, 1862. Wiley Sword Collection, Suwanee, Ga.

Matson, Corporal John S. B., Company I, 120th Ohio Infantry. Letter to Friend Lyman, January 20, 1863. Wiley Sword Collection, Suwanee, Ga.

McCornack, Sergeant Andrew, Company I, 127th Illinois Infantry. Letters 1862–1865. Wiley Sword Collection, Suwanee, Ga.

McWayne, Sergeant Eugene A. "Casey," Company E, 127th Illinois Infantry. Letters 1862–1865. Wiley Sword Collection, Suwanee, Ga.

Miller, Private Isaac, Company E, 93rd Ohio Infantry. Letter December 2, 1864. Wiley Sword Collection, Suwanee, Ga.

Miller, Sergeant Martin V., Company E, 7th Illinois Infantry. Letters April 5, 19, 1862. Wiley Sword Collection, Suwanee, Ga.

Moore, William S., Confederate soldier. Letter July 23, 1863 (copy dated June 19, 1939). Wiley Sword Collection, Suwanee, Ga.

Morgan, Captain William C., Company F, 3rd Maine Infantry. Letter July 22, 1863. Wiley Sword Collection, Suwanee, Ga.

Morse, Private William H., Company C, 3rd Michigan Volunteer Infantry. Letters July 28, November 18, 1861, to wife; Lucy Morse letters to husband, August 7, 1861, June 12, 13, 1862. Wiley Sword Collection, Suwanee, Ga.

———. Military service and pension records. National Archives, Washington, D.C.

Nevill, Robert, Company E, 103rd Ohio Infantry. Letter June 1, 1864. Wiley Sword Collection, Suwanee, Ga.

Norton, Captain David W., Company E, 42nd Illinois Infantry, assistant inspector general (a.i.g.) staff of Major General John M. Palmer. Original letters

1861–1864, and journal transcript of letters (1894). Wiley Sword Collection, Suwanee, Ga.

Opdycke, Colonel Emerson, 125th Ohio Infantry. Letter to wife, October 25, 1863. Ohio Historical Society, Columbus, Ohio.

Ranger, Captain Fred E., Company F, 22nd New York Infantry. Letter December 17, 1862. Wiley Sword Collection, Suwanee, Ga.

Shafter, Colonel William R., 17th U.S. Colored Troops. Letter December 19, 1864. Wiley Sword Collection, Suwanee, Ga.

Shafter, Mrs. William R. "Hattie" Shafter. Letter December 20, 1864. Collection no. 838, Library of Congress, Washington, D.C.

Shedd, Lieutenant Calvin, Company A, 7th New Hampshire Infantry. Letter November 15, 1862. Wiley Sword Collection, Suwanee, Ga.

Sofield, Captain Alfred J., Company A, 149th Pennsylvania Infantry. Letters May 29, June 3, 1863. Wiley Sword Collection, Suwanee, Ga.

———. Personal military service and pension records. National Archives, Washington, D.C.

Srofe, Sergeant William R., Company K, 48th Ohio Infantry. Letters September 22, 1862, June 21, 1863. Wiley Sword Collection, Suwanee, Ga.

Stevens, Surgeon George T., 77th New York Infantry. Letter August 4, 1863. Wiley Sword Collection, Suwanee, Ga.

Tallman, Sergeant George W., Company E, 20th Iowa Infantry. Letters September 30, December 29, 1862. Wiley Sword Collection, Suwanee, Ga.

Unknown. Letter fragment, n.d. [ca. 1866, New Orleans]. Wiley Sword Collection, Suwanee, Ga.

Vance, Captain James, Jr., Company K, 37th Virginia Infantry. Letter to Kate Fulkerson, August 22, 1861. Wiley Sword Collection, Suwanee, Ga.

Waltner, Sergeant Jesse, Company K, 49th Ohio Infantry. Letter November 28, 1863. Wiley Sword Collection, Suwanee, Ga.

Waterhouse, Private Winfield S., Company I, 17th Maine Infantry. Letter November 14, 1862. Text quoted in eBay no. 2160941705, February 27, 2003.

Webb, Major General Alexander S. Papers. Yale University Library, New Haven, Ct.

Webb, Private Henry, 50th Virginia Infantry, CSA. Letters to Mrs. Jacob Smiley, May 20, June 10, 1864. Historical Collectible Auctions, Graham, N.C., Catalog, November 6, 2003, item 141; eBay auction item no. 2173137005, May 9, 2003.

Wilcox, Lieutenant Edgar N., 18th U.S. Infantry. Diary 1863. Wiley Sword Collection, Suwanee, Ga.

Winston, Private William H. H., Company G, 11th Virginia Infantry. Letter June 13, 1863. Wiley Sword Collection, Suwanee, Ga.

Wolcott, Private Samuel W., Company F, 7th Connecticut Infantry. Letters, November 19, 1863, June 12, 1864. Wiley Sword Collection, Suwanee, Ga.

Younger, Lieutenant Joseph G., Company F, 53rd Virginia Infantry. Letter August 18, 1864. Wiley Sword Collection, Suwanee, Ga.

BOOKS AND OTHER PUBLISHED MATERIALS

Abernethy, Byron R., ed. *Private Elisha Stockwell, Jr., Sees the Civil War.* Norman: University of Oklahoma Press, 1958.

Anderson, William M. *They Died to Make Men Free: A History of the 19th Michigan Infantry in the Civil War.* Barrien Springs, Mich.: Hardscrabble Books, 1980.

Anonymous. "The Pinch of the Fight at Gettysburg." Soldier's letter dated July 23, 1863. *Cincinnati Daily Commercial,* August 11, 1863.

———. *The True Story of David Owen Dodd.* Memorial Chapter no. 48. Little Rock, Ark.: United Daughters of the Confederacy, 1929.

Bates, David Homer. *Lincoln in the Telegraph Office.* New York: Century Company, 1907.

Baumgartner, Richard A. *Yankee Tigers II: Civil War Field Correspondence from the Tiger Regiment of Ohio.* Huntington, W.Va.: Blue Acorn Press, 2004.

Baumgartner, Richard A., and Larry E. Strayer, eds. *Echoes of Battle: The Atlanta Campaign.* Huntington, W.Va.: Blue Acorn Press, 1991.

Bever, Walter F., and Oscar F. Keydel. *Deeds of Valor: How America's Heroes Won the Medal of Honor.* 2 vols. Detroit: The Perrien-Keydel Company, 1901.

Briggs, John Ely, ed. *Palimpsest,* vol. 4, no. 2 (February 1923).

Broadhead, Thornton F. Newspaper clipping: "Col. Broadhead's Last Letter," n.d., n.p., ca. 1862.

Brown University. *Alumni Quarterly,* November 1990.

Castel, Albert. *Tom Taylor's Civil War.* Lawrence: University Press of Kansas, 2000.

Coddington, Edwin B. *The Gettysburg Campaign: A Study in Command.* New York: Charles Scribner's Sons, 1968.

Confederate States Navy Research Center. Internet copy of the *Southern Historical Society Papers* 32 (1904). www.csnavy.org.

Connecticut Adjutant General's Office. *Record of Service of Connecticut Men in the Army and Navy of the United States During the War of Rebellion.* Hartford: State of Connecticut, 1889.

Connelly, Thomas Lawrence. *Autumn of Glory: The Army of Tennessee, 1862–1865.* Baton Rouge, La.: Louisiana State University Press, 1971.

Cozzens, Peter. *This Terrible Sound: The Battle of Chickamauga.* Urbana: University of Illinois Press, 1992.

Daniel, Larry. *Soldiering in the Army of Tennessee; A Portrait of Life in a Confederate Army.* Chapel Hill: University of North Carolina Press, 1991.

Davis, Jefferson. *Rise and Fall of the Confederate Government.* 2 vols. New York: D. Appleton & Co., 1881.

Davis, William C. *Jefferson Davis: The Man and His Hour.* New York: HarperCollins, 1991.

Dowdey, Clifford, and Lewis H. Manarin, eds. *The Wartime Papers of Robert E. Lee.* Boston: Little, Brown and Co., 1961.

Fleet, Betsy, ed. *Green Mount After the War: The Correspondence of Maria Louisa Wacker Fleet and Her Family, 1865–1900.* Charlottesville: University Press of Virginia, 1978.

Fleet, Betsy, and John D. P. Fuller, eds. *Green Mount: A Virginia Plantation Family During the Civil War, Being the Journal of Benjamin Robert Fleet and Letters of His Family.* Charlottesville: University Press of Virginia, 1962.

Gibbon, John. *Personal Recollections of the Civil War.* New York: G. I. Putnam's Sons, 1928 reprint, Dayton, Ohio: Morningside Press, 1988.

Grant, Ulysses S. *Personal Memoirs of U. S. Grant.* 2 vols. Charles Webster & Co., 1885.

Hallock, Judith Lee. *Braxton Bragg and Confederate Defeat.* Vol. 2. Tuscaloosa: University of Alabama Press, 1999.

Haskell, Frank Aretas. *The Battle of Gettysburg.* Madison: Wisconsin History Commission, 1908.

Herndon, Dallas T. "Letters of David O. Dodd, with Biographical Sketch" (pamphlet). n.d., n.p. [ca. 1930].

Hess, Earl J. *The Union Soldier in Battle: Enduring the Ordeal of Combat.* Lawrence: University Press of Kansas, 1997.

Hood, John Bell. *Advance and Retreat: Personal Experience in the United States and Confederate Armies.* 1889. Reprint: Bloomington: Indiana University Press, 1959.

Hull, Mark M. "Concerning the Emancipation of the Slaves." In *A Meteor Shining Brightly: Essays on Maj. Gen. Patrick R. Cleburne,* edited by Mauriel Phillips Joslyn, Milledgeville, Ga.: Terrell House, 1997, 143–177.

Johnson, Mark W. *That Body of Brave Men: The U.S. Regular Infantry and the Civil War in the West.* Cambridge, Mass.: Da Capo Press, 2003.

Ladd, David L., and Audrey J. Ladd. *The Batchelder Papers: Gettysburg in Their Own Words.* 3 vols. Dayton: Morningside Press, 1994–95.

Lamers, William. *The Edge of Glory: A Biography of General William S. Rosecrans, U.S.A.* New York: Harcourt, Brace & World, 1961.

Lewis, G. W. *The Campaigns of the 124th Ohio Volunteer Infantry.* Akron: The Werner Co., 1894.

Linderman, Gerald. *Embattled Courage: The Experience of Combat in the American Civil War.* New York: Free Press, 1987.

Livermore, Thomas L. *Numbers and Losses in the Civil War in America, 1861–1865.* 1900. Reprint: Bloomington: Indiana University Press, 1957.

Markens, Isaac. *President Lincoln and the Case of John Yates Beall.* New York, 1911.

McCain, John, and Marshall Salter. *Why Courage Matters: The Way to a Braver Life.* New York: Random House, 2004.

McMurry, Richard M. *John Bell Hood and the War for Southern Independence.* Lexington: University Press of Kentucky, 1982.

Moran, Lord. *The Anatomy of Courage.* 1945. Reprint: Garden City Park, N.Y.: Avery Publishing, 1987.

Porter, Horace. *Campaigning with Grant.* New York: The Century Co., 1897.

Purdue, Howell, and Elizabeth Purdue. *Pat Cleburne, Confederate General.* Hillsboro, Tex.: Hill Junior College Press, 1973.

Richmond [Va.] Examiner, Wednesday, March 1, 1865 (article on the execution of John Yates Beall).

Ripley, Amanda. "How to Get Out Alive." *Time,* May 2, 2005, 59–62.

Rowland, Dunbar, ed. *Jefferson Davis, Constitutionalist: His Letters, Papers, and Speeches.* 6 vols. Jackson, Miss.: Jackson Department of Archives, 1923.

Roske, Ralph J., and Charles Van Doren. *Lincoln's Commando: The Biography of Commander William B. Cushing.* New York: Harper Bros., 1957.

Rye, Scott. *Men and Ships of the Civil War.* Stamford, Ct.: Longmeadow Press, 1995.

Sandburg, Carl. *Abraham Lincoln, the War Years.* 2 vols. New York: Harcourt, Brace and Co., 1939.

Sexton, James A. "The Observations and Experiences of a Captain of Infantry at the Battle of Franklin, November 30, 1864." In *Military Essays (MOLLUS,* Illinois Commandery), Chicago, Illinois, vol. 4, 1907.

Sherman, Nancy. *Stoic Warriors: The Ancient Philosophy Behind the Military Mind.* New York: Oxford University Press, U.S.A., 2005.

Simon, John Y., ed. *The Papers Of Ulysses S. Grant.* 26 vols. Carbondale: Southern Illinois University Press, 1967–2003.

Smith, Theodore Clarke. *The Life and Letters of James Abram Garfield.* 2 vols. New Haven: Yale University Press, 1925.

Stearns, W. A. [*Memorial of*] *Adjutant Stearns* [First Lieutenant Frazar A. Stearns, 21st Massachusetts Infantry]. n.p.: H.O. Houghton Co., 1862.

Stewart, George R. *Pickett's Charge: A Microhistory of the Final Attack at Gettysburg, July 3, 1863.* Boston: Houghton Mifflin, 1959.

Sword. Wiley. "Capt. William C. Morgan, 3rd Maine Infantry. Hero or Scoundrel at the Peach Orchard." *Gettysburg Magazine*, no. 25 (2001), 75ff.

———. "Carried Under Two Flags." *North South Trader* 8 no. 2 (January–February 1981), 16ff.

———. *Embrace an Angry Wind: The Confederacy's Last Hurrah; Spring Hill, Franklin, and Nashville*. New York: HarperCollins, 1992.

———. *Mountains Touched with Fire: Chattanooga Besieged, 1863*. New York: St. Martin's Press, 1995.

———. *Sharpshooter: Hiram Berdan, His Famous Sharpshooters, and Their Sharps Rifles*. Lincoln, R.I.: Andrew Mowbray, 1988.

———. *Shiloh: Bloody April*. 1974. Reprint: Dayton: Morningside Press, 2001.

———. *Southern Invincibility: A History of the Confederate Heart*. New York: St. Martin's Press, 1999.

Tennessee General Web Project. Tennesseans in the Civil War. 13th U.S. Colored Infantry Regiment. www.TNGenWeb.org.

Underwood, Robert, and Clarence C. Buel, eds. *Battles and Leaders of the Civil War*. 4 vols. New York: Century Company, 1887–88.

U.S. Congress. House. "Barbarities of the Rebels at Manassas." 37th Congress, 2nd sess., [1861–1862].

U.S. War Department. *War of the Rebellion: A Compilation of the Official Records of the Union and Confederate Armies*. 128 vols. Washington, D.C.: U.S. Government Printing Office, 1891–1902.

Venner, William T. *Hoosier's Honor: The Iron Brigade's 19th Indiana Regiment*. Shippensburg, Pa.: Burd Street Press, 1998.

Wainwright, Charles S. *A Diary of Battle: The Personal Journals of Col. Charles S. Wainwright, 1861–1865*. New York: Harcourt, Brace & World, 1902.

Ward, Joseph R. C. *History of the 106th Regiment Pennsylvania Volunteers*. Philadelphia: F. McManus, Jr., & Co., 1906.

Webb and His Brigade at the Angle Gettysburg: In Memoriam, Alexander Stewart Webb, 1835–1911. Albany, N.Y.: n.p., 1916.

Wilson, James Harrison. *Under the Old Flag*. 2 vols. Westport, Conn.: Greenwood Press edition of 1912 edition, published by D. Appleton & Co., 1971.

Wyeth, John Allan. *Life of Nathan Bedford Forrest*. 1901. Reprint: Dayton: Morningside Press, 1988.

Index of Military Units

Note: (CSA) stands for Confederate States of America; (USA) stands for United States of America. Numbered units appear before named units.

General Index

Note: (CSA) stands for Confederate States of America; (USA) stands for United States of America. See also separate Index of Military Units.

absenteeism, 90, 98
Alabama, 20, 75, 211
Albemarle, Confederate ironclad, 109–13
Albemarle Sound, North Carolina, 109
Aldrich, Ann Shafter, 126–32
Aldrich, Capt. Job (USA), 126–31
Allatoona, 197
Allegan, Michigan, 184, 187
ambushes, 20
American Civil War
   changing tactics of, 33, 42
   end and aftermath of, 262
   historical importance of, 269, 275
   South's hope to win peace from North,
     226, 229
   total casualties of, 65, 144–45
Ames, Brig. Gen. Adelbert, 89
amphibious operations, 8
amputations, 195
Anatomy of Courage (Moran), 32
Anderson, Lt. Charles W. (CSA), 186
Anderson, Gen. Patton (CSA), 256
anger
   as coping method, 147–50
   at the enemy, 148, 167

   as motive for fighting, 167–68
   at officers, 149–50, 171–72
Angle on Cemetery Ridge, 231
animals, response to danger by, 31
Antietam, Battle of, 33, 195
Arkansas Post, 164
Arkansas River, 155
Armistead, Brig. Gen. Lewis ("Old Lo")
   (CSA), 95–96, 98, 144, 231
Army, U.S., 239
   regular, 14, 173
artillery
   enemy's, attacking, 55
   own, support from, 54–55, 229,
     230–31
Asbury, Pvt. Fouts (USA), 154
Ashburton Treaty, 104
Atlanta, Georgia
   Battle of, 60
   fall of, 196, 259
Atlanta Campaign, 3, 24, 35–36, 43,
    44–51, 60, 86, 158, 196, 234
atrocities of the enemy, anger at, 148,
   167
Ayers, Capt. Gideon (USA), 167

Morgan, Col. Thomas J. (USA), 128
Morgan, Capt. William C. (USA),
    188–92
Morse, Lucy, 124–26
Morse, Pvt. William H. (USA), 124–26
Mosby, John S. (CSA), 266
"Mule-Shoe Salient," 99
Murfreesboro, Tennessee, 115–21, 160,
    171–72, 235, 238
Murfreesboro Pike, 127–28, 154
mutiny, 173–74

Napoleon, 29
Napoleonic warfare tactics, 32, 42, 56, 215
Nashville, Tennessee, 20, 116–17, 127,
    199, 211, 212, 236
    siege of, 154, 234, 235
Nashville, Tennessee, Battle of, 63, 167
    wreck of Hood's army at, 238
Naval Academy, 108
naval warfare during the American Civil
    War, 101–14
Navy, U.S., 102
Nevill, Pvt. Robert (USA), 35–36
New Berne, North Carolina, Battle of,
    29–30
New England, 121–22
Newnan, Georgia, 263
New York City, 107
Niagara River, 106
Nichols, Mate D. C. (USA), 104
noncombat assignments, dissatisfaction
    with, 9
noncommissioned officers, authority
    exercised by, 174
Norman aristocrats, 121
North, the
    peace party of the, 226
    South's hope that it would tire of war,
        224–26, 229
North Anna River, 191
North Missionary Ridge, 59, 177–78
Norton, Capt. David W. (USA), 16–26
Norton, Sgt. Wallace E. (USA), 10, 11

oath of obedience, 6
officers
    anger at, and desire to kill, 149–50,
        171–72

soldiers' hostility to, 171–74
textbook education of, 42
unpopular with men, 90, 172
Ohio, 242
Ohio River, 234
Opdycke, Col. Emerson (USA), 176, 198
Orchard Knob, 177, 178
orders
    discretionary vs. peremptory, 46
    "foolish" or unreasoned, 42
    refusal to carry out, 3–7, 44–50, 270
Overland Campaign, 191
Overton Hill, 117–18
Owen, Brig. Gen. Joshua T. "Paddy"
    (USA), 90
Owl Creek, 215

pain, overcoming, 99–101
Palmer, Maj. Gen. John M. (USA), 22–26
patriotism
    as reason for enlisting, 8, 16–17
    as reason for soldiering, 166
peace party, of the North, 226
Peach Orchard (Gettysburg), 151, 189,
    229
Pecos River, 131
Pender, William D. (CSA), 93
Peninsula Campaign, 88, 134
Pennsylvania, invasion of, 148, 156
Perryville, Kentucky, Battle of, 56, 58,
    84–88, 233n., 245
Petersburg, Virginia, 234, 259
    Battle of, 150, 167
Peterson, Capt. Samuel G. W. (USA), 207
Pettigrew, Gen. James Johnston (CSA),
    93, 230
Philo Parsons steamboat, 104–6
physical courage, 83–200, 270
Picket Boat No. 1 (USA), 110
Pickett, Maj. Gen. George E. (CSA), 93,
    230
Pickett's Charge, 108, 144, 148, 189, 198
Pickett's Mill, Georgia, 25
    Battle of, 158
Pillow, Gen. Gideon J. (CSA), 211
Pittsburg Landing, Tennessee, 54, 210,
    211–13, 219, 220; See also Shiloh
Plymouth, North Carolina, 109, 113
Point Lookout Prison, Maryland, 149, 168

World Trade Center Towers, terrorist
 attack on, 31
wounded, being, the feeling of, 29
wounds
 disfiguring, 195
 mortal, 78, 87–88
 recovery from, 24, 94, 158
 temporary survival from, 100, 135–38

Wright, Brig. Gen. A. R. (CSA), 91,
 228

Yandell, Dr. D. W. (CSA),
 217
Yankees, 121–22
Younger, Lt. Joseph G. (CSA),
 144

DISCARD